SOCIAL DEVELOPMENT IN ASIA

Social Indicators Research Series

Volume 5

This new series aims to provide a public forum for single treatises and collections of papers on social indicators research that are too long to be published in our journal *Social Indicators Research*. Like the journal, the book series deals with statistical assessments of the quality of life from a broad perspective. It welcomes the research on a wide variety of substantive areas, including health, crime, housing, education, family life, leisure activities, transportation, mobility, economics, work, religion and environmental issues. These areas of research will focus on the impact of key issues such as health on the overall quality of life and vice versa. An international review board, consisting of Ruut Veenhoven, Joachim Vogel, Ed Diener, Torbjorn Moum and Wolfgang Glatzer, will ensure the high quality of the series as a whole.

The titles published in this series are listed at the end of this volume.

SOCIAL DEVELOPMENT IN ASIA

Edited by

KWONG-LEUNG TANG

University of Northern British Columbia, Prince George, Canada

KLUWER ACADEMIC PUBLISHERS

DORDRECHT / BOSTON / LONDON

A C.I.P. Catalogue record for this book is available from the Library of Congress.

ISBN 0-7923-6256-X

Published by Kluwer Academic Publishers,
P.O. Box 17, 3300 AA Dordrecht, The Netherlands.

Sold and distributed in North, Central and South America
by Kluwer Academic Publishers,
101 Philip Drive, Norwell, MA 02061, U.S.A.

In all other countries, sold and distributed
by Kluwer Academic Publishers,
P.O. Box 322, 3300 AH Dordrecht, The Netherlands.

Printed on acid-free paper

Printed in the Netherlands.

ACKNOWLEDGEMENTS

This edited text originates from the World Congress of Quality of Life held at the University of Northern British Columbia in the summer of 1996. Not long afterwards, Professor Alex Michalos, the renowned authority on quality of life research, sent out invitations for book proposals to conference participants. He told us that Kluwer Academic Press had agreed to publish a book series to complement Social Indicators Research, the leading journal for quality of life research. I took up this challenge and sent him my ideas. He liked my proposal and immediately offered me much advice and suggestions. In retrospect, the completion of this book was not possible without the active support of Alex. Here I wish to express my deepest appreciation to Professor Alex Michalos who freely gave of his expertise and provided the major impetus which culminated in this book.

For a book of this sort, I have naturally had to depend on experts from many countries. In the course of preparing this text, I have been most fortunate to work with a group of academics from Asia. I am grateful to the contributors of the book's chapters for the wealth of research experience and understanding that is reflected in their work: Joe C. B. Leung, James K. C. Lee, Yeun-wen Ku, Sunwoo Lee, In-Jae Lee, Voravidh Charoenloet, Pradeep Agrawal, P. V. Srinivasan, and Gerard Greenfield.

I am grateful to the following reviewers for reading and commenting on various chapters of this book: Paul Bowles, Shereen Ismael, Suresh Kurl, James Leiby, Apo Po-lam Leung, Gordon Ternowetsky, and Evaon Wong.

I am grateful especially to the late Professor Gordon Ternowetsky for his helpful comments and editorial assistance. Professor Ternowetsky passed away suddenly this fall. I am certain that his contributions to the field of Canadian social policy and poverty research will be long remembered.

I owe a special debt to some of my finest students at the University of Northern British Columbia who spared their precious time before the final examination proofreading the entire manuscript. They include: Dawn Hemingway, Paula Hunter, Stephanie Peckford, Ava Temple, and Tracy Yuill. Special thanks are due to Carroll Ternowetsky for reading parts of the manuscript. Jennifer Studney, Terry McBride and my wife, Jacqueline Cheung once again have given me much secretarial and editing support. Many thanks to all of them! Finally, I am appreciative of the assistance and patience of the professional staff at Kluwer Academic Press, especially Sabine Wesseldijk, the publishing editor. None of those named is responsible for any view expressed or any remaining deficiencies in the book.

Kwong-leung Tang
Prince George, British Columbia

CONTENTS

ABOUT THE CONTRIBUTORS

Pradeep Agrawal is an Associate Professor at the Indira Gandhi Institute of Development Research, Bombay, India. He holds a Ph.D. in economics from Stanford University, California and has taught at several universities in the United States. His main research interests are in the areas of economics of development and growth, financial markets, and East Asian and Indian Economies. He has several publications in professional international and national journals in these areas. He has also co-authored two comparative studies of East Asia and India: (1) *Economic Restructuring in East Asia and India: Perspectives on Economic reform*, 1995, published by Macmillan Press, United Kingdom and St. Martin's Press, New York and, (2*) Policy Regimes and Industrial Competitiveness: A Comparative Study of East Asia and India*, forthcoming from Macmillan, United Kingdom.

Voravidh Charoenloet is an Associate Professor of comparative labour economics at Chulalongkorn University in Thailand. He is director of the Political Studies Centre at his university. He obtained his doctorate from University of Paris X in France. He is the author of numerous chapters and articles on various issues of labor economics and social policy in Asian journals. His latest book, *Comparative Economic Development*, came out in 1992.

Gerard Greenfield is a labour research activist working in East and Southeast Asia. He was formerly a Research Coordinator for Asia Monitor Resource Center, a regional labour NGO based in Hong Kong and was until recently the Education Program Organiser in Indonesia for the International Union of Food Workers Association (IUF) Asia-Pacific. He also served as an associate lecturer in Asian Studies at Murdoch University. His main fields of interest and publications are comparative labor welfare, human rights, and the role of international organizations in socio-economic development in Asia. Recently, he has written a book chapter on social development in post-war Vietnam, which will be published by Routledge, New York.

Yuen-wen Ku is an Associate Professor of Social Policy at the Department of Social Policy and Social Work, National Chi Nan University, Taiwan. He was awarded his doctorate from the University of Manchester in 1995. Before that, he published many books and papers in Taiwan, and taught at the Soochow University and the National Taiwan University respectively. His most recent book in English is *Welfare Capitalism in Taiwan* (London: Macmillan, 1997). At the present, Ku is embarking on a comparative study on East Asian social security systems. He is also the Secretary General of the Association of Social Policy, ROC, and an editor of Social Policy and Social Work, an important academic journal in this field in Taiwan.

James Kin-Ching Lee is currently an Associate Professor in the Department of Public and Social Administration of the City University of Hong Kong. He has been involved in the teaching of social policy in the last fourteen years in a number of Hong Kong tertiary institutes, including Polytechnic University, Chinese University, Shue Yan College and City University. He has completed research in social indicators, housing policy, and elderly care and housing, as well as comparative social policy. He has published in local and international journals in the field of social policy and housing policy. He completed his undergraduate education in Hong Kong and obtained his doctorate in policy studies from Bristol University, England.

In-Jae Lee is an Associate Professor in the Division of Social Welfare at the Hanshin University in South Korea. He teaches community organization and social research. He had his undergraduate education in Korea. He obtained his Ph.D. in social welfare from the Seoul National University in 1994. His academic interests include community action, social welfare policy, and agency evaluation. He is the author of *Social Security in Korea.*

Sunwoo Lee is a research fellow at the Korea Institute for Health and Social Affairs in Seoul, South Korea. He holds an undergraduate degree and a master's degree from Seoul National University. He obtained his Ph.D. in social welfare from the University of California at Berkeley in 1995. He previously taught social welfare at Seoul National University. His academic interests include community welfare, social safety nets, and research and statistics. He is the co-author of the book: *Statistics in Social Welfare* (Seoul, South Korea: Nanam Publishing Company, 1997).

Joe Cho-Bun Leung is an Associate Professor in the Department of Social Work and Social Administration at the University of Hong Kong. He holds a Ph.D. in social work. His publications focus on social security, social work training, community services, family support for the elderly, and the work of nongovernmental organizations in China. He is the co-author (with Richard Nann) *of Authority and Benevolence; Social Welfare in China* (New York: St. Martin's Press, 1995).

P.V. Srinivasan is an Associate Professor at the Indira Gandhi Institute of Development Research in Bombay. He holds a Ph.D. from the Indian Statistical Institute, New Delhi. His areas of interest include poverty, food policy, and public sector pricing and tax policies. He has several publications in professional international and national journals in these areas. He has conducted extensive studies related to food price stabilization, food security and analysis of poverty based on household sample survey data, including some for the UNDP and the World Bank.

Kwong-Leung Tang is an Associate Professor in the College of Arts, Social & Health Sciences at the University of Northern British Columbia, Canada. He received an Master of Science in social policy from the London School of Economics and Political Science and his doctorate in social welfare from the University of California at Berkeley. He is the author of *Colonial State and Social Policy: Social Welfare*

Development in Hong Kong 1842-1997 (Lanham, Maryland: University Press of America, 1998). His academic interests include law and social policy, human rights and international organizations, and comparative social policy analysis.

FOREWORD

Although the idea of development only became an integral part of academic and indeed public discourse after the Second World war, it is not a new one. It is rooted in ancient beliefs about social change and social progress. These beliefs are found in the religions and cultures of diverse civilizations, including those of Asia. In some of the ancient civilizations, change was viewed as a retrogressive decline from a previously golden age of perfectibility. In others, change was regarded as an never ending process of cycles of progress and decline. Yet others took a more optimistic view believing that change was progressive and that social conditions would steadily improve.

Many ancients regarded change as a property of divine intervention. Disobedience or compliance with the will of the Gods could trigger change for the worse or for the better. Others believed that change could be affected by human action. The achievements of the ancient civilizations demonstrated the ability of human beings to rise above subsistence poverty, alter their situation and create unimagined wealth. Of course, this prosperity also relied on power. The ability to subjugate others, exploit labor and extract wealth was a primary source of splendor.

While development engendered progress, it also oppressed and exploited. Despite their great achievements, the ancient civilizations were built on subjugation, slavery and violence. Progress for some thus depended on the misery of others. Although much mitigated, the paradox remains a real one today. While development has transformed traditional economies, promoted impressive technological innovations, and raised standards of living, it has not eradicated human misery. Economic modernization in many parts of the world has been achieved through low wage industrialization, the exploitation of agricultural labor and the employment of women and children under appalling working conditions. In addition, the benefits of economic development have not been evenly or justly distributed.

Many urban centres in the developing world brashly reveal the inequalities of modernization. High-priced European cars compete in the traffic with buffeted taxis, motorized rickshaws and bicycles; ragged street vendors sell their wares outside luxury boutiques stocked with Western goods; and child beggars frequent the entrances to modern hotels and restaurants. While social conditions in many countries, particularly in Asia, have improved dramatically over the last fifty years, poverty, ill-health, illiteracy and homelessness persist on a huge scale.

There is growing recognition that the distortions of development must be addressed. After half a century of unprecedented economic progress, greater efforts are needed to deal with the poverty and attendant social ills that still characterized the lives of hundreds of millions of human beings. There is growing recognition that economic development cannot, on its own, create prosperity for all. While economic development generates wealth, and is the source of dynamic change, it fails to promote social progress for all citizens.

The 1995 United Nations World Summit on Social Development presented an opportunity for the international community to make a renewed commitment to progress by seeking to harmonize social and economic development policies and ensure that basic human needs are met. Most of the world's leaders attended the Summit and endorsed its call, but few would claim that the Summit's recommendations have been widely adopted. The challenge of responding to massive social need is as urgent as ever before.

The challenge is particularly great in Asia which has the highest proportion of the world's poor, marked inequalities in income and wealth and some of the most spectacular contrasts in affluence and poverty both within countries and in the region as a whole. The recent economic crisis in East Asia has also demonstrated the social vulnerability of many ordinary people who were enjoying the benefits of high rates of economic growth. In East Asian nations such as Japan and South Korea, unemployment and a serious decline in living standards caught many by surprise and governments were thrown into disarray. The need for coherent policies that promote economic development in conjunction with social development is only too obvious.

As the need for social development is being recognized, this important book builds on the growing international literature on the subject. Edited by Kwong-leung Tang, it explores diverse aspects of the topic in the Asian region. The authors of the various chapters present up to date information on social development in a variety of Asian nations including China, Hong Kong, India, Thailand, Singapore, South Korea and Taiwan. They demonstrate their extensive knowledge of the field, and show how the social development perspective can inform policy making. The book will be a major resource for scholars and students concerned with social development in Asia. It also informs those working in the field of social policy and development in other parts of the world. Developments in Asia affect the global world system in its entirety.

The authors also provide valuable lessons for social policy in other nations. With increased economic pressures, fiscal difficulties and electoral disenchantment with conventional social programs, new perspectives such as social development offer promising alternatives to current social welfare thinking. As this book reveals, the social development perspective can facilitate the emergence of new approaches to social welfare that will promote the well-being of all the world's citizens.

James Midgley
Dean of the School of Social Welfare &
Harry and Riva Specht Professor of Public Social Services
University of California, Berkeley

KWONG-LEUNG TANG

INTRODUCTION

SOCIAL DEVELOPMENT IN ASIA

Until the onset of the Asian economic crisis in 1997, the world was amazed by the phenomenal economic development in many Asian countries. This occurred in four waves. Japan, which recovered quickly from the Second World War, had been prominent since the late 1960s. The four Asian tigers of Hong Kong, Singapore, Taiwan and South Korea excelled economically from the 1970s onwards. Following closely on their heels were the second-tier Asian countries like Thailand, Malaysia and Indonesia which have had equally spectacular economic growth in the last two decades (Grandea, 1995). Finally, since the early 1990s, poorer Asian countries like China and India have embarked on similarly rapid economic reforms.

Asia is a large and diverse continent and it is clear that economic miracles do not take place in every country (for example Cambodia, Nepal, Burma, etc.). Nevertheless, taken as a whole the Asian countries have the highest GNP per capita in the developing world. Excluding Japan and considering the small cluster of East Asian tigers alone, their economic performance has indeed been miraculous. Since the early 1970s the average rate of growth of real per capita income has exceeded 6 percent in each of the four tigers. Had it not been for the Asian economic meltdown in 1997-98, these countries would be doing very well. They registered a growth rate of 7.4 percent in 1994 compared to 6.3 percent in 1990. Economic development in Asia is even more surprising in view of the fact that the 1980s was a period of decline in Africa and Latin America. As noted, both China and India, which usually rank low in the economic league of Asian countries, have been experiencing very fast growth in the last decade.

The case of China is particularly illustrative: despite the lingering Asian crisis, natural disaster and failing state-owned enterprises (SOEs), it managed to achieve a 7.8 percent growth rate in 1998. Such economic miracles have become objects of study and models for replication in other transitional societies (such as Eastern European and Latin American countries) which are eager to achieve a comparable level of development. Across Asia people have come to expect sustained, rapid growth and increasing prosperity as a constant. The economic goal of wealth creation has become an end in itself and there are few countries in the region that do not adhere to this principle of thought and action. In the wake of such success stories,

K.-L. Tang (ed.), Social Development in Asia, 1–9.

there has been a burgeoning literature on the economic performance of these Asian states. Yet there have been relatively few studies which examine their social development and developmental problems.

One central theme of such studies is that social development lags behind economic development in Asia. A related theme is that the fruits of economic development are not spread equally. These voices (Estes, 1987), though not often heard, express rising concern about social development problems. However, until recently, the discourse in development has been dominated by economic studies. More often than not the key message from economic analyses of East Asian states is that economic growth is conducive to a better society. Hence there has been talk among Asian countries of the new millennium being an 'Asia century'. There is a strong belief that economic growth and social development will advance together in the coming century. Reports from international organizations like the World Bank and the International Monetary Fund tend to reinforce this euphoria. The World Bank, for instance, has touted the East Asian economic miracle as a prime example of how growth can be obtained with equality. Country reports on social development which are submitted to these international organizations usually present a rosy view of the social reality. For a long time, official optimism from many countries has painted a very positive picture of their social achievement. There is an assumption that the fruits of economic development will be filtered evenly through the entire population so that eventually all citizens will benefit from it. Thus the first task in national planning is to ensure wealth creation. Not surprisingly, many outsiders to the region have taken social development in Asia for granted.

SOCIAL DIMENSIONS OF DEVELOPMENT

As we approach the new millennium, this would seem to be an opportune time to consider how much social progress has been made and to identify what major development problems still remain. The major objective of this volume is to bring together different contributors from different disciplines (economics, labor welfare, social administration, public policy) to examine and document what levels of social development (based mostly on social conditions and social services measures) their countries have attained. Have these countries come closer to the goal of 'growth with equity'? What developmental problems are lingering and posing a threat to their future stability? To what extent could state intervention in this region resolve some of these social problems? Is privatization a viable option for improving social development?

A central theme runs through the all chapters in this book. Behind the facade of rapid economic development, the Asian countries analysed in this volume are facing some serious problems in their social development. Despite their recent progress, they have a number of social problems, notably poverty, inequality, low social spending and rising unemployment. Unfortunately, official responses in many countries have been to ignore, downplay or dismiss these problems (with the exception of unemployment which is an important concern to countries like Indonesia, Japan, Hong Kong and Singapore in the aftermath of the 1998 Asian economic collapse). Hence, social development as a policy issue is often understated. It has not occupied an important place in the developmental agenda. While acknowledging that social development is an important objective and paying lip service to it, most Asian countries see it as an inevitable outcome of economic growth. By implication, this book also taps into the social costs of rapid economic development.

Despite public euphoria, contributors in this volume note various significant social problems arising from economic growth. The stakes are enormous since such problems are a threat to social stability. In short, economic growth and affluence do not guarantee a parallel achievement in social development.

DEVELOPMENT IDEOLOGIES IN THE 1990s

The lagging of social development behind economic development needs to be put in context. Two factors which help to explain the underemphasis on social development in Asia are developmental ideologies and the notion of social rights. In development studies discourse, two divergent approaches are evident: modernization school and the neoliberal approach.

Immediately after the Second World War and until well into the 1960s, the main thrust of development theory focused on the dynamic of national income growth, usually measured by change in GNP per capita. Rising from the war-torn context, many Asian countries have subscribed to this principle in the belief that social development spending is wasteful and unproductive. Hence, the seeds of a welfare state (in the Western sense of the word, which champions full employment, a comprehensive social safety net and universal social services) were never sewn in the soil of Asia. Also known as the trickle-down theory of development, the dominant ideology called for a development policy which would focus on the infrastructural development of a country. The eventual distribution of its economic fruits would enable everyone to benefit from the economic successes of the country.

With the onset of the welfare state crisis in the mid-1970s, a neoconservative paradigm has become increasingly dominant in many industrialized countries, including the United States, Britain and Canada. This ideology accuses welfare states of having failed and gives primacy to the marketplace as the determinant of individual choice, freedom and well-being. Followers of neoliberalism argue that government spending, especially on welfare, undermines the market, drains the economy and reduces individual initiative (Mullaly, 1998). This ideology has found its way into the Asian countries which have adopted an adverse attitude toward social welfare -- an attitude that blends well with the dominant ideology for modernization in the 1960s. The result is that there has been an apology for non-action in the social sphere in many Asian countries.

In many Western democracies, labour movements and organized interests have been pushing their governments to invest in social welfare development as a way of dealing with issues of poverty, wage disparities and social inequality. Often, such movements have been backed by a notion of social rights. By contrast, Asia's development is taking place in a context where demands for human rights are much less respected, even disparaged. Thus, a number of Asian states are either authoritarian or tightly controlled by a ruling party (Hong Kong, China, Indonesia, Taiwan, Singapore, etc.). Civil and political rights are not extended to people in these authoritarian Asian countries and violations of such rights/principles are not infrequent.

For countries like South Korea, Thailand and Taiwan which have liberalized their political system, democracy is still in its infancy. Overall, there is a clear absence of the notion of social rights in the political discourse of most Asian countries. Many governments foster a sense of "compassionate conservatism", i.e. they uphold the view that people should resort to assistance from their families or social networks. This has implications for the future of social development in Asia and by all accounts the lack of a solid foundation for social rights means that Asian people are less likely than their counterparts in developed regions to press for social spending in order to achieve better social development. In this respect, Asia defies those theoretical analyses which assume there is a certain linear evolution of citizenship rights. Such a notion of citizenship rights has been extensively examined by T.H. Marshall (1963).

In his analysis, which is based on English history, there are three kinds of rights. First to be adopted are civil rights which refer to guarantees of individual liberty and equality before the law. Second come political rights relating to political enfranchisement. Last are social rights which refer to ‘a modicum of economic welfare and security’. All three constituent rights of citizenship are expanding. In the British case, its historical development involved an expansion from civil rights to political rights and, in the twentieth century, to social rights. The latter were at first restricted to the needy as social services, but were later extended to the working classes and eventually to the whole population (Mishra, 1977; Rodgers et al., 1995).

Essentially, Marshall supported an egalitarian notion of social provision but he was concerned with the potential conflict between a regime of social rights and a social order governed by the rules of the capitalist market. Marshall's citizenship theory could be seen as a way to advance and legitimize the welfare state within a liberal democratic context (Jayasuriya, 1996). His citizenship theory attempts to overcome the inequalities of free market capitalism through an emphasis on community-oriented political and social rights that stresses citizen participation in shared communities. This would provide moral foundation for social welfare which would be grounded in community rather than individual rights. Obviously, Asian social development is not fuelled by a parallel development of social rights. At present, the notion of social rights is still not embraced by a wide audience in Asian states. It is still imperfectly developed, occasionally entering into national debate only through social work academics or activists pushing for social changes.

SUMMARY OF CHAPTER CONTRIBUTIONS

We turn now to highlight the major arguments of the contributors in this volume. First of all, Joe Leung, examining social development in post-market reform China, concludes that despite impressive economic development large segments of the population are excluded from the benefits of the economic miracle. Existing problems of social income inequality, poverty and unemployment have actually been exacerbated by the economic growth. The government's ability to respond to these problems is undermined by the massive economic problems China is facing with respect to perennial budget deficits, soaring international debts and a declining share of national revenue. Such problems pose a threat to the government if it really wants to move toward a situation of Xiaokang, a social development level equivalent to that of a middle-income nation by the year 2000.

James Lee examines the debate between individualism and collectivism in Hong Kong, an affluent city now under the control of Mainland China. Historically, the Hong Kong colonial government has shown much pragmatism in constructing a residual social welfare system which has been rather functional. He notes: "the pragmatic mix of social policies such as those found in Hong Kong could actually amount to a form of social corporatism, where the state plays a key role in social resources distribution and yet succeeds in not tampering with individual responsibility and the spirit of capitalism" (Chapter 2). The key question for him (and policy makers) is whether the state should now withdraw from the social market or not. Reviewing the social service indicators, there are signs of universalism (housing, education and hospital care) and selectivism (social welfare). Both before and after Hong Kong was badly hit by the economic crisis, there have been calls for the privatization of social services and cutbacks in social spending for the poor. The social service system is under severe strain now, since both the lower economic class and the middle class are badly affected.

In his study of Taiwan, Ku notes that although education and public health are well developed and social insurance is expanding to cover more and more people, the government welfare effort is still too low to be available to all the public. Situating his study of Taiwanese social welfare development in the politico-economic context, he finds a general hostility towards state welfare in Taiwan on the part of bureaucrats, who place a strong emphasis on economic development. However, there are alternative views which present social welfare in a better, more positive light. He further notes that the present-day Taiwanese state is facing a great challenge with respect to balancing two requirements: deregulation of the economy under globalization and the establishment of a social safety net under democratization. Despite such tensions, the ruling party, under the pressure of increasing democratization and contest from its major rival party (the DPP), has been active in its social agenda; it has already set up a national health insurance in 1995 and a national pension system will be introduced in the year 2000. The degree of state intervention is set to increase, though the advantages of privatized social services are being weighed. In welfare delivery terms, there is a close parallel between Hong Kong and Taiwan: both have a residual system.

Likewise, one could find a residual welfare system in South Korea. In Chapter 4, Sunwoo Lee and In-Jae Lee look at social welfare development in South Korea which is deemed to be underdeveloped. They review government policies on income maintenance, health insurance, industrial injury insurance, employment insurance and housing. The social welfare system has been under considerable strain in the aftermath of the Asian economic crisis. Unemployment has risen alarmingly and the residual social welfare structure is not able to cope with the escalating problems from the crisis. Social conditions are likely to decline when the government single-mindedly engages in economic recovery to the neglect of social development.

In the next chapter on Singapore, Kwong-leung Tang notes the rapid economic development this small city-state has achieved. Other than massive investment in housing and the implementation of a central provident fund, however, the Singapore Government has paid little attention to social development. A more humanitarian approach would take into consideration the human costs of its rapid economic development. Noting the disparity between its ranking in human development and per capita ranking (United Nations, 1998), it is clear that the state in Singapore has considerable financial and political leverage to effect the kind of social development needed.

Like most Asian countries under examination in this volume, Thailand has been badly affected by the economic crisis in 1997. This was particularly painful considering that there was an economic boom in the early 1990s. A host of factors contributed to this boom: foreign investment, increased tourism and the opening-up of foreign markets. Thailand integrated well and early in world capitalism and participated actively in liberalization. Liberalization was championed by the government and international organizations in the early 1980s and structural adjustment programs were accordingly introduced. In his study of labour welfare and practices in Thailand (the 'fifth Asian tiger'), Charonenloet notes the weak and fragmented union movement in a country with a population of 60 million (half of whom are employed). Due to weak unionization, the use of temporary and casual workers is common to save production costs. A number of other problems are found in employment: long working hours, job insecurity, union busting, the prevalence of child labour, a high industrial injury rate, an unrealistically low minimum wage, the downward deregulation of labourers and lack of statutory labour protection. As Thailand's economy becomes internationalized, it is not easy for the government to regulate international capital which exerts a strong presence since it is borderless. Despite such weaknesses and the prevalence of problems in employment, there are some stories of success. After the tragic fire in Kader factory in 1993 which resulted in heavy casualties, workers became mobilized and pressed for compensation which led to improved industrial safety regulations on the part of both employers and the government. Specifically, the employers were blamed for their neglect of fire prevention facilities in the factories.

The Kader tragedy demonstrated that multinational companies which are relocated to Thailand are not always the country's best employers. Though only limited successes in the area of victims' compensation and campaigning for workers' rights have been achieved, organizing (backed by NGOs and academics) in the wake of the Kader tragedy is an encouraging example of workers' empowerment, a feat not easily achieved under Asian authoritarian governments.

The final country under examination is India. While East Asian countries and Thailand are performing rather well economically, India has been a latecomer, with economic growth picking up only recently. It achieved some 7 percent growth in the early 1990s for the first time since independence. With 300 million in poverty, it is still a poor country, even by Asian standards. Pradeep Agrawal and P.V. Srinivasan conclude that social indicators such as safe drinking water and the infant mortality rate have been slowly improving over the years. But poverty was given prominence in their study and they found that poverty alleviation was a function of economic growth, which harked back to the modernization trickle-down theory. Overall, the Indian government was not able to spend much on education and health (in per capita terms). Yet the positive role of the state is affirmed by Agrawal and Srinivasan when they note that 'the government will have to strive hard to not only allocate more funds but to improve the institutions to carry out social development more efficiently'.

The issue of privatized welfare against state welfare in the context of international influences is addressed fully in the last chapter. Arguing from a critical perspective, Greenfield studies the ideological influences wielded by the international organizations in the region, including the World Bank and the International Monetary Fund. He challenges the notion of an effective state advanced by the Bank in its 1997 World Development Report and professed to be drawn from the experience of the miracle's economies of East Asia. He notes the hidden but strong neoliberal emphases in their agenda: social fundamentals such as education, health and environmental protection can be secured through market-driven competition and privatization. This can be achieved through political authoritarianism and elite-centred policy-making.

The outcome will be very problematic as far as social development is concerned. The World Bank's notion of an 'effective state' will only exacerbate existing social problems of poverty and unemployment and raise the social costs of rapid economic growth. Instead, the tremendous social, economic, political and environmental problems faced by the people of the region, and the demands made by popular social movements in response to these problems, require an effective state that is democratic and capable of protecting the rights and interests of the people. The state in various countries should be able to re-regulate markets and place the long-term interests of society before the short-term interests of private business. As such, the concept of an effective state is here redefined. It must be based on democratic policy-making and an administration that gives substance and true meaning to citizenship rights and participation.

DEVELOPMENT PROBLEMS--COMMON THEMES

Despite the strong emphases on economic growth and a repression of labour rights and movements in these countries, invariably, all contributors note marked improvements in general social conditions in those Asian countries under review. Of the various sectors of social policy, education is afforded the utmost attention in most of the countries. Those in support of state intervention who search for good news in social development will be delighted to see the expansion of unemployment insurance in South Korea as well as a 97% rate of NHI coverage in Taiwan. Some of the social issues noted in the subsequent chapters include the following:

1. Problems of poverty and social inequality are found to be either severe or worsening in countries like Hong Kong, Taiwan, Singapore and South Korea.

2. Selected groups of beneficiaries from social initiatives can be identified. In the case of Taiwan, for example, Ku suggests that military servicemen, veterans and government employees stand to gain most from the provision of social goods.

3. Social assistance schemes are underdeveloped in Taiwan and Singapore. Since the end of 1998 there has been a strong public backlash against welfare recipients in Hong Kong which is partly due to the worsening economic conditions.

4. In most of these countries, the external environment is a factor too important to ignore. The ideology of privatization which has been the prevalent motivation in policy analysis is making considerable inroads in some Asian countries, i.e. Hong Kong, China, Taiwan and India. Notably, the central provident fund in Singapore is moving toward private investment and promising more choices for the beneficiaries.

5. There are new social policy initiatives which aim at bettering human development: National Health Insurance in Taiwan, a Mandatory Provident Fund in Hong Kong, Unemployment Insurance in South Korea, and the reform of SOEs in China which has implications in terms of welfare for employees.

6. Unique political and economic contexts have engendered these different kinds of initiative. Ku notes the intense rivalries between the ruling KMT Party and the DPP, giving rise to a situation in which the leading opposition party to some extent contributes to the growth of social policy.

ADVERSITY AND CHANGE

With the recent unprecedented Asian economic woes, systematic analyses of the social impacts are only just emerging. A few worrying trends can be identified. First of all, unemployment has been on the rise in most countries. Furthermore, latest research reports tell of suffering among specific groups of people (for instance women and children). With a number of Asian countries (Japan, Hong Kong, Singapore, Thailand and Indonesia) now in recession, a prolonged period of adversity with high unemployment, rising poverty and greater income disparity is a real possibility. Finally, in spite of the economic crisis, there have been calls for more privatized social services in Hong Kong, China, South Korea and Singapore. A degree of apathy has set in on the part of the government in the aftermath of the economic crisis and there is no telling whether Asian governments will be looking at their development problems in earnest.

Historically the West has shown that social spending is increased in times of acute social or economic crisis (Cloward and Piven, 1972). Adversity resulting in greater social and political tensions spur changes. In the wake of the economic storm, international organizations like the International Labour Organization have called on governments to be attentive to social conditions which have been rapidly deteriorating since the crisis. These governments are urged to introduce or expand their social protection provisions to lessen human suffering and enhance social stability. At the time of writing there is no sign that these Asian countries are heeding this advice.

On the contrary, there are increasing governmental efforts in some countries to narrow the social safety net in order to reduce social spending as well as the number of people on statutory welfare. The recent example of the Hong Kong Special Administrative Region (SAR)'s effort to reduce social assistance benefits to larger families on welfare is a case in point. This shows that unlike in the pre-crisis era, there is no sense of complacency on the part of the government after the 1997 handover. Instead, there is a general sense of urgency to reinforce financial stability at the expense of social spending. This is a strong endorsement of limited government and a manifest call for self-help.

REFERENCES

Ahuja, Vinod, Bidani, Benu, Ferreira, Francisco & Walton, Michael (1997). Everyone's Miracle? Revisiting Poverty and Inequality in East Asia. New York: World Bank.

Cloward, R. & Piven, F. (1972). Regulating the Poor. New York: Columbia University Press.

Esping-Andersen, Gosta (1997). Welfare States in Transition: National Adaptations in Global Economies. Thousand Oaks, California: Sage.

Estes, Richard (1987). Social Development Trends in the Pacific.Social Development Issues, Volume 11, Number 2, pp. 3-19.

Grandea, Nona (1995). Overview. In Robert Clarke (ed), Partnerships for a New Agenda: Human Resource Development and Poverty Alleviation in the APEC Region (pp. 1-10). Halifax, Canada: Lester Pearson International Institute & the North-South Institute of Ottawa.

Ismael, Jacqueline & Hill, Enid (Eds) (1997). Social Work and Social Development: Asian Experiences. Calgary: Detselig Enterprises Ltd.

International Labour Organization (1998). The Asian Financial Crisis: The Challenge for Social Policy. Geneva: Author.

Jayasuriya, Laksiri (1996). Citizenship and Welfare: Rediscovering Marshall. Australian Journal of Social Issues, 31(1): February, 19-38.

Marshall, T.H. (1963). Sociology at the crossroads and other essays. London: Heinemann.

Midgley, James (1996). Towards a Developmental Model of Social Policy: Relevance of the Third World Experience. Journal of Sociology and Social Welfare, Volume 23, Number 2, 59-74.

Midgley, James (1995). Social Development. Thousand Oaks, California: Sage.

Mishra, Ramesh (1977). Society and Social Policy. London: MacMillan.

Mulluly, Bob (1998). Structural Social Work. New York: Oxford University Press.

Rodger, Gerry, Gore, Charles & Figueiredo, Jose (1995). Social Exclusion: Rhetoric, Reality and Responses. Geneva: International Institute for Labor Studies.

Tang, Kwong-leung (1996). Social Security and Social Development: East Asian Newly Industrializing Countries, Canadian Review of Social Policy/Revue canadienne de politique sociale, Issue 38, November, pp. 56-71.

World Bank (1997). World Development Report 1997: The State in a Changing World. New York: Oxford University Press.

JOE C. B. LEUNG

CHAPTER ONE

MOVING TOWARD XIAOKANG IN CHINA

INTRODUCTION

Between 1978 and 1995, China's GDP grew at an average rate of 9.4% a year, and an average growth rate of 6.5% is expected in the coming decade. Indisputably, China's economic performance has been phenomenal. Yet with a GNP per capita of US$655 in 1996, China is still classified as a poor nation. Rapid economic reforms have posed an intriguing question for social development analysts: What happens to social development in a country with a market-oriented economy and a socialist political structure? At first glance, great strides have been made in social development, notably in life expectancy (70 years), mortality rate (6 per 1000 population), infant mortality rate (36 per 1000 population), and literacy rate (75%) (State Statistical Bureau, 1997). Indeed, the success of economic reforms has brought along substantial improvement in the quality of life of the majority of the people in China. With the rapid liberalization of the economic structure, however, social concerns such as poverty, family breakdown, rural migrants, school drop-outs, unemployment, prostitution, drug addiction, juvenile delinquency, the care of abandoned children, the elderly, the physically disabled and the mentally ill have become more critical. This chapter introduces the philosophy and strategy of social development espoused by Deng Xiaoping, and focuses on some of the unresolved issues, namely demographic crises, declining poverty and widening income disparities.

MARKET-ORIENTED REFORMS: DISMANTLING THE 'IRON RICE BOWL'

For decades after coming to power in 1949, China adopted a Soviet model of social welfare which centered on the workplace. Whether a factory in an urban area, or a commune in the countryside, the work unit (collectives) functioned as a self-sufficient 'welfare society' within which an individual received life-long employment and basic income protection, and enjoyed benefits and services in areas such as housing, food, education, recreational activities and health care (Schurmann, 1971; Walder, 1986; Oi, 1989; Leung and Nann, 1995; Shaw, 1996). Most of these services were either free of charge (non-contributory) or inexpensive. The commitment of the work units to 'high welfare' was perceived as necessary to

K.-L. Tang (ed.), Social Development in Asia, 11–22.

compensate for the inadequacy of the economic system which pursued a policy of 'low wages and high employment.' While there were substantial differences between rural and urban welfare, and between different work units, the basic policy within each work unit was largely egalitarian, and attempts were made to minimize differences in wages, welfare and employment.

As this welfare system is 'collective-centered' rather than 'state-centered', the role of the state at the macro-level was to provide a stable order within which the collectives could develop and fulfill the functions of political education, economic production and welfare service provision. The collectives were controlled by the state through central planning and redistribution, and also were somewhat protected. For example, the state would provide subsidies or credits to cover losses. At the individual level, the state ensured that citizens belonged to a collective through household registration which limited rural-urban migration, and job assignment which controlled the recruitment and mobility of workers. For the few people outside a collective, the state provided a remedial welfare program for the 'three nos': those with no family, no source of income, and no working ability. The domination of the work unit-centered welfare had rendered social services organized by non-governmental charities and government departments unnecessary.

Under Mao Zedong, social problems such as prostitution, begging, venereal diseases, illiteracy, delinquency, drug addiction, and unemployment were either eliminated or substantially reduced. Through the policies of full employment, reduced income differentials, control over wages and prices of essential commodities, China attained high levels of public health, education, and social welfare (1). Furthermore, income inequalities were low, especially in cities. The Gini coefficient in 1978 was only 0.31 (0.19 in cities) (Griffin and Zhao, 1994). These achievements were better than those of countries with similar levels of economic development. According to estimates by the United Nations, the economic development of China was ranked only 107th among 150 countries in 1970-75, but the Physical Quality of Life Index (literacy rate, infant mortality, and life expectancy) was 68th (Wu, 1995, p.42).

With the market-oriented economic reforms after 1978, the egalitarian-oriented and needs-based welfare system established by Mao has come under severe criticism. The major assaults are on the 'iron rice bowl', or job security, which is regarded as an impediment to the promotion of economic productivity and work incentives. Distribution, according to Deng Xiaoping, can no longer be based on need, but on labor effort, supplemented by other means of distribution such as ownership of land and capital. Furthermore, differences in pay should be widened so as to encourage individual enthusiasm and speed up the development of production, and the major policy is to allow some people to become wealthy first, as part of the goal of common prosperity (Beijing Review, April 15-21, 1991, p.v).

Under the primacy of economic growth, Deng designed a 'three-stage' development strategy. The first stage was to double the 1980's per capita GNP by the year 1990, and the basic problem of feeding the population should then be resolved. By the year 2000, China, after doubling the 1990's GNP per capita, would attain Xiaokang, a level of living standard marked by a relatively comfortable standard of living with adequate, though not extravagant, food, housing and clothing. The traditional Confucian ideal of Xiaokang refers to a society which has eliminated poverty. In the third step, China aims to become an affluent society comparable to other middle-income nations by the middle of the next century (Lu, 1991; State Statistical Bureau, 1992; Yin, 1994; Yan, 1996; Zhao, 1996).

Meanwhile, the term Xiaokang has been mentioned in the Eighth Five-Year Plan (1990-1995) and the 14th Party Congress in 1992, referring to a level of living standard where the basic livelihood, consumption patterns, housing conditions, cultural life, health levels, and social services have been improved (Yin, 1994, p.2). The Ten-Year Program Plan of Development (1990-2000) stipulated the goals of Xiaokang:

> The standard of living will improve, with China having comfortable levels of food and clothing. The means of subsistence will be plentiful and consumption patterns more reasonable. Housing conditions will be remarkably improved, cultural life further enriched and the people's health continuously improved. Social service facilities will be continuously developed (Beijing Review, May 6-12, 1991, p.14).

China accepts that social development is an integral part of economic development, and economic growth is a prerequisite to improvement in the quality of life. Apparently, the national development of China focuses primarily on economic growth through improving productivity and attracting foreign investment. But in practice, Chinese leadership also stresses social stability, and social development is considered a mechanism to mitigate social tensions brought on by rapid economic reforms.

INCREMENTAL AND DECENTRALIZED REFORM STRATEGIES

To facilitate market reforms, China disbanded the communes in 1983, and individual families then had to bear the brunt of responsibility for protection against contingencies. In urban areas, employment guarantees were removed in 1986 through the introduction of the contract worker system, bankruptcy law, open market for labor recruitment, and dismissal procedures. In social security, individuals were encouraged to contribute to social insurance schemes for retirement and medical care (Leung and Nann, 1995; Chow, 1996).

On the whole, Chinese social reform is guided more by pragmatic concerns than by a clear visionary direction and comprehensive developmental blueprint. In launching the reforms, Deng's method was to 'grope for stones to cross the river.' In China, reform tends to be incremental, trial and error and piecemeal, rather than employing a 'shock therapy' approach based on introducing radical changes. Assuming the role of macro-control at the top, the central government delineates broad guiding principles for reform. These principles are indicative rather than mandatory and universal. As the government explains the shift in the function of state planning:

> Government plans have been geared to the market, with guidance planning replacing compulsory planning, a shift in government emphasis from direct to indirect control, and a focus on long- and medium-term planning (Beijing Review, September 18-24, 1995,

p.14).

At the bottom level, local governments are encouraged to experiment with different solutions and models according to local conditions and capacity. After some years of continuous experimentation and evaluation, the government publicizes and promotes successful experiences or models through legislation, which often can be implemented flexibly according to local schedules (Guo, 1996). The strength of this approach is that it can minimize resistance and facilitate readjustments through feedback from program implementation. The shortcoming is that regional disparities in social development can be substantial.

In the 1990s, the central government issued a series of laws and white papers related to social development. Examples of these laws include: The Law on the Protection of the Disabled (1991), the Law on the Protection of the Juvenile (1991), the Law on Adoption (1992), the Law on the Protection of the Rights of Women (1992), the Labor Law (1994), the Law on Maternal and Infant Health Care (1994), and the Law on the Protection of the Rights and Interests of the Elderly (1996). Examples of the white papers and program plans include: National Program of Action for Child Development in China (1992), White Paper on the Situation of Women in China (1994), The Report of the People's Republic of China on the Implementation of the Nairobi Forward-looking Strategies for the Advancement of Women (1994), and White Paper on the Situation of Children in China (1996). These laws and plans acknowledge the rights and needs of vulnerable populations. For example, according to the Labor Law (1994), all enterprises should conform to a prescribed standard in working conditions (minimum wage, holidays, working hours, safety standards, etc.), welfare (pensions and unemployment insurance), and protection of women and children . However, they also prescribe that the primary responsibility for providing care to those people in need lies with the family. For example, the Law on the Protection of the Rights and Interests of the Elderly reiterated the legal obligations of adults to take care of the financial, medical, housing and social needs of their elderly parents and parents-in-law (Leung, 1997).

In pursing an open door policy, China is linked not only economically and politically to the outside world, but also in social life as well. In abandoning the traditional policy of self-reliance, it is now more open to assistance from international organization such as Oxfam, the Red Cross and World Vision whose programs include relief in natural calamities, agricultural loans, educational sponsorship, medical operations, staff training, equipment donations, and overseas adoption. According a report from the World Bank, China is now its largest borrower. In receiving outside assistance, the plight of the disadvantaged is open to scrutiny by foreign journalists and human rights groups. China has reiterated that the right to subsistence is regarded as the foremost human right, as compared with political and economic rights. Yet because of international pressure, the Chinese Government has to pay more attention to the rights of the poor, the disabled, the unemployed, orphans, victims of natural disasters, prisoners and women.

SOCIAL DEVELOPMENT INDICATORS: ACHIEVEMENTS AND SHORTFALLS

Since 1987, the Chinese Academy of Social Sciences has used social development indicators as a basis for measuring national development as a whole and development in different regions and provinces. The first set of 16 indicators is divided into three major areas, namely economic conditions, living standards, and consumption patterns. These indicators are used to evaluate the development of China as compared with other nations in the world. China's ranking among 120 countries has moved upwards slightly from 70th in 1987 to 66th in 1993 (Zhu, 1996). The areas of social development that China has done well in are life expectancy, literacy, natural growth, and per capita fat consumption. China has performed poorly in the level of urbanization, proportion of the labor force in the tertiary industry, proportion of GDP allocated for education, protein consumption, and the Engel coefficient. For instance in 1995, only 30% of the population was officially classified as living in cities, and 24% of the labor force was employed in tertiary industry. These figures are low even when compare with other developing countries. Another project carried out by Chinese demographic researchers on the quality of life showed that China ranked 36th among 58 nations which had provided complete data on quality of life indicators. China belonged to the middle-lower category, similar to the Philippines, Mexico, Brazil and Peru (Feng and Dai, 1996).

Based on the Human Development Index, the United Nations Development Program ranked China at 111st among 174 countries in human development (Zhu, 1996). The report, Progress of Nations, published by UNICEF, praised the advances of China in improving primary school enrollment, in providing basic health care services and in advancing the status of children. But it claimed that nearly 400 million people do not have access to safe drinking water, and 76% of the population still lacks access to safe sanitation. Among developing nations, China has the highest number of cases of diarrhea per year among children under five (South China Morning Post, July 25, 1997, p.10).

Another set of 36 indicators is used to assess and compare social development among provinces. These indicators are divided into six categories, namely, social structure, level of education, economic efficiency, quality of life, social order, and social stability. The coastal provinces and the three municipalities (Beijing, Shanghai and Tianjin) were top on the list, whereas the interior provinces of Guizhou, Yunnan and Gansu were at the bottom (Zhu, 1995a; 1995b; 1996).

According to official estimates, China's large cities have already attained Xiaokang in terms of the social development indicators targeted for the year 2000. Even though social development expectations for the rural areas are much lower than those in the urban areas, Chinese officials have admitted that it is an unrealistic target for the rural areas to attain Xiaokang even by the year 2000 (Hong Kong Economic Journal, December 5, 1994, p.6). As they have in economic development, the coastal provinces and the municipalities have made greater strides than other areas in social development too. These widening differences, particularly among provinces is a worrisome concern to the central government.

Notwithstanding some significant improvement, the level of education remains low. In 1995, there were only 2,040 persons per 100,000 people with college education. Although the Nine-Year Compulsory Education Law has been in effect since 1986, 18.3 million children aged between 6 and 14 left school without completing their primary education in 1995. Among the Chinese, the average number of years of education received is only 5.1 (6.1 for male and 4 for female). In cities, the number is 7.1 years, whereas it is only 4.3 years in villages (Wu, 1995, p.45). Some 145.4 million people over the age of 15 remain illiterate, and 70% of them are female. Even though the Chinese Government has pledged to wipe out illiteracy among young people by the year 2000, government expenditures allocated to education in 1996 were only 2.4% of the GDP, or 16.3% of annual government expenditures (Hong Kong Economic Journal, October 13, 1997, p.7).

In 1996, the official urban unemployment rate was only 3 per cent, representing only 5.5 million people. But some estimates put the figures at 18 per cent, or 27.5 million people who are either out of work or not being paid by their ailing state-owned enterprises (South China Morning Post, June 8, 1997, p.5). Even worse, if the 150 million surplus rural workers who are ready to move into cities for jobs are included, the problem of unemployment reaches a crisis level (Leung, 1996). Among the unemployed, the situation is more critical for vulnerable populations such as women, the young, the old and the disabled. To alleviate the intractable problem of rising unemployment, the government has established job referral and re-training centers, introduced the five-day work week, facilitated the export of workers to overseas countries, and encouraged the development of rural industries which already employ over 130 million peasants.

DEMOGRAPHIC CRISIS

In the coming decade, China is approaching a demographic crisis which affects the quality of social development. The One-child Policy implemented in the 1980s has gradually changed China's demographic structure (Banister, 1987; Peng, 1991; Goldstein and Wang, 1996). In 1996, the birth rate has been stabilized at 16.98 per 1000, and the death rate at 6.56 per 1000, resulting in a natural growth rate of 10.42 per 1000 (State Statistical Bureau, 1997). Still, because of the enormous population base (1,224 million people), China has a net annual population increase of 13 million people. Given the present rate of increase, the population of China will inevitably reach 1.3 billion by the year 2000. Their enormous population has often been perceived by the Chinese Government as an impediment to achieving a higher pace of economic and social development.

Since China is geographically so large, regional variations in population characteristics reflecting the difference in socio-economic development are inevitable. In natural growth rate, Shanghai, due to the effectiveness of the One-child policy, has seen negative population growth since 1993 (-1.3 per 1000 in 1995), whereas in Tibet, the growth rate was 16.1 per 1000 in 1995. Life expectancy at birth in Shanghai was 75 years, but only 59 in Tibet, a difference of 16 years. On average, life expectancy in the countryside is lower than the city by 4 years (Wu, 1995, p.5).

The declining mortality rate has extended life expectancy to 70.8 years (male, 68.71; female, 73.04). The proportions of the population aged 0-14, 15-64, and 65 and over are 26.4%, 67.2%, and 6.4% respectively. The implications are threefold. First, the supply of labor and the demands for jobs in the coming years will be tremendous. Second, now almost three quarters of families are nuclear families; the average household size in 1996 was 3.7 persons, down from 4.4 persons in 1982. Smaller family size means there are fewer potential caregivers to dependents in the family. Third, the elderly population will rise to 7% of the national population by the year 2000, and to 12.9% by the year 2025. China will soon become an aging society, and the implications for health and social services are colossal. The dependency ratio, that is, the ratio between the aged population and the number of people in the labor force, increased from 8.33 in 1989 to 10.06 in 1995 (State Statistical Bureau, 1996, p.73). What worries the Chinese Government most is the rate of increase in the proportion of elderly people. It took only 20 years for China's elderly population to inrease from 5% to 7% of the national population. In the early days of other developed countries, similar increases took at least 50 years (Tian, 1990, p.42). A recent World Bank report claimed that China is facing a pension crisis as more people are retiring in the coming years (South China Morning Post, September 19, 1997, p.1).

China is convinced that only economic growth can provide the country with sustainable development. Yet improvement in the quality of life can only be achieved when population growth is under control. Otherwise, population increases, with its accompanying increases in demands for food, education, and employment, will inevitably jeopardize the benefits of economic growth (Yi, 1996). Yet the draconian population policy has other unintended consequences. Riots have been reported in the countryside of Guangdong because officials had imposed heavy fines on families violating the One-child Policy (South China Morning Post, September 8, 1997, p.8). Because of the tenacious traditional desire for sons, incidents of infanticides, neglect, maltreatment and malnutrition of female infants have been reported (South China Morning Post, September 26, 1997, p.12).

DECLINING POVERTY AND WIDENING INCOME DISPARITIES

One major concern that has come with the economic reform is the widening of income disparities. The policy of intensive development in coastal provinces, Special Economic Zones and cities has created significant disparities in the income and the living standards between rural and urban areas, geographical regions and economic sectors. In the mid-1980s, the income of the top 20% income group was only 5 to 6 times the bottom 20%. But the difference has increased to 12 times by 1994. Likewise, the Gini coefficient, as a measurement of income inequality, has increased from 0.31 in 1979 to 0.38 in 1988, and further to 0.43 in 1994 (Wu, et al., 1995; Li, 1996).

Except in the first few years of the decollectivization reforms, the income of the peasant population did not seem to improve significantly. The ratio of the annual per capita income in the cities and in the rural areas widened from 1.24: 1 in 1978 to

2.27: 1 in 1996. Most peasants are not entitled to pensions and medical care insurance. Per capita expenditure on the medical care of urban residents is four times that of peasants (Ming Pao, September 22, 1997, p.11).

In terms of regional differences, the ratio between peasants in eastern, central and western provinces in 1980 was 1.39: 1.11: 1. The ratio became 2.25: 1.75: 1 in 1993. In cities, the ratio was widened from 1.15: 0.88: 1 to 2: 1.32: 1 in 1995. Likewise, the differences between regions in social development are expected to widen further in the coming years (Guo, 1996, p.58). The Chinese leadership has pledged to increase support for the central and western regions by giving them priority in planning infrastructure and resources development projects, instituting, step by step, a standard payment transfer system, and encouraging both Chinese and overseas investors to invest in the regions (South China Morning Post, September 13, 1997, p.8).

Among different economic sectors, employees in joint ventures are getting higher salaries and welfare benefits than those in state-owned and collectively-owned enterprises. In 1995, the average per capita annual wages in joint ventures and privately-owned enterprises, state-owned enterprises, and collectively-owned enterprises were 7,463 yuan (1 US$ is equal to 8.3 yuan), 5,625 yuan and 3,931 yuan respectively; and in pensions, 5,682 yuan, 5,575 yuan and 3,356 yuan respectively (State Statistical Bureau, 1996, p.116). Currently, a group of high-income, middle-class people, composed of individual entrepreneurs, joint venture managers, and recreational performers (singers and movie stars) is burgeoning (Chinese Academy of Social Sciences, 1997).

Under Mao, there was no official measurement of the extent of poverty. Based on an annual average cost of 120 yuan for a minimum caloric intake, and using Engel's coefficient which defines basic expenses exceeding 60% of total income as poverty-stricken, the government set the poverty line at 200 yuan in 1984. Accordingly, 15.1% of the rural population, or 128 million people were living in poverty at that time. Based on a similar calculation, the poverty line in 1978 was set at 100 yuan, and 250 million people, representing 26% of the national population, were defined as being poverty-stricken at that time (Zhao, 1996; Beijing Review, August 12-18, 1996, pp.12-15). As such, the official poverty line refers to an absolute subsistence level of living.

In 1986, the State Council established the Leading Group Office of Poverty Alleviation and Development. The primary task of the Group was to formulate policies and plans to assist those underdeveloped regions. In some poverty-stricken regions, local leading groups on poverty alleviation were established. The coordinating work of the Office at the national level, which focuses on regional poverty alleviation, is described as 'macro-level poverty alleviation'. The work with specific poverty-stricken households is the responsibility of the civil affairs departments, and is called 'micro-level poverty alleviation'.

In 1991, the Office worked jointly with the World Bank to conduct a survey on China's poverty-stricken areas (World Bank, 1992). The survey identified 679 counties (31% of the total 2,194 counties) with 100 million people (13.4% of the rural population) as poverty-stricken. Their annual per capita income was between

150 and 300 yuan. Some 80% of the poverty-stricken population lived in the western (45.7%) and central provinces (31%). Ethnic minorities only constitute less than 8% of the national population, but they account for 40% of the poverty-stricken population (Kang, 1996, p.5). More importantly, the criteria used by the Chinese Government to define a poverty-stricken region is not solely based on income level. In fact, old revolutionary bases and areas with high numbers of ethnic minorities, for political reasons, are often included in the list of poverty-stricken regions requiring direct state assistance (Zhu, 1994; Kang, 1996).

China proudly claimed that between 1978 and 1995 some 185 million poverty-stricken people had been assisted out of poverty (Beijing Review, August 12-18, 1996, pp.12-15; March 24-30, 1997, p.16-23). In 1996, the number of people living in poverty has dropped further to 58 million (The poverty line was set at a per capita income of 530 yuan a year). But the World Bank estimated, using the international poverty standard of US$1 per person per day, that 350 million people, just under one-third of the Chinese population lived in poverty (South China Morning Post, 10 May 1997, p.9). The work of the government in poverty-stricken regions includes investment in transportation, industrialization, electricification and irrigation work. Assistance to individual poverty-stricken households includes the provision of loans, information, technologies, training and employment, tax exemption and reduction, and subsidized school education.

In 1994, the Chinese Government pledged to launch a seven-year program to eliminate poverty in the rural areas before the year 2000. The 'Chinese War on Poverty' campaign identified 592 impoverished counties which required direct state assistance (Wei, 1996, p.323). To this end, an average of 11 million poverty-stricken people have to be assisted out of poverty each year. Based on the experiences of the first two years, only 5 million people are likely to be out of poverty each year, and often many of them can easily fall back into poverty conditions (Ming Pao, September 24, 1996, p.12). Furthermore, it is reported that about one-quarter of the relief fund in 1994 due to mismanagement and corruption has not been properly spent on relief work (Oriental Daily, 19 July 1995, p.9).

According to figures from the State Statistical Bureau, the number of poor people living in cities reached 11.76 million, or 3.3% of the urban population in 1996. The poverty line for urban areas was set at a per capita annual income of 1,700 yuan. Their average per capita annual income was only 1,321 yuan which was equivalent to 30% of the per capita income of an average urban resident. Some 85% of these urban poor lived in economically backward cities in central and western regions. Some 84% of them became poor because of unemployment (Beijing Review, May 19-25, 1997, p.6).

In recent years, the government has improved traditional social assistance program which only provided assistance to 'three nos people'. The new program, called the 'Minimum Living Standard Guarantee System' provides assistance to the unemployed and low-income families with income falling below the defined poverty line. Up to now, 116 cities, mainly coastal and economically more prosperous ones, have established the program, representing one-sixth of the total number of cities in China. About 900,000 people have received assistance from the program, 62% of them in Shanghai (Hong Kong Economic Journal, April 11, 1997, p.9; Ministry of Civil Affairs, 1997, p.240).

CONCLUSION

With the collapse of socialism as the guiding developmental ideology and the emergence of a more pluralistic and market-oriented economy, work units, organizations, local governments, neighborhoods and individuals can now have more autonomy. In a gradually depoliticizing society, political ideology has been playing a less central role in defining social problems and their solutions. The government can no longer rely on vague political promises, political education, propaganda, mass mobilization or top-down coercive disciplinary action to alleviate social problems and satisfy social needs. Economic decentralization and marketization has also reduced the capacity of the central government to control societal resources, and has in a way, even discouraged government intervention. Facing perennial budget deficits, soaring international debt, and a declining share of national revenue, the ability of the central government to direct social development in a unified and concerted direction is rapidly eroding. Meanwhile, the government, in diminishing its regulatory role in the livelihood of the ordinary people, is more willing to share its responsibility in social development with the family, individuals, neighborhoods and private enterprises. This developmental direction is summarized under the slogan of 'small government and big society' and 'socialization'. In practice, the government has to rely more on private charities, non-governmental organizations and self-help initiatives to cope with unmet social needs. For example, the China Youth Development Foundation launched Project Hope to help dropouts in deprived areas return to school. The China Charity Foundation raises funds for work with orphans and disabled children (Beijing Review, March 25-31, 1996, p.13-15).

Rapid economic reforms can create social tensions leading to social instability. Not surprisingly, industrial and rural unrest has been reported from time to time. In the countryside, peasants are complaining about excessive taxes, fees and fines, as well as the inability of the local governments to pay contracted prices for their grain (South China Morning Post, November 9, 1996, p.8; August 26, 1997, p.1). In cities, workers are protesting against massive layoffs, delayed payment of wages and pensions, soaring food prices, and land requisitions for redevelopment (South China Morning Post, November 28, 1996, p.9; August 31, 1997, p.8; October 13, 1997, p.8). Because of the social risks it is facing, the Chinese Government has to slow down economic reforms and must intervene from time to time using social welfare programs to mitigate social conflicts. Yet most of these emergent welfare programs are decentralized, operated by local and neighborhood governments. Therefore, social development will only just muddle through, with piecemeal and pragmatic steps, and profound regional variations are inevitable. Finally, the legitimacy and governing mandate of the Communist Party will be at stake if it fails to deliver the promise of an abundant future and meets the rising expectations of the people.

ENDNOTES

(1) The World Bank praised the effort of the Chinese Government in limiting urban poverty to extremely low levels through a system of full employment, linked to narrow ranges of earned income, coupled with heavy subsidization and price controls on basic foodstuffs and housing and near universal access to education and health care (World Bank, 1992, p.2).
(2) The Human Development Index is used by the United Nations Development Program to assess relative levels of human development in various countries. It combines three measures: life expectancy, literacy rate and average income based on purchasing power parity.
(3) This figure only includes the urban population (with non-agricultural household registration status), aged between 15 and 50 years old, who although willing to work, were unemployed and registered in local employment centers.
(4) Expenditures on welfare in work units jumped from 7.8 billionyuan in 1978 (13.7% of total wages) to 236.1 billion yuan in 1995 (29.2% of total wages). Money spent onretirees accounts for 65.3% of total welfare expenses. The number of retirees receiving pensions grew from 3.1 million in 1978 to 30.9 million in 1995, and the ratio of employees to retirees decreased from 30:1 to 4.8:1 over the same period (State Statistical Bureau, 1996, pp.733-735).
(5) The Chinese government does not use the same income measurement for peasants and urban residents. Therefore the measurement of income difference here represents only a general picture. The annual per capita disposable income for urban households was 4,377yuan in 1996, up 13 per cent over the previous year, or a real growth of 3.8 per cent after excluding inflation. The per capita net income of rural households was 1,926 yuan, up 22 per cent, and the real growth was 9 per cent (State Statistical Bureau, 1997).
(6) The success in reducing the poverty-stricken population was phenomenal, particularly in the beginning years. Poverty rates declined from about one-third of the rural population in 1978 to one-tenth by 1985. However, reductions have slowed since the mid-1980s.
(7) In a strict sense, there are no non-governmental organizations inChina which enjoy a high degree of autonomy, and with leaders not appointed by the government (Leung, 1994; Yamamoto, 1995).

REFERENCES

Banister, J. (1987). China's Changing Population. Stanford: Stanford University Press.

Beijing Review. Beijing.

Chow, N. (1996). Social Security Reform in China - An Attempt to Construct a Socialist Security System with Chinese Characteristics. In Wong, L. and MacPherson, S. (Eds.). Social Change and Social Policy in Contemporary China. Aldershot: Avebury, pp.27-49.

Chinese Academy of Social Sciences (1997). Study on the Problem of Income Distribution. Management World (Guanli Shijie), 2, 64-71.

Feng, L. T. and Dai, X. Y. (1996). The Quality of Life of the Chinese Population Revisited (Zhongquo Renhou Shenhuo Ziliang Zhai Yanjiu). Beijing: Higher Educational Publishers.

Goldstein, A. and Wang, F. (1996). The Many Facets of Demographic Change. Boulder, Col.:Westview Press.

Griffin, K. and Zhao, R. W. (1993). The Distribution of Income in China. New York: St. Martin's Press.

Guo, J. Y. (1996). Social Development in China: The Blueprint (ZhongquoShehui Fazhen Lanpishu). Kunming: Yunnan People's Publishers.

Hong Kong Economic Journal. Hong Kong.

Kang, X. G. (1996). The Problem of Poverty in China and Anti-poverty Theories (ZhongquoPinkun yu Fan Pinkun Lilun). Nanning: Guangxi People's Publishers.

Leung, J. (1994). The Emergence of Non-governmental Welfare Organizations in China: Problems and Issues. The Asian Journal of Public Administration, 16.2, 209-223.

Leung, J. (1996). The Emergence of Unemployment Insurance in China: Problems and Issues.Canadian Review of Social Policy, 38, 5-17.

Leung, J. (1997). Family Support for the Elderly in China: Issues and Challenges. Journal of Aging and Social Policy, 9.3. (in press)

Leung, J. and Nann, R. (1995). Authority and Benevolence: Social Welfare in China. Hong Kong: Chinese University Press.

Li, Q. (1996). An Analysis on the Income Disparity, Poverty Class, and Social Equity. New Horizon (Xin Shiye), 5, 15-18.
Li, P. L. (1995). Social Stratification in the Market Transition in China (ZhongquoXin Shiji Jieji Jieceng Baogao). Shenyang: Liaoning People's Publishers.
Lu, X. Y. (1991). China's Xiaokang Society in the Year 2000 (2000Nian Zhongquo de Xiaokang Shehui). Nanchang: Jiangxi People's Publishers.
Ming Pao. Hong Kong.
Ministry of Civil Affairs (1997). China Civil Affairs Statistical Yearbook (ZhongquoMinzheng Tongji Nianjian). Beijing: Ministry of Civil Affairs.
Oi, J. (1989). State and Peasant in Contemporary China: The Political Economy of Village Government. Berkeley: University of California Press.
Oriental Daily. Hong Kong.
Peng, X. (1991). Demographic Transition in China: Fertility Trends since the 1950s. New York: Oxford University Press.
Schurmann, F. (1971). Ideology and Organization in Communist China. Berkeley: University of California Press.
Shaw, V. (1996). Social Control in Chinaz: A Study of Chinese Work Units. Westport: Praeger Publishers.
South China Morning Post. Hong Kong.
State Statistical Bureau (1992). China Xiaokang Standard (Zhongquo Xiaokang Biaozhun). Beijing: State Statistical Publishers.
State Statistical Bureau (1996). China Statistical Yearbook 1996. Beijing: State Statistical Publishers.
State Statistical Bureau (1997). "Statistical Communique on Socio-economic Development in 1996," Beijing Review, March 10-16, 23-34.
Tian, X. Y. (1990). China's Elderly Population and Society (Zhongquo Laoren Renhao yu Shehui). Beijing: China Economic Publishers.
Walder, A. (1986). Communist Neo-traditionalism, Work and Authority in China's Industry. Berkeley: University of California Press.
Wei, L. Q. (1996). 1996-2010 Research Report on the Comprehensive Development Strategies in China (1996-2010 Nian Zhongquo Shehui Quanmian Fazhan ZhanlueYanjiu Baogao). Shenyang: Liaoning People's Publishers.
World Bank (1992). China, Strategies for Reducing Poverty in the 1990s. Washington, DC: The World Bank.
Wu, C. P. (1995). The Report on Changing Popûlation and Development in China (ZhuanbianZhong de Zhongquo Renkou yu Fazhan Zong Baogao). Beijing: Higher Education Publishers.
Wu, A. G., Wang, S. G. and Kang, X. G. (1995). Regional Disparities in China (ZhongguoDiqu Chaju Baogao). Shenyang: Liaoning People's Publishers.
Yamamoto, T. (1995). (ed.). Emerging Civil Society in the Asia Pacific Regional Community. Singapore: The Institute of Southeast Asian Studies.
Yan, L. T. (1996). Discussion on China's Xiaokang Society (Zhongguo Xiaokang Shehui Lun). Beijing: People's Publishers.
Yi, L. Q. (1996). A Study on the Full-scale Development Strategies of China (Zhongquo Shehui Quanmian Fazhan Zhanlue Yanjiu Baogao). Shenyang: Liaoning People's Publishers.
Yin, S. J. (1994). Study on China's Xiaokang Level (Zhongquo Xiaokang Shuiping Yanjiu). Changsha: Wunan Publishers.
Zhao, Z. K. (1996). Deng Xiaoping: Social Development Strategy (Deng Xiaoping Shehui Fazhan Zhanlue). Kunming: Yunnan People's Publishers.
Zhu, L. (1994). Use of Work to Replace Relief and the Relief of Poverty (Yi Gong Dai Zheng yu Huanjie). Shanghai: Sanluen Publishers.
Zhu, Q. F. (1995a). The Modernization Ranking of China in the World. Modernization (Xiandaihua), 11, 4-5.
Zhu, Q. F. (1995b). An Assessment on China's Social Development Level in 1992. China's Population Resources and Environment (Zhongquo Renkuo Ziyuan yu Huanjing), 1, 81-85.
Zhu, Q. F. (1996). An Assessment on the Level of Socio-economic Development in the 188 cities in China. City Problems (Chengshi Wenti), 1, 38-42.

JAMES K. C. LEE

CHAPTER TWO

BALANCING COLLECTIVIZATION AND INDIVIDUAL RESPONSIBILITY: HONG KONG SOCIAL POLICY UNDER THE CHINESE REGIME

INTRODUCTION

The social welfare system in Hong Kong is widely acknowledged as rather residual in nature, where social policies are meant for the unfortunate few who happen to be least able to help themselves during a certain vulnerable point in life (McLaughlin, 1993; Chow 1995). The social assistance system (the Comprehensive Social Security Assistance scheme) merely serves to provide a basic level of financial and material help to ailing families on a temporary basis. The government has always stressed that the welfare system should not create dependence and work disincentives. It is there to help unfortunate individuals, but not to be relied upon as a means of livelihood. A wage-earning job and a full employment policy are still widely regarded as the most important welfare guarantee for individuals and families. Sustainable economic growth and a highly productive labor force are still considered the keys to welfare and quality of life. 'Hong Kong is not and would not want to claim that it is a welfare state, since the very term is regarded as distasteful and dangerous' (Wilding, 1997).

Although the above description was to a great extent true in the colonial era (and in many ways is still true of the new Special Administrative Region [SAR] government), the change of sovereignty on 1 July 1997 did bring about unprecedented and unanticipated changes to both the society and the economy. The downward trend in the socio-economic paths of the Pacific Rim countries in the 1990s and, in particular, the Asian economic turmoil in the latter part of 1997, have fundamentally changed the growth path of these once active economies. Since May 1998, Hong Kong has seen unemployment rising to 4.2%, the highest since 1975, with 128,000 people laid-off for the period March 1997 through May 1998 (1). The Government has recently revised the 1998 growth estimate from 3.5% to -2%, the first negative growth year since 1985 (2). While the Financial Secretary suggested that Hong Kong has perhaps been the first to get back to its feet since October 1997, many now believe it will take some years before the economy will fully recover from the economic turmoil. To quote a Newsweek feature, 'Hong Kong has lost its edge

K.-L. Tang (ed.), Social Development in Asia, 23–38.

with the opening up of China' (3). This time the direct impact of the Asian meltdown on Hong Kong has not simply affected the low-income class. The middle class has also been hard-hit, particularly when property values have shrunk by nearly 50%, with a small number of people experiencing negative equity for the first time.

How does the economic downturn affect social life? Does Hong Kong's social policy live up to the challenges of this trying period? This chapter will explore the answers to these questions. In particular, it is argued that the existing residual welfare system that has been workable for the last three decades might not be able to meet the needs of a declining economy. The reason lies in the fact that a welfare model that is so dependent on full employment and economic growth makes social policy highly vulnerable and negates the very nature of social protection. To fully explore the fragility of the Hong Kong social welfare system, this chapter will examine three major aspects of social policy: (1) the uniqueness of the Hong Kong social policy model (why it worked); (2) balancing collectivization and individualization in welfare (how it works) (3) the dilemma and vulnerability of the current social policy model (whether it will continue to work). In particular, three major policy areas will be examined: housing, education and health. It is suggested that in order to maintain social stability, the government has deliberately chosen these three policy areas to be more universalistic and collective in their mode of consumption. However, with the onset of privatization and public-sector reform in the early 1990s, the government has been placing more emphasis on individualizing welfare. The paper will also examine social security and poverty. It is argued that social security is the most vulnerable part of social policy since the economic maelstrom in 1998 could have done lasting damage to the economy. Individuals and families are now left behind to take up more welfare responsibility. Unless the government begins to establish a new balance in social security consumption, the existing system will soon be overburdened. How should the government respond to this dilemma?

THE UNIQUENESS OF THE HONG KONG SOCIAL POLICY MODEL

'Hong Kong is not a welfare state and it would not be in the interest of the society to become one'. Time and again government officials have reiterated this clear policy statement. What the government is referring to is, of course, the welfare state in a western context, particularly those welfare regimes prevalent in Europe, Canada and Australia, where the state takes over major collective responsibilities for the provision of social services, relying on revenues from a relatively high income tax. Public welfare in Hong Kong, on the other hand, is limited by the very low tax rate and a revenue system banking on substantial receipts from speculative land sales. The Hong Kong welfare model primarily relies on two basic principles: minimalism and economism. The first principle embodies a highly pragmatic approach where public welfare is made available only to those who are least able to help themselves. With the exception of an old age allowance and subsidized hospital services, social policy in Hong Kong is largely selective and means-tested. Thus far, welfare expenditure has been kept at a comparatively low percentage of the economy, and the government has taken great care not to exceed its spending limit. The second principle of economism is more fundamental. Social expenditure must not exceed economic growth. Social policy is practically considered a sub-system of the economy and therefore social welfare should in no way undermine the working of the economy. Any welfare policy which carries the slightest hint of burdening or obstructing the market is seen as antithetical and hence insupportable. The society, the economy and the state have thus developed a clear and consistent anti-welfare rhetoric, effectively forestalling any major change in the welfare function. The lengthy debate on the Central Provident Fund issue in the last two decades is a classic example (4).

The above two principles clearly rest on some important assumptions about the way in which society works, two of which in particular are worth mentioning: first, an emphasis on the work ethic for self and family survival; and second, economic growth through market capitalism. These two sets of belief thus constitute the core value of Hong Kong society. To further elaborate, Wilding (1997) suggested six characteristics which distinguish the Hong Kong welfare model from other welfare systems: (1) work and full-employment must be the central element of welfare since it is the way most people secure income and independence; (2) economic growth must be seen as the basis of welfare; (3) government expenditure must be in line with the rate of economic growth; (4) economic growth is the lubricant of the social system; (5) social policy must be integrated in and adapted to Chinese culture and values; and (6) social policy must only aim at providing a safety net and should set itself a limit. This limit is guided by the belief that there is an equilibrium situation in social expenditure, beyond which dependency and work disincentives would result. The last colonial governor Chris Patten's 1996 Policy Address encapsulates the spirit of Hong Kong social policy most succinctly:

> the Hong Kong welfare system does not exist to iron out inequalities. It does not exist to redistribute income. Our welfare programmes have a different purpose. They exist because this community believe that we have a duty to protect the vulnerable and the disadvantaged members of society, the unfortunate minority, who through no fault of their own, are left behind by the growing prosperity enjoyed by the rest of Hong Kong (The Governor's Annual Policy Address, 22 October 1966).

While Patten's policy statement flies the flag of neo-conservatism and free capitalist pragmatism, some would argue that there is an emerging welfare model in its own right in Hong Kong (Wilding et al., 1997). Although government expenditure in social services does not follow the universalistic pattern of western welfare states, a careful examination actually reveals a pattern of highly collectivized consumption in welfare. In the case of Hong Kong, a collective mode of welfare consumption can be found in public housing, free education and a highly accessible hospital service. Following a unique trajectory, collective provision of subsidized housing is very much characterized by active state intervention. Hong Kong prides itself on the fact that 50% of its housing is subsidized and 38% of its citizens live in public rental housing (see Table 1). Hong Kong spends 2.8% of its GNP on education, taking up 17.4% of total public expenditure. In terms of higher education, Hong Kong now admits 18% of young people reaching university entrance age. This is in stark contrast to only 2% in the early 1970s and represents a major step forward in the collective provision of higher education. Hong Kong now provides universal access to subsidized hospital and clinic services, with provisions largely distributed on the basis of citizenship.

Table 1: Housing Indicators in Hong Kong %

	86	91	96
Home Ownership Rate	38	48	50
(1) private home ownership	62	74	72
(2) government home ownership	11	18	24
Average Household Size (no. of persons)	3.7	3.5	3.4
(1) public housing	4.3	3.9	3.6
(2) private housing	3.3	3.2	3.1
Housing Stock	1.4 m	1.7 m	1.9 m
(1) public rental flats	0.573 m	0.667 m	0.693 m
(2) public home ownership flats	0.066 m	0.131 m	0.21 m
(3) private housing	0.74 m	0.88 m	1.03 m
Living Space			
(1) median occupation density (per person)		7.2 sq m	8.3 sq m
(2) proportion of overcrowded households (per person space below 4.5 sq m)	13.9 sq m	5.1 sq m	2.0 sq m

Source: Housing Authority Housing in Figures 1996

How could all this happen in a capitalism thriving on individualism and opportunity? The theoretical question to be raised here is why a welfare system so much influenced by a residual philosophy and with so much emphasis on self-reliance and government non-intervention should resort to a selective mode of collective consumption. The answer lies in the fact that in order to achieve a high degree of social stability and economic growth within a small city-state, the state has only limited choice in social policy. In order to ensure the smooth reproduction of labor power needed for capitalist production, the state needs to take the lead in the collective provision of some social services which have a direct bearing on labour productivity. To maintain legitimacy, it is essential for the state to collectivize some social polices while maintaining a high degree of selectivity in others (e.g. social security). We shall explore in turn the detailed development of housing, education, health and social security policies in the last two decades.

BALANCING COLLECTIVIZATION AND INDIVIDUALIZATION: THE RELUCTANT COLLECTIVIST IN PUBLIC HOUSING

From the outset, the Hong Kong colonial government took an extremely disinterested and passive attitude towards public housing provision and would have continued to do so had it not been for two very significant historical events: first, the massive influx of immigrants from Mainland China during and after 1949; and second, a fire that broke out on Christmas eve of 1953 at Shek Kip Mei --- an urban slum which for some writers has come to symbolize the genesis of the housing story in Hong Kong (Castells et al., 1990) --- which made thousands of families homeless. The government quickly responded by erecting H-shaped seven-storey resettlement blocks with only communal toilet facilities and water supply in order to resettle the first fire victims and later the large influx of refugees from Mainland China.

The government only began to take housing more seriously in the mid-1960s when the first phase of economic development was badly in need of industrial land which had hitherto been occupied by illegal squatters erecting their own makeshift huts (Smart, 1989). This began a decade of slum clearance around the city fringe, with some of those areas subsequently developed into huge industrial townships, for example Tsuen Wan, Kwai Chung and Kwun Tong. Continuous economic growth and rising income in the early 1970s created more demand for resettlement housing and compelled the government to think more seriously about housing for the future. This period saw the arrival of a new governor, MacLehose, whose government sought to improve both the quality and design of public rental blocks. These blocks had individual toilet and kitchen facilities and marked the first phase of low-cost public rental housing. Throughout the 1950s, 1960s and early 1970s, social housing with state subsidies was seen as the main thrust of the housing system, with home ownership remaining almost entirely the preserve of the private market.

With rising affluence and the hard lessons learnt from the 1967 Riots, the government first started to become involved in the production of public home ownership for the middle-income group in the mid-1970s. The Home Ownership Scheme (HOS) was founded in 1976 on two grounds: first, there was a sector of the community with aspirations to be home owners but who could not afford private housing, and second, a group of better-off tenants needed to be screened out of the public rental sector in order to make way for others on the long waiting list.

Although it proved extremely popular amongst the marginal middle-income group, the government was very cautious about HOS expansion (in 1997 it constituted only 11% of the total housing stock). This reluctance later surfaced in the first housing policy statement in 1987, the Long Term Housing Strategy, which made explicit the government's intention to leave the production and distribution of middle-income housing to the private market. In fact, administratively, the government had already laid down the future commodification of housing by severing the Housing Authority (HA) from the mainstream state bureaucracy in the mid-1970s. The Housing Authority then became an independent statutory organization with full financial autonomy. It received a development loan from the government and acquired land from the state with zero development costs. The Authority is responsible for planning and designing housing developments, determining the level of housing subsidies in rent and generally setting the price level of the HOS. Production is left to private contractors under an open bidding system. In some ways the HA acts like a major developer who seeks to influence housing consumers at the lower end of the housing ladder. However, as our analysis proceeds, it becomes clear that the HA does not really act like a developer because of the underpinning policy that constrains it from competing with private developers.

The above description provides a rough trajectory of housing policy in Hong Kong, characterized first by unplanned responses to critical phases of urban development. Starting out as a process of decommodification, public housing development was seen as instrumental to labour reproduction and development needs during an acute period of economic development. Decommodification shifted to a low gear in the 1980s with the process of commodification emerging during a period of political instability. Home-ownership promotion was largely left to the private market in the mid-1980s. The acute growth of middle-class housing demand in the 1980s fuelled one of the most speculative eras in the private home-ownership market, lasting almost a decade during which house prices fluctuated immensely, rocketing to ten times the prices in the mid-1980s.

The commodification of public housing was expected to continue under the new Chinese government after 30 June 1997. However, somehow this policy was eclipsed by a new policy to create more land and to build many more new houses (85,000 new housing units per year) until the year 2007. Housing policy has become highly politicized and is now deemed to be a necessary platform to achieve political stability and legitimacy. While the Director of Housing further reiterated the intention of the government not to intervene so much in the housing system, it is widely recognized that underpinning the housing system still lies a major state effort to ensure that both the lower economic class and the middle class will be adequately housed (5). Henceforth, the dilemma facing the new government is how to increase the role of the state in housing responsibility and yet not overburdening the state bureaucracy.

Since 1998, one of the ways of achieving this has been through the Sale of Public Rental Flats Scheme, where sitting tenants are allowed to purchase their rental units at substantially discounted prices. This will increase the home-ownership rate quickly while involving minimum state effort. At the same time the government also provides home loans to middle-class households in the form of the Sandwich Class Home Loan. Through these policies the Housing Department is able to shed part of its public housing burden and can therefore concentrate more on new housing projects in middle-class home ownership. Likewise, a housing NGO --- the Housing Society --- has also been given the task of developing an executive type middle-class housing scheme and hence is helping to offset some of the supply stringency in HOS for the middle classes. Through these policies and the housing agency, collectivized housing provision and consumption are minimized and concealed under institutional innovations, hence striking a better balance between the two opposing processess: collectivization and individualization.

EXPANSION IN EDUCATION: FROM ELITIST TO MASS EDUCATION

The education system in Hong Kong has undergone two major changes in the last two decades. The first of these was the provision of free and universal elementary education in the 1970s and the second was the rapid expansion of the higher education sector in the late 1980s. Hong Kong started to provide free and universal elementary education up to the age of 12 in 1971. In 1978 this was extended to Form III, three years beyond elementary education. In 1996-97, the government spent about 17.4% of public expenditure on education, giving it first place in public expenditure ranking. Before 1974 the education system had been very much an elitist system, with less than 50% of primary school leavers offered subsidized school places. Consequently, many children could not afford secondary education. The introduction of nine-years compulsory education in 1978 began to turn secondary schooling into mass education. Chan and Leung (1997) suggest that the new Secondary School Places Allocation System (SSPA) first broached the question of education equality. SSPA is a system in which school place allocation is based on internal assessments of schools and Academic Aptitude Test results. It is more equitable than the old elitist system on two grounds. First, it guarantees everyone access to junior secondary school education with an acceptable standard of quality. Second, the randomization of allocation to some extent successfully evens out inequality arising from the best students being concentrated only in elitist schools. However, this attempt to promote equity has met with great resistance from famous secondary schools. Both the school and parent associations strongly propose more autonomy in school choice. This situation is somewhat remedied by the allowance of a feeder system whereby schools are permitted to allocate a private quota of 10-15% of school places to primary school students. The adverse consequence of this policy is that it encourages better-off families to move to better school districts with feeder schools, making school places in these school district fiercely competitive and hence resulting in educational equity much less accessible to many.

One of the often criticized areas of education is the availability of university places. In the early 1970s Hong Kong had only two universities, The University of Hong Kong and the Chinese University of Hong Kong. During this period only 2% of the relevant age groups were admitted to universities. Access to higher education for the masses was thus extremely limited. In 1980, the government established the Committee to Review Technical and Higher Education which recommended that university places should be increased to 8% (Chang, 1992). Pressure to further increase the number of degree places remained high throughout the 1980s. The City Polytechnic was established in 1984 to augment the increasing need for technical qualifications at university level. In 1988, a third university, the Hong Kong University of Science and Technology, was inaugurated. This marked the most rapid period of expansion in higher education. In 1989, the then Governor David Wilson launched a program to increase the number of university first-year places from 7,000 to 14,500, i.e. 18% of the relevant age groups, by 1995. In order to recruit sufficient manpower for university teachers, large-scale staff development and extensive overseas recruitment were launched from the early 1990s.

Two situations have resulted from this rapid expansion. First, rising costs in university education led the University Grants Committee to begin tightening university budgets in the latter part of the 1990s. A series of managerial measures were introduced to improve management quality and enhance the efficiency of university operations (e.g. the Research Assessment Exercise, the Appraisal System and Institutional Accreditation Exercise). These measures are characterized by a widespread use of formal student feedback through form-filling, to the extent that many teachers find the teacher-student relationship increasingly instrumental. In addition, the proliferation of quality control mechanisms often means an additional administrative workload for teachers and university administrators. This, in turn, affects the overall productivity of the university sector. At the same time, there has been a marked degradation of the personal and intellectual relationship between student and teacher that forms the most important part of university education. Second, the rapid increase in university places has also resulted in a lowering of admission standards. Judging by the performance of students in examinations and coursework, it is evident that the average academic standard of university students in the 1990s has declined. It is a widely acknowledged fact that the standard of language and communication skills has fallen, largely as a result of declining standards in primary and secondary schools. Language skills enhancement is now a priority amongst schools and universities. School teachers are given salary incentives if they can achieve better language standards (6).

From Table 2, it can be seen that the education picture in Hong Kong in 1996 comprises 81% of the population having at least primary or secondary level education, while only 16% managed to get beyond the secondary ladder. Degree holders have doubled from about 4% two decades ago to more than 8% of the population. Although education expansion was criticized as slow and inadequate in the 1970s, the 1980s and 1990s have successfully turned around the elitist model. The provision of mass education also shows that the government was shifting from a selective to a universalistic stance in education policy. Although reluctant and slow to act in the beginning, the government gradually recognized the primacy of educational input in fostering economic growth and social stability. Empirical studies of the effect of mass education on income distribution indicate a positive relationship between the two. In a recent study on income distribution and education expansion, Lui (1997) argues that change in educational composition as reflected in Table 2 comes close to explaining all the increases in overall income distribution. Lui further predicts that in the long term, educational investment will lead to greater disparity and inequality in income. Scott (1989) argues that the expansion of higher education opportunities in the 1980s was part of a set of corporatist strategies employed by the departing colonial government to regain ruling legitimacy in the last days of a changing sovereignty. In addition, higher education expansion was also conceived as an effective means to woo the emigrating middle classes to remain in Hong Kong. Therefore, it could be argued that a shift to a more collective mode of intervention was all part of a state strategy to maintain both economic and social stability.

However, the rapid increase in educational expenditure has become a sensitive economic and political issue since the early 1990s. This is coupled at the same time with the efficiency drive of public sector reform during the same period. Since 1997, universities have been earmarked for an annual cutback of 3% of the budget. With the Asian economic crisis still looming large, the University Grants Committee (UGC) is already cutting back on student bursaries and loans. From Fall 1998 onwards, students are no longer entitled to means tested interest-free loans. They will only be allowed to take out a loan from the UGC with interest repayment. Uneven performance in schools has also led the government to introduce quality education concepts. The Quality Education in School White Paper published in 1997 reflects the more recent drive of the government to realign resource efficiency in the secondary sector.

Table 2: Working Population by Education, 1986, 1991, 1996

	1986	1991	1996
No Schooling	214,516	152,714	88,868
Primary	771,123	622,066	550,219
Lower Secondary	527,760	572,071	619,886
Upper Secondary	709,097	830,817	988,117
6th form	128,317	153,905	203,298
Tertiary:Non-Degree	151,494	181,362	188,029
Tertiary: Degree	140,966	202,168	405,281
Total	2,643,273	2,715,103	3,043,698

Source: 1996 Population By-census Main Report

Table 3: Expenditure in Social Policy 1986-1997

Component	1986/87	87/88	88/89	89/90	90/91	
Economic	2,525	2,996	3,516	4,065	5,222	
Security	7,454	8,090	9,598	11,544	13,843	
Social Welfare	2,576	2,863	3,485	4,379	5,318	
Health	4,366	4,979	5,673	7,254	9,230	
Education	8,598	9,450	11,654	13,392	16,542	
Environment	397	413	525	1,198	2,025	
Community & External Affairs	3,279	3,737	4,346	5,387	6,591	
Infrastructure	6,707	7,406	8,783	13,96	11,943	
Support	6,244	6,672	7,464	9,196	12,067	
Housing	5,785	7,032	9,755	11,569	12,416	
Public Expenditure	47,930	53,636	64,799	81,945	95,198	
	91/92	92/93	93/94	94/95	95/96	96/97
Economic	5,849	7,563	12,447	7,374	9,637	10,542
Security	14,899	16,286	17,322	18,975	21,323	24,733
Social Welfare	6,352	7,299	9,170	10,948	14,558	18,277
Health	10,693	13,636	18,458	19,322	23,852	25,051
Education	19,431	22,158	25,409	28,878	33,781	39,163
Environment	2,675	3,129	3,134	4,401	6,167	6,550
Community & External Affairs	6,754	6,973	8,326	9,229	11,006	13,016
Infrastructure	14,279	17,484	23,051	26,231	27,040	24,180
Support	14,504	16,034	21,284	20,891	26,621	29,887
Housing	12,577	12,932	16,607	19,701	21,259	25,845
Public Expenditure						

Source: Finance Branch, government secretarial, 1996: Hong Kong Annual Report 1997
Notes: All figures are expressed in HK$ Million at current market prices.

In sum, while the 1980s marked the end of elitism and inaugurated an era of rapid education expansion, the 1990s have evidenced much more cautious progression and budgetary contraction. The balancing act between collective consumption and individualization has begun to swing back towards the individual side. The School Management Initiative (SMI) launched in 1991, as well as the Quality Education drive in 1997, are indicative of the trend to bring individual responsibility back into the education sector.

HEALTHCARE FOR ALL?

A full 80% of public-sector healthcare in Hong Kong comes under the umbrella of the Hospital Authority, which controls all government hospitals and aided hospitals, while primary healthcare is largely left to the private market. The healthcare budget comes second only to education, comprising approximately 13% of total public expenditure. By any international standard, Hong Kong has an impressive list of health indicators. Infant mortality has reached an all time low of 4% since 1996, while life expectancy is 76 for males and 82 for females (see Table 4). While the number one cause of death is still malignant tumors, death arising from heart disease has been reduced from 92 per ten thousand of the population to 74, although death arising from pneumonia has been on the rise since 1992. Understandably, this is attributable to the large number of single elderly people who died during the severe winter in 1996 and 1997. Pneumonia is therefore more a disease of aging and poverty, rather than bad healthcare.

Underlying this impressive series of statistics, however, healthcare in Hong Kong has been going through a very trying period. Over the last few years, there have been numerous cases of bad hospital management and professional negligence by medical personnel which have caused fatalities and negative publicity, notably cases such as wrong prescription, negligent pharmacy and unjustified surgery. With the formal establishment of the independent statutory Hospital Authority in 1990, both the public image of healthcare services and the doctor-patient relationship have markedly improved. However, such improvements have often been portrayed by the media as piecemeal, and it is evident that the fundamental flaws of the healthcare system cannot be cured in an instant.

In theory the Hong Kong healthcare system represents an ideal balance between collectivization and individualization. Some 70% of all primary healthcare needs are provided by private practitioners in the market in the form of GP services. The government takes up supplementary out-patient services in district clinics and hospitals as a safety net for those who cannot afford primary healthcare in the market, but who, nevertheless, can afford the time to queue up in government clinics. In practice, the government is finding it increasingly difficult to sustain a collectivized mode of provision under the present system.

Broadly, the healthcare sector can be clearly differentiated into a 2-tier system: the government takes up almost all hospital care (secondary care) while the market takes up primary healthcare. The government provides basic subsidized curative care through hospitals and clinics, always at a point below actual community needs. Healthcare expansion will always be inadequate and the government hospitals take good care not to compete with services being provided by the private market. This extremely cautious and conservative attitude to healthcare created enormous efficiency and equity problems in the early 1980s. Urgent reform was badly needed. The government conceived of the problems largely in terms of an efficiency framework. Doctors were bad administrators and besides, they were too powerful. In 1984, the government appointed an international consultancy firm (W.D.Scott and Co. of Cooper and Lybrand) to consider ways of: (1) integrating government and subvented hospitals under a new structure; (2) improving the management efficiency of hospitals; and (3) introducing differential charges for different classes of hospital services. The famous 1985 Scott Report (Scott & Co, 1985) recommended the setting up of a new Hospital Authority and the appointment of professional hospital executives. The Hospital Authority has been in operation since 1991, and while the image of public hospital care has improved over the past few years, critics suggest that the HA has reached a crossroads. Gould (1997) argues that the setting-up of a Hospital Authority as a new bureaucracy was an 'uncontrollable reinvention of the former Medical and Health Department: the head office of the organization now controls the operational data necessary for informed central government decision-making, is unwieldy and frequently accused of being bureaucratic' (7).

The Director of Audit's 1996 Report also criticized doctors as being overpaid (8). With 98% of its funding coming from tax revenues, the HA is actually outcompeting the private sector. Private hospitals are now facing a diminishing market share. The upshot of all this is that with the continuing domination of medical professionals and western medical technology, there is a tendency for the healthcare sector to continue its growth unimpeded, to the extent that financing healthcare will overburden government expenditure. The policy dilemma now is how to put the individual back into an already over-collectivized public sector. Using a differential pricing strategy, or even a cost-recovery principle might ease the problem temporarily, but would have little effect on escalating medical costs. An active consideration in recent years has been the option of health insurance, which is seen as an effective way of putting the individual back into the equation. Hay (1992) argues that the traditional method of pouring money into healthcare by the government could never meet the people's eventual healthcare needs, whereas a comprehensive healthcare insurance plan in the market should give people better choice. His proposal is echoed by Ho (1997) but modified into a Universal Excess Burden Health Insurance Plan where all citizens would pay an annual threshold contribution to get full coverage. The advantage of the Plan is that while the main thrust of the health budget still comes from public revenues, the individual is also required to contribute to medical costs. When the Chief Executive promised to conduct a comprehensive review of healthcare delivery and financing in late 1998, he indicated that healthcare insurance options would once again be one of the main items on the agenda.

Table 4: Health Indicators in Hong Kong

	1992	1996	1997
Expectation of life at birth (1)			
Male	75	76	76
Female	81	82	82
Infant mortality rate (per 1 000 live births)	5	4	4
Deaths per 1000 000 of 45-64 years old (1)			
Male	848	646	580
Female	410	304	285
Death rates (per 100 000 population) (1)			
Malignant neoplasms	156	161	159
Heart diseases	92	77	74
Pneumonia	35	63	58
Cerebravascular disease	53	49	47
Injury and poisoning	29	26	26

Note: (1) Figures for 1992 were re-compiled using the revised population estimates released in September 1996.
Source: http:www.info.gov.hk/censtatd/hkstat/hkinf/health.h

SOCIAL SECURITY AND POVERTY

'Hong Kong's material progress on the economic front has not been fully transformed into improvements in the quality of life.' That was the concluding statement of a South China Morning Post survey in October 1997, three months after the handover of sovereignty (9). While Hong Kong is ranked sixth internationally in per capita GDP at $189,985 (even higher than Britain, Canada and Australia), it is disheartening to note that economic growth has not brought with it a concomitant rise in affluence for the people, or at least not for the most disadvantaged groups in society. For much of the 1980s, the standard social security payment was kept at an extremely low level, so low that it created disincentives for claimants. It is interesting to note that the number of Comprehensive Social Security Assistance (CSSA) cases has been maintained at a very low level, from 0.3% of the population in 1971 to about 2.5% of the population in 1997. To determine whether CSSA recipients get an adequate level of life assistance, Macpherson (1994) carried out a survey and concluded that even though welfare recipients spend over 70% of their income on food, they are still not able to adequately feed themselves. In order to put aside money for nutritional requirements, social activities considered basic in Chinese culture (e.g. an occasional visit to a dim-sum breakfast or an annual school outing) become unattainable. This has serious implications for the normal growth and development of young schoolchildren as well as for elderly people trying to maintain a minimal social network for survival.

With unemployment rising to 6.2% in the third quarter of 1999, one of the main issues of social policy debate is whether or not the social assistance system will become overburdened (South China Morning Post, Front Page, November 15, 1999). This concern is evidenced by a rapid increase in the number of unemployment cases in CSSA applicants. In August 1994 there were only 4,415 unemployed applicants, making up 4.37% of the total number of applicants, while in 1997 the number of unemployed had increased to 16,152 cases (8.98%). Unemployed CSSA applicants have doubled within three years. At the same time, numerous abuse cases have been discovered, particularly amongst new immigrants from China. In early 1998, a family of four managed to receive more than HK$10,000 per month, whereas the monthly salary of a working-class breadwinner is only HK$6,000. The public began to raise questions about possible abuses and dependency. Moreover, such cases provide the government with a strong justification for not increasing the level of social security payment. At the same time, Hong Kong has been occupied with the whole social debate over the inclusion or exclusion of legal and illegal new immigrants from China on grounds of family reunion (Lee, 1996). At present Hong Kong allows a daily intake of 150 people from China to settle in Hong Kong. The majority of these new immigrants are women and children coming to join their working-class husbands in Hong Kong. It is generally predicted that most of them are economically inactive, hence presenting a potential burden to the existing social service system.

The CSSA is essentially a means-tested social assistance scheme. In principle, all those in financial difficulties are eligible, including those in employment with very low earnings. A cursory analysis of CSSA recipients shows that 61% of them are elderly people. Unemployed claimants only constituted 7.4% in 1996. Since 1992, the number of CSSA recipients has grown more than threefold, from around 80,000 to 187,000 in 1997 (see Table 5). This increase reflects two fundamental policy issues. First, with the current economic downturn and the gradual process of social aging, the trend will be for an increasing demand for CSSA. Second, Hong Kong still lacks a comprehensive social insurance system based on individual contributions. Since the mid-1970s, there have been endless political debates within the Legislative Council about the setting up of an income-related Central Provident Fund scheme. The proposal has time and time again been rejected by the government. It was not until 1994 that the government took the initiative of proposing the first contributory Old Age Pension Scheme. The essence of the proposal lies in relieving the present government burden of social security by asking those of working age to make a contribution to the pension so that it can be used immediately to pay out to elderly people. No sooner was the proposal put forward than it was turned down by the Chinese government for fear that its implementation would mean a departure from the existing philosophy on social security. Simply put, the government thought that a city-wide pension scheme would mean too much of a burden for a retreating polity. It was later substituted by a new proposal to adopt a Mandatory Provident Fund Scheme, which would require employers to set up a transferable private provident fund scheme. While this scheme is still in the planning stage, it has been widely criticized as financially risky for participants since the government refuses to act as the final guarantor. In the face of a highly volatile international money market in 1998, money invested under the new scheme could face enormous financial risk in the near future.

Table 5: Social Security Indicator in Hong Kong

		1992	1996	1997
Comprehensive Social Security Assistance Scheme				
No. of case (2)	thousands	80	160	187
Amount of payment (3)	HK$ million	1,136	4,831	7,128
Social Security Allowance Scheme (4)				
Disability Allowance				
No. of cases (2)	thousands	77	71	76
Amount of payment (3)	HK$ million	695	915	1,037
Old Age Allowance				
No. of cases (2)	thousands	424	436	440
Amount of payment (3)	HK$ million	1,848	2,768	3,005
Traffic Accident Victims Assistance Scheme				
No. of cases (2)	hundreds	49	56	54
Amount of payment (3)	HK$ million	60	111	123

Notes: (1) As from 1.7.93 onwards, the Public Assistance Scheme was replaced by Comprehensive Social Security Assistance (CSSA) Scheme. Hence, figures as from 1993 and those of previous years are not strictly comparable.
(2) Figures are as at end of the year.
(3) Figures for 1991/92, 1995/96 and 1996/97.
(4) As from 1.7.93 onwards, the Special Needs Allowance Scheme was renamed as the Social Security Allowance (SSA) Scheme and cases in receipt of CSSA are no longer eligible for SSA. Hence, figures as from 1993 and those of previous years are not strictly comparable.
Source: http:www.info.gov.hk/censtatd/hkstat/hkinf/health.htm

CONCLUDING REMARKS

The history of social policy in Hong Kong has been one of pragmatism and incrementalism. Starting out as a highly residualized mode of provision, it gradually transformed into a more collective mode, encompassing such policy areas as public housing, mass education and subsidized hospital care. The mix of welfare in Hong Kong is thus highly reflective of the domination of the ideology of capitalism. The linking theme within the entire development history of social policy-making is full employment and economic growth. Social expenditure must be subsumed under economic surplus. In weaving the social welfare safety net, the state has taken great care not to create work disincentives and dependency. In some ways, Hong Kong even lives up to the expectations of the theoretical project suggested by Esping-

Andersen — that a pragmatic mix of social policies such as those found in Hong Kong could actually amount to a form of social corporatism, where the state plays a key role in social resources distribution and yet succeeds in not tampering with individual responsibility and the spirit of capitalism. To the ordinary man or woman on the street, this all sounds quite trivial since 1997. The pragmatic approach to social expenditure was planned on the assumption of a buoyant economy and full employment. The hitherto satisfactory balance between collective provision and individual responsibility is no longer easily attainable. Through no fault of their own, many people are being laid-off for the first time in their lives. If the economy bounces back within a few months, individuals may be able to adapt and adjust, or even take time out to retrain. But if the downturn continues for some years, the safety net may not be safe anymore. The rapid increase in the demand for unemployment benefit among CSSA recipients has already exposed the stresses on the system. Unfortunately, Hong Kong's social policy has not been planned for sustained economic downturn. The collapse of the economy has already brought enormous difficulties for the working class and the middle classes. Yet the social policy system only caters for those with transient hardship. The discordance between the social security system and economic reality is likely to emerge in the form of social unrest, creating a further burden and strain on an already besieged social system.

ENDNOTES

(1) South China Morning Post , 19 May, 1998.
(2) "Economy slides into negative growth", South China Morning Post , 27 May 1998: front page.
(3) "Hard Times in Hong Kong", Newsweek,, 13 July 1998: 15.
(4) The two representative debates on the feasibility of CPF took place on 13 May 1987and 10 July 1991, in the Legislative Council, Hong Kong Hansard: p. 1531-1611; p. 2779-2833.
(5) News release on the "Corporate Plan of the Housing Department," July, 1998.
(6) Ming Pao Daily, 6 July 1998, p. A10.
(7) Gould, R. (1997). 'Health' in Wilding et al. (1997), p. 33.
(8) Director of Audit (1996), Annual Report, Hong Kong: Government Printer.
(9) Lau, C. K. (1997). 'What figures in our life?' South China Morning Post, 12 October 1997, p.9.

REFERENCES

Castells, E., et. al. (1990). The Shek Kip Mei Syndrome, London: Pion.

Chan, H.M. & Leung, J. (1997). EducationIn Wilding, P. et. al (eds.) Social Policy in Hong Kong (pp.55-77). London: Edward Elgar.

Chang, K. M. (1992). Educational Policiy-making in Hong Kong: The Changing Legitimacy. In Gerald, A. Postiglione (ed.) Education and Society in Hong Kong: Towards One Country and Two Systems, Hong Kong: HKU Press.

Chow, N.S. (1995). Social Welfare: Concepts and Institutions, Hong Kong: ChungHwa Publishing Co. (in Chinese).

Esping-Andersen, G. (1990). Three Worlds of Welfare Capitalism, Cambridge: Polity Press.

Hay, J. W. (1992). Health Care in Hong Kong: An Economic Policy Assessment, Hong Kong: Chinese University Press.

Ho, L .S. (1997). Health Care Delivery and Financing: A Model for Reform, Hong Kong: City University Press.

Hong Kong Government (1966). The Governor's Address, Hong Kong: Government Printer.

Lee, J. (1996). Belong to the same root ? The social inclusion and exclusion of new immigrants from China. Unpublished paper presented at the Hong Kong Government Annual Policy Forum in August, 1996. (in Chinese)

Lui, H.K. (1997). Income Inequality and Economic Development, Hong Kong: City University Press.

MacPherson, S. (1994). A Measure of Dignity: Report on the adequacy of Public Assistance Rates in Hong Kong, Hong Kong: Hong Kong Council of Social Service.

McLaughlin, E. (1993). Hong Kong: A Residual Welfare Regime. InCochrane, A. and Clarke, J. (eds) (1993). Comparing Welfare States: Britain in International Context, pp. 105-140.

Midgley, J. (1986). Industrialization and Welfare: The Case of the Four Little Tigers. Social Policy and Administration, Volume 20, Number 3, Autumn 1986, pp225-238.

Scott & Co. Ltd (1985). The Delivery of Medical Services in Hospsitals: A Report for the Hong Kong Government, Government Printer.

Scott, I. (1989). The Legitimacy Crisis in Hong Kong, Hong Kong: Hong Kong University Press.

South China Morning Post, 19 May 1998: front page.

Wilding, P. et. al. (1997). Social Policy in Hong Kong, London: Edward Elgar.

YEUN-WEN KU

CHAPTER THREE

SOCIAL DEVELOPMENT IN TAIWAN: UPHEAVALS IN THE 1990s

Since the publication of Esping-Andersen's (1990) book on welfare capitalism, the issue of whether there are, in fact, three welfare regimes in accordance with his classification — i.e. liberal, conservative and social democratic — remains controversial (e.g. Castles and Mitchell, 1992). Since most of the modern welfare states on which Esping-Andersen's study is based are European, this could prevent his explanation from extending to other cases with very different politico-economic contexts and historical backgrounds, especially those from the dynamic economies in East Asia. Even so, Esping-Andersen's concept of welfare regime, which refers to the systematic interweaving of state, economy and welfare, remains helpful for analyzing potential and distinctive types of welfare capitalism.

This chapter will look at recent social development in Taiwan to gauge its social performance as well as the efforts of state policy and expenditure on welfare. We will concentrate on the political and economic contexts in Taiwan in order to explore further the dynamics of such development. In particular, the aim of expanding state welfare in the face of growing concerns about the possible damage to the economy will be examined, showing that the Taiwanese state is facing a great challenge to balance two requirements: deregulation of the economy under globalization and the establishment of a safety net under democratization. The discussion will end with a brief assessment of the Taiwanese welfare regime.

ECONOMIC GROWTH VS. STATE WELFARE: A LONG DEBATE

The prodigious economic growth in the Asian Newly Industrialized Countries (NICs) has attracted a great deal of scholarly attention exploring the dynamics behind this success story. A distinctive developmental model is now being recognized, which emphasizes the role and capacity of the state in managing conditions favoring production. The themes of 'developmental state' and 'governing the market' are therefore the keynotes explaining the outstanding economic performance in East Asia.

However, some scholars have observed a dark underside to the East Asian 'miracle', manifest in extreme political subordination and exclusion of laborers,

K.-L. Tang (ed.), Social Development in Asia, 39–59.

alongside an incomplete social security system (e.g. Deyo, 1989; Ku, 1995). The term 'reluctant welfarism' is used by Midgley to describe the fact that East Asian states are reluctant to increase their role in social welfare. According to him:

> the four Asian NICs have been congruent with a marked reluctance on the part of the political elite to expand social programs. They have consistently affirmed their faith in the virtues of free enterprise, self-reliance and hard work and frequently declared an aversion to welfarism (Midgley, 1986: 234).

For this reason, the plausible explanation that the rapid economic growth in East Asia is due to the slow progress of state welfare which has enabled the state to spend more on matters directly linked to economic growth is exaggerated. MacPherson argues that four extreme methods of economic adjustment have been widely applied by the Asian NICs in response to changes in the world market: (1) a reduction in government expenditure; (2) the shifting of resources from consumption to investment; (3) the adoption of macro-economic policies favoring international trade; and (4) the raising of productivity levels through reliance on market mechanisms (MacPherson, 1992: 56). In pursuit of economic growth and restructuring there is no way of completely avoiding social costs. The poor are the hardest hit by government policies and practices for speeding economic growth because there is little national wealth left to improve their living conditions.

In contrast to MacPherson's point, Deyo's recent paper provides a very different insight. He argues that social and economic development goals are often compatible and closely linked under the development strategy of export-oriented industrialization (EOI) — the basic model of development in the Asian NICs. EOI calls for more effective utilization of human resources, such as low wages and compensation levels, high productivity and low levels of labor conflict. For it to succeed there must be some social policy to maintain or reproduce human resources, particularly in the areas of education, health and housing. Furthermore, a low level of labor conflict relies on state intervention in wage negotiation and control over trade unions. Although there may be different components of social policy in the Asian NICs, they all perform well in terms of enhancing labor productivity, encouraging enterprise training, and subsidizing wages in favor of economic growth (Deyo, 1992: 304--5).

Both perspectives have interpreted one side of the coin only. It is true that state welfare in the Asian NICs still lags far behind the levels attained in the European welfare states, whether in terms of government expenditure or social programs. But we also note a significant improvement in living conditions with the increasing incomes resulting from economic growth. Although there may well be a dilemma between economic growth and social progress, some social programs were developed even before the economic take-off in the Asian NICs, such as the Central Provident Fund in Singapore in 1953, the labor insurance scheme in Taiwan in 1950, and compensation on work injury in Hong Kong and Korea in 1953. In particular, we find a gradual but important expansion of state welfare in the Asian NICs in more recent decades (Social Security Administration, 1997).

Interestingly, a similar debate has also taken place in Sweden, a social democratic welfare state far removed from East Asia. Some leading Swedish economists promote the 'Welfare State Jeopardy Hypothesis', as it is called by Korpi, and claim that the Swedish welfare state has had serious negative effects on economic growth (Korpi, 1993). Although Korpi has discovered many problems with the methodology and data reliability of these economists, this century-old debate between the economy and welfare, market and state has not yet reached a conclusion.

Nevertheless, some Taiwanese economic bureaucrats still persist in their negative view of social welfare, particularly the welfare role of the state. Generally, they argue that state welfare (Ku, 1997a):

- is consumptive, rather than productive, which decreases wealth creation
- damages the flexibility of the labor market and therefore constrains the growth of jobs
- increases expenditure and decreases savings, which in turn exhausts resources for investment
- raises tax levels for financing its development
- makes people dependent, retards work motives and condemns recipients to a life of poverty.

Others provide a very different view. They note the positive impacts made by state welfare, such as (Ku, 1997a):

- contributing to the formation of human capital, such as improved levels of education and health, which are fundamental to EOI development strategy
- enhancing social integration and therefore stabilizing productive relationships in favor of economic growth
- maintaining domestic consumption power as a policy tool to manage supply-demand at a macro-economic level
- public spending which favors domestic production and therefore contributes to economic growth.
- increasing employment opportunities, especially in the public sector and related service providers, profitably and non-profitably.

In an attempt to combine these two opposing views as well as to find a practical way of integrating economic and social policies in pursuit of general social welfare objectives, Midgley proposes the social development approach, which means 'a process of planned social change designed to promote the well-being of the population as a whole in conjunction with a dynamic process of economic development' (1995: 25). He regards economic and social processes as equally important components of the development process. Social development cannot take place without economic development, and economic development is meaningless if it fails to bring about significant improvements in the well-being of the population as a whole. Based on this theme, Midgley identifies some important features of the social development approach: an organizational framework assuming responsibility for social development programs; the promotion of human well-being through economic development to secure employment and incomes; and a preference for social programs that are positively linked to economic development (1995; 1997).

Moreover, the realization of these goals needs an activist style of state intervention called managed pluralism, in which 'governments play a positive role in facilitating, coordinating and directing the efforts of diverse groups of individuals, groups and communities and effectively utilizing the market, community and state to promote social development' (1995: 175).

Midgley's points are highly thought-provoking, particularly his suggestion that the state should not avoid a positive role in this process. However, to some extent he oversimplifies the nature of a global system whose constraints are beyond the control of the nation state, and the levels of competition, conflict and contradiction within it which are even more significant than cooperation and harmony. We would argue that the real interaction between economic growth and state welfare and their possible impacts on each other should not be linear and dichotomous. We have to locate social policy in the politico-economic context that has given rise to it, before arbitrarily assuming that economic growth and state welfare are compatible or incompatible, able or unable to be integrated. This approach will be examined in the case of Taiwan. First of all, we need to have a general understanding of social development in Taiwan.

SOCIAL DEVELOPMENT IN TAIWAN: A PROFILE

A surprising fact of Taiwanese state welfare has been identified by Ku (1995), who reports that although education and public health are well developed in Taiwan, and social insurance is expanding to cover an increasing number of people, the government's welfare effort is still too low to be universally available. This is especially pertinent given that military servicemen and civil servants received over 70% of the welfare expenditure of the central government while the disadvantaged received only around 3% in 1991 (Ku, 1995). Under the pressures of democratization since the 1980s, the Taiwanese state has been expanding its welfare efforts in order to win support from the public. The first nationally universal social program, National Health Insurance (NHI), was proposed in 1987 and finally introduced in 1995. This section focuses mainly on the development of Taiwanese state welfare in the most recent decade, using the figures to draw up a profile.

Table 1 shows some selected social indicators in Taiwan, through which a significant improvement in social conditions can be observed. Successful economic growth has brought Taiwanese people great prosperity. Average income rose from US $3,297 in 1985 to US $12,872 in 1996. This, combined with a low unemployment rate, has prolonged life expectancy, improved literacy and widened the availability of medical resources, indicating that Taiwan has escaped from mass poverty and become a developed economy. Infant mortality is fluctuating slightly, but is lower than most of the developing countries and is comparable to Western industrial countries, where the infant mortality rate is about 7 per thousand births (Midgley, 1997: 55-67). The aging process is accelerating in Taiwan: 7% of the population were 65 years old or older in 1993 and this proportion is expected to increase to 10.3% in 2011, according to estimates by the Council for Economic Planning and Development (CEPD) (CEPD, 1996b: 7). It is anticipated that the growing aged population will be an important pressure group in the near future, pushing for the realization of related social programs such as pensions and community care.

Table 1: Selected Social Indicators in Taiwan, 1985-1996

Year	GNP Per Capita (US$)	Life Expectancy		Literacy (%)	Infant Mortality Per 1,000	No. of Hospital Beds per 10,000	Unemployment (%)	65+ as % of population
		Male	Female					
1985	3,297	70.82	75.81	91.6	6.78	38.47	2.9	5.1
1986	3,993	70.97	75.88	92.0	6.29	41.84	2.7	5.3
1987	5,298	71.09	76.31	92.2	5.08	43.88	2.0	5.5
1988	6,379	70.99	76.21	92.6	5.34	44.50	1.7	5.7
1989	7,626	71.10	76.48	92.9	5.71	43.12	1.6	6.0
1990	8,111	71.33	76.75	93.2	5.27	43.80	1.7	6.2
1991	8,982	71.83	77.15	93.6	5.05	45.14	1.5	6.5
1992	10,470	71.79	77.22	93.9	5.18	46.30	1.5	6.8
1993	10,852	71.62	77.52	94.0	4.80	47.90	1.5	7.1
1994	11,597	71.81	77.76	94.2	5.07	48.98	1.6	7.4
1995	12,439	71.85	77.74	94.4	6.43	52.62	1.8	7.6
1996	12,872	71.87	77.92	94.7	6.66	53.39	2.6	7.9

Sources: 1. CEPD (1996a), *Taiwan Statistical Data Book.*
2. DGBAS (1997), *Social Indicators in Taiwan Area of the Republic of China, 1996.*
3. MIA (1997), *Statistical Data Book of Interior Affairs.*

Is the state playing a significant role to improve living conditions and secure the well- being of the people through the intervention of social policy? The answer to this question may be found in Table 2, which shows total government expenditure according to different functions. Originally, social welfare expenditure was a very general figure in Taiwan, containing many items hardly regarded as social welfare, such as environment protection, a lump sum pension to retired politicians and some parts of salaries to civil servants (Ku, 1995). This exaggerated the real welfare efforts of the Taiwanese state and incurred serious criticisms from scholars and the opposition. To obtain the real figure for social welfare expenditure, the government has limited its total expenditure to nine functions since 1990, as shown in Table 2. The most significant change is the division of social welfare expenditure into three functions: social security, community and environment protection, and the pension fund for civil servants, so that social security expenditure is more likely to be consistent with so-called 'social welfare' or 'state welfare'.

Following the adjustment, we learn that the welfare efforts of the state fell sharply from 15.7% in 1985 to 8.2% in 1990. However, the first half of the 1990s was a significant growth period for social security expenditure, increasing to 14.4% in 1996. This figure is closely linked to the commencement of NHI in 1995. It is still

Table 2: Total Government Expenditure by Functions, 1985-1996

Unit: NT$ million, %

Year	Total			General Administration	Defense	Education, Science & Culture	Economic Development	Social Security	Community & Environment Protection	Pension Fund For Civil Servants	Debts	Others
	Amount	% of GNP	%									
1985	563,729	23.0	100.0	11.0	24.0	19.8	24.5		15.7		4.2	0.8
1986	632,661	23.6	100.0	11.1	24.2	20.5	24.4		15.6		3.4	0.8
1987	662,135	21.2	100.0	10.9	22.5	20.3	25.9		15.5		4.1	0.9
1988	751,930	21.8	100.0	10.7	21.3	19.7	25.5		17.5		4.5	0.8
1989	1,239,554	32.6	100.0	7.8	15.2	16.7	43.7		12.2		3.5	0.9
1990	1,166,747	27.6	100.0	10.8	18.1	19.5	25.9	8.2	2.7	6.5	7.4	0.9
1991	1,416,625	30.6	100.0	10.8	16.0	20.4	22.8	8.3	2.3	6.2	12.3	0.9
1992	1,696,117	32.7	100.0	11.7	14.1	19.1	27.3	8.0	3.7	5.6	9.9	0.6
1993	1,859,294	32.6	100.0	11.2	13.6	18.9	29.4	7.3	3.9	5.5	9.0	0.7
1994	1,913,742	30.8	100.0	11.3	16.8	20.0	24.5	8.3	4.3	5.8	8.5	0.5
1995	2,074,204	30.9	100.0	10.7	13.0	17.2	21.1	11.2	3.1	5.7	17.3	0.6
1996	2,005,897	26.6	100.0	12.2	14.2	18.7	16.4	14.4	3.4	6.8	13.4	0.5

Sources: 1. CEPD (1996a), *Taiwan Statistical Data Book.*
2. DGBAS (1997), *Social Indicators in Taiwan Area of the Republic of China, 1996.*
3. MIA (1997), *Statistical Data Book of Interior Affairs.*

below the level of Western welfare states, due to the lower percentage of total government expenditure as a proportion of GNP. In addition, Table 2 also reveals the policy priority of the Taiwanese state. Economic development and defense were usually the top two priorities, though education expenditure exceeded both of these in 1996. It should be noted that education expenditure in Taiwan includes funds allocated to science and culture, the former being particularly important to technology and economic development. Education expenditure in Taiwan is not put purely into education at all, as Ku has argued (1995).

A further question claims our attention. At the beginning of this section we mentioned a radical imbalance in welfare allocation between various groups in favor of those who are deemed important to the stability of the government, such as military servicemen and civil servants. Has this changed? Tables 3 and 4 provide an answer to this question. Table 3 shows central government expenditure on social security, distributed by different governmental departments. We find the Commission for Veterans is still the biggest beneficiary, and the share to the Ministry of Interior Affairs, which is the major department in charge of national welfare services, only accounts for around one-third of the expenditure on the Commission for Veterans. If we put the shares of veterans, civil servants (the Ministry of Examination) and military servicemen (the Ministry of Defense) together, this figure amounts to over 50% of the total social security expenditure of the central government.

Table 3: Social Security Expenditure of the Central Government by Departments, 1992-1996①

Unit: NT$Billion, %

Year	Commission for Veterans	Ministry of Interior Affairs	Agriculture Council	Dept of Health	Labor Council	Ministry of Examination	Ministry of Defense	Others	Total
1992									
Amount	97.1	20.2	6.1	7.4	2.2	5.2	5.8	25.4	169.5
%	57.3	11.9	3.6	4.4	1.3	3.1	3.4	15.0	100.0
1993									
Amount	102.8	26.3	6.3	8.2	3.0	6.0	5.5	20.3	178.4
%	57.7	14.8	3.5	4.6	1.7	3.4	3.1	11.4	100.0
1994									
Amount	112.8	25.7	6.0	7.0	3.9	5.6	5.9	17.5	184.4
%	61.2	14.0	3.3	3.8	2.1	3.0	3.2	9.5	100.0
1995②									
Amount	110.0	50.5	12.5	25.3	5.1	8.2	6.8	19.3	237.8
%	46.3	21.2	5.3	10.6	2.2	3.5	2.9	8.1	100.0
1996②									
Amount	116.6	36.6	35.0	20.0	18.4	12.9	6.1	20.4	266.0
%	43.8	13.8	13.2	7.5	6.9	4.8	2.3	7.3	100.0

Notes: ① Calculated by the CEPD with data from various governmental departments (including pension fund for civil servants), so the total figures in selected years are slightly different from Table 2, due to errors.
② Projected figures.
Source: CEPD (1996b), Table 2-6.

Table 4: Social Security Expenditure of the Central Government by Various Groups, 1996

Unit: NT $ Thousand, %

Groups	Social Insurance	Social Assistance	Welfare Services	Employ-ment Services	Health Care	Sub-Total	As % of Total
Civil Servants & Teachers	5,248,810	27,000	111,752	--	--	5,387,562	4.5
Veterans	10,142,110	535,187	20,858,773	--	--	31,536,070	26.6
Military Service-men	6,704,775	--	--	--	--	6,704,775	5.7
Laborers	11,970,510	--	2,517,799	1,316,593	--	15,804,902	13.4
Farmers	21,801,639	10,000,000	11,559,300	69,970	--	43,430,909	36.7
Poor	747,463	6,665,500	--	3,564	184,421	7,600,948	6.4
Handicap ped	3,000	--	2,316,209	49,266	1,434,000	3,802,475	3.2
Children	--	--	744,713	--	202,743	947,456	0.8
Youths	--	--	436,202	624,268	50,000	1,110,470	0.9
Women	--	--	192,818	--	45,664	238,482	0.2
Elders	--	--	1,589,530	--	266,586	1,856,116	1.6
Sub-Total	56,618,307	17,227,687	40,327,096	2,063,661	2,183,414	118,420,165	
As % of Total	47.8	14.6	34.1	1.7	1.8		100.0

Source: Adapted from Hsiao-hung Nancy Chen et al. (1996), Table 2-3-6.

In order to obtain a more accurate figure on the distribution of social security expenditure, a legislator defined social security more specifically as comprising social insurance, social assistance, welfare services, employment and healthcare. He then calculated its distribution across various groups according to the budget of the central government submitted to him in 1996. Table 4 is the result. Although veterans, civil servants and military servicemen received the largest share as usual, farmers have had a nearly equal share. Other groups such as laborers, the poor, the disabled, children, young people, women and the elderly were far behind. The possible reasons for this situation will be explored in the next section. Another dimension revealed in Table 4 is the importance of social insurance in social security expenditure, which accounted for 47.8% in 1996, compared with social assistance expenditure of only 14.6%. Welfare services ranked second at 34.1%. The result seems to indicate that the Taiwanese state prefers social insurance programs for the productive groups, and welfare services, mostly in kind, for the disadvantaged, supplemented by employment services and healthcare. Social assistance in the form of cash benefits receives less attention from the state. Table 5 demonstrates this finding more clearly.

Table 5: Percentage of Population Covered by at least One Social Insurance Program and Social Assistance, 1985-1996

Unit: 1,000 persons, %

Year	Insurance Programs excluding NHI		National Health Insurance (NHI)		Social Assistance	
	No. of Insured Persons	% of Population	No. of Insured Persons	% of Population	No. of Low-Income Persons	% of Population
1985	4,950	25.47	--	--	118	0.61
1986	5,603	28.80	--	--	114	0.59
1987	6,355	32.30	--	--	112	0.57
1988	7,489	37.62	--	--	112	0.56
1989	8,964	44.58	--	--	101	0.50
1990	9,634	47.33	--	--	114	0.56
1991	10,171	49.48	--	--	116	0.56
1992	11,252	54.22	--	--	115	0.55
1993	11,757	56.14	--	--	119	0.56
1994	12,172	57.62	--	--	116	0.55
1995	10,070	47.28	19,124	92.34	115	0.54
1996	9,892	46.07	20,041	95.96	116	0.54

Source: DGBAS (1997), *Social Indicators in Taiwan Area of the Republic of China, 1996*

Before 1995, there were about fourteen social insurance programs in Taiwan, among which labor insurance, insurance for civil servants and insurance for military servicemen were three major systems, covering a variety of risks including maternity, injury and sickness, medical care, disability, old age, death and funeral allowances (Ku, 1995). Along with the expansion of these social insurance programs, the proportion of the population covered by at least one of them grew very fast over the last decade, from 25.47% in 1985 to 57.62% in 1994 (see Table 5). Since 1995, some piecemeal health insurance programs have been integrated into the NHI, causing a decline in the proportion of the population covered by social insurance other than NHI, to 46.07% in 1996. However, the proportion of the population covered by the NHI is very high, starting out in 1995 at 92.34% and rising to 95.96% in 1996. This figure is projected to be about 98% by the end of 1997. In other words, nearly all of the population will have come under the protection of the NHI in just three years. This marks the most impressive achievement of state welfare development in Taiwan to date. In contrast to the remarkable development of social insurance, social assistance remains underdeveloped. People receiving social assistance constitute around 0.5% of the population, and no significant improvement has been made in the past ten years. As Ku argues, although rapid economic growth has provided job opportunities for the poor, enabling them to extricate themselves from poverty, another reason for the low take-up is that the government has pushed down the official poverty line level to less than one-third of per capita income, thereby dramatically reducing the number of low-income people (Ku, 1995). The uneven development between social insurance and social assistance implies an incomplete safety net for the Taiwanese people, particularly as regards the risk of losing ones income because of the lack of unemployment benefit in social insurance.

To summarize our findings from the above discussion: economic growth in Taiwan has been accompanied by an improvement in general social conditions, that puts Taiwan on a par with the developed countries. However, aging of the population is also accelerating, probably because of prolonged life expectancy and increasing medical resources, and this will put pressure on the Taiwanese economy as well as the social support system.

It is difficult to say whether the state has placed enough emphasis on state welfare in terms of government social security expenditure, which lags far behind the Western welfare states, or too much emphasis on groups such as veterans, civil servants and military servicemen who are still the biggest beneficiaries of welfare spending.

Although education expenditure is not used solely for education purposes, it is clearly the most preferred policy in the social domain as its share of total government expenditure in 1996 moved beyond both defense and economic development for the first time. Apart from education, social insurance programs are gradually expanding to cover increasing numbers of the population, the most remarkable development in social insurance being the establishment of the NHI in 1995, which is projected to cover 98% of population by 1997, making it virtually universally available to all Taiwan's residents. However, due to the absence of unemployment benefit and the underdevelopment of social assistance, an economic safety net does not yet exist to secure incomes from risk.

How has the profile of social development in Taiwan taken this form? And how is it linked to Taiwan's past economic performance? In order to account for its development we need to locate it in the Taiwanese politico-economic context. Thus, we turn to these issues in the next section.

INTERNAL DYNAMICS

In Ku's (1997b) comprehensive study on welfare capitalism in Taiwan, he traces its development from 1895 to 1990, searching for internal dynamics from a Marxist perspective which would integrate four factors: the capitalist world system, state structure, ideology and social structure. He argues:

> The capitalist world system, as a form of international politics, introduces Western welfare measures to Taiwan which gradually replace traditional and informal provision, on the one hand; but, as it is also a global system of intensely competitive economics, it places limits on Taiwan's welfare development in order to speed up economic growth, on the other hand. In particular, Taiwan suffers from political isolation in the international community because of China's repression, and economic growth has been the most important means to consolidate its links with the external world. This is even more apparent as we learn that economic growth in Taiwan is mainly dependent on the competitiveness of its products in the world market. Taiwan cannot afford the cost of

> economic isolation, especially now that it has been isolated politically. Its limited resources are therefore poured into areas which will benefit economic growth, especially infrastructure in the economic domain, and public health and education in the social domain.

This may explain why the disadvantaged are neglected most. In order to stabilize the production relationship in favor of economic growth, and more particularly to repress potential unrest because of constrained working conditions, social control, rather than social welfare, is employed by the state through its bureaucrats. This may also explain why veterans, civil servants and military servicemen benefit most. Even though welfare programs have been initiated and expanded to include more disadvantaged groups, as the state faces political crisis, these efforts are limited to piecemeal provision and are not allowed to consume too much in the way of national resources, so long as the existing social controls remain in force.

Education policy is preferred by the state for two reasons. Firstly, it can train necessary labor forces for production; and secondly, it can be an important ideological tool for disseminating propaganda. Hostility to the European-style welfare state is deliberately publicized by the Taiwanese state and its economic elite in order to legitimize an 'economics first' policy, using exaggerated claims of the negative effects of social welfare on the economy as a deterrent, such as 'A welfare state encourages people to be unemployed in order to claim benefits'.

At the start of the 1980s, Taiwan's political isolation in the international community showed no signs of improving, due to China's repression. However, its capitalist development has been maturing and has created a private sector that is strong enough to wield political influence, particularly because the state needed the private sector to consolidate its links with the outside world through trade. At the same time, radical social movements were provoked into action against long-term social underdevelopment. Without support from abroad, the Taiwanese state found these developments difficult to suppress. A more democratic political environment and an institutional welfare system became important to win the support of society. This explains the introduction of the NHI. In light of the farmers' protest in Taipei on 20 May 1988 which required 2,000 policemen to contain 18 hours of rioting, it also accounts for the relatively large share of social security expenditure on farmers in 1996.

In the 1990s, the process of democracratization has been established in Taiwan. Political elections are no longer limited to the local level and Taiwanese people can now vote for their president. Since the foundation of the Democratic Progressive Party (DPP) in 1986, it has become the major opposition party against the KMT, the ruling party since 1945. With each coming election, the KMT faces greater challenges to its policy style. Issues relating to social welfare are often advocated by the DPP against the 'economics first' principal of the KMT. For example, in the election of legislators in 1992, a debate on whether or not Taiwan should become a welfare state was provoked between the two sides, in which social welfare occupied first place on the political agenda for the first time. This also heightened people's awareness of the welfare role of the state. In 1993, the DPP published its white paper on social welfare, proposing: (DPP, 1993):

- Establishment of a universal social insurance system, covering pension, health, work injury and unemployment benefits
- Family allowances for children and young people
- Increased cash benefits for social assistance
- Expansion of welfare services to disadvantaged groups
- A comprehensive medical care system and network
- A housing policy for everyone
- Collectively bargained working conditions.
- Establishment of a ministry responsible for social welfare at central government level
- Inclusion of social welfare in national development plans
- Proceeding with resources redistribution across the nation.

In the election of local authorities at the end of 1993, the DPP's policy proposal of a universal pension scheme became a political platform for winning the election. The DPP announced that citizens who were 65 years old and over would receive NT $5,000 every month from 2 October. The KMT fiercely criticized the policy as a collective bribe for elderly voters, but it pressed ahead nevertheless with its own launch of a series of measures for elderly people. On 2 October, the Ministry of Interior Affairs announced that a policy draft on a national pension scheme would be published in November, and on 6 October the allowance for low-income elderly people was increased from NT $3,000 to NT $5,000 per month. On 7 October, the DPP proposed a further pension scheme specifically targeted at farmers, prompting President Lee Teng-hui, the leader of the KMT, to ask the Executive Yuan to enact a comparable scheme as soon as possible. The cabinet meeting on 21 October announced that the allowance for low-income elderly people would increase further to NT $6,000 per month and promised an extra NT $3,000 for the middle-to-low income elderly. The DPP held a public hearing of its pension policy on 22 October, while the Ministry of Interior Affairs also published its draft policy on a national pension scheme.

In a very short period — less than one month — the pension scheme had become a major issue throughout the island and the size of the allowance kept increasing. This case attests to the fact that social welfare is now an important issue in Taiwanese politics, and the KMT has to take the social policy proposals of the opposition seriously, especially when faced with the growing challenge with every election. The first half of the 1990s in Taiwan has been a period of intense policy debates, alongside the continuing revision and expansion of the existing welfare schemes. Policy competition between political parties has become a main theme of the electoral process.

In response to this change, the KMT has been trying to achieve a more consistent social policy, resulting in the publication of The Guiding Principles of Social Welfare Policy in 1994. The nine principles for Taiwanese welfare development aim to:

- Emphasize the balance between economic and social development
- Establish a proper social administration system
- Put the family at the center of social welfare policy
- Facilitate teamwork among the various governmental departments and emphasize the importance of professional social workers
- Promote harmony and cooperation between employers and employees
- Establish a financially independent social insurance system
- Meet the satisfaction of needs through a mixed economy of welfare
- Provide public housing for lower income families
- Provide equal opportunity for access to medical care.

This is indeed the most comprehensive statement on social policy since the KMT first began to rule in Taiwan. However, in comparison with the DPP's white paper, we can see that the KMT's policy orientation still holds true to the philosophy of 'economics first' in these principles. It still strongly emphasizes the importance of (a) economic growth in supporting social welfare; (b) sharing welfare responsibilities with the family and the private sector; (c) harmonizing industrial relationships; and (d) financially independent social insurance that will not increase government burdens. Economic concerns are still the priority of the KMT, though it has been forced to expand state welfare in the face of competition from the main opposition party.

It was expected that the first presidential election in early 1996 would push some welfare issues or policies to the fore. This did not actually happen because China's military exercises turned public attention away from domestic affairs to the external threat. The public has been made aware of the urgent need to safeguard the island's security and this is pursued through Taiwan's consolidation in the international community, particularly by its strong economic links with the rest of the world. To some extent, then, economic growth must not be weakened for the sake of more welfare consumption, though this would not necessarily be the outcome. Ironically, crude policy-making like that fueling the pension debate in 1993 does risk abusing and wasting public resources. This could in turn increase hostility to social policy and undermine the nature and necessity of social welfare. Under such conditions, the debate on the need for economic growth and social welfare will become even more conflictive in Taiwan.

For the reasons outlined above, we find that social security expenditure in Taiwan has risen very rapidly, from 8.3% of total government expenditure in 1994 to 14.4% in 1996 (as shown in Table 2). But this has not radically changed the original structure in favor of veterans, civil servants and military servicemen, who are still the biggest beneficiaries of state welfare. During the first half of the 1990s, welfare development in Taiwan was carried out on a piecemeal rather than a systematic basis, so that the government could push forward specific welfare programs which would win the support of select groups.

A further question is whether or not the Taiwanese state, or the KMT's policy orientation, will be able to continue along past lines. In fact, some signs of structural problems appear to be creating more pressure for change. These could present major challenges to the Taiwanese state.

CHALLENGES TO FACE

In 1979, three scholars co-authored a book advocating Taiwan's development as a model of growth with equity (Fei *et al.*, 1979). However, this model is now being severely criticized. Table 6 demonstrates income distribution, tax burden and crime rates from 1985 to 1996. Although disposable income per household has increased significantly, from NT $320,495 in 1985 to NT $826,378 in 1996, testifying to the strong economic performance of the Taiwanese state, social inequality is expanding at a faster rate than ever before. The ratio of the wealthiest to the poorest quintile in Taiwan has increased from 4.5 in 1985 to 5.38 in 1996, showing the same development in terms of Gini coefficient. As social inequality widens, people become increasingly dissatisfied with existing conditions, especially in the context of a growing awareness of relative deprivation. This could in turn lead to risky economic ventures and criminal acts in pursuit of quick money (Lin, 1995). The following two social problems may be linked to the widening income gap.

The first is the rise in the crime rate from 317.3 cases per 100,000 of the population in 1985 to 933.4 in 1996, nearly three times higher than ten years ago (Table 6). The most notorious example of the crime problem is the so-called 'three heaviest criminal cases' at the turn of 1996 and 1997, when eight officials and councilors of Taoyuan county, including the mayor himself, were murdered on the same day; a feminist leader of the DPP was raped and killed; and the only daughter of a famous actress was kidnapped and killed. Of the three heaviest criminal cases, only the kidnapping case was finally resolved in November 1997 after a dramatic event in which the last surviving kidnapper held a South African diplomat and his family hostage, bargaining with the police for a better trial. The domestic criminal case was shocking not only because it had become a diplomatic issue, attracting international media attention, but also because such a situation had never occurred before, clearly demonstrating the incapacity of the government and the police to maintain social order. This provoked a surge of popular protest which led to a forced reshuffle of the cabinet. Notably, the other two cases are still unsolved.

The second is the rise of social movements struggling for better living conditions. Popular protest and labor activism induce uncertainty in production relations and slow down the rate of capital accumulation, causing concern among capitalists who put pressure on the government to restore social order in favor of economic production. For example, a survey in 1990 found that 72% of enterprises in Taiwan were dissatisfied with economic conditions, especially with social disorder and the labor movement. In addition, 49.5% of the surveyed enterprises thought that the KMT, as the enduring ruling party, should take responsibility for improving this problem. Another survey of capitalists in the same year revealed that social disorder was felt to be the most critical problem affecting economic growth, since it would force enterprises to move out of Taiwan (Wang, 1992: 12-13). The general public are not satisfied with existing conditions either, though not for the same reasons as the capitalists. A survey of public opinion in 1992 revealed the criticism that the government does not pay enough attention to improving income distribution. Corruption and deals between politicians and businessmen that clearly neglected social conditions in favor of economic growth were considered particularly damaging. Additionally, the public called upon the government to do more to improve income distribution, particularly through education and social welfare measures (The 21st Century Foundation, 1992; 1993).

Table 6: Income Distribution, Tax Burden and Crime Rate, 1985-1996

Year	Disposable Income Per Household (NT$)	Ratio of Wealthiest to Poorest Quintile	Gini Coefficient	Per Capita Tax Burden as % of Income	Crime Rate in 100,000 Population
1985	320,495	4.50	0.290	17.7	317.3
1986	341,728	4.60	0.296	16.5	481.4
1987	366,487	4.69	0.299	16.1	457.3
1988	410,483	4.85	0.303	17.8	445.8
1989	464,994	4.94	0.303	19.5	451.6
1990	520,147	5.18	0.312	21.9	453.6
1991	587,242	4.97	0.308	19.1	600.1
1992	639,696	5.24	0.312	20.4	674.5
1993	707,879	5.42	0.316	20.1	674.6
1994	769,755	5.38	0.318	20.0	577.7
1995	811,338	5.34	0.317	20.2	802.6
1996	826,378	5.38	0.317	18.2	933.4

Source: DGBAS (1997), *Social Indicators in Taiwan Area of the Republic of China, 1996.*

Whatever the people and the capitalists claim, the state is always at the core of policy. Under democratization, the Taiwanese state is no longer able to satisfy people with solely economic growth. Social development is therefore an urgent and important policy for the legitimacy of the state, and a necessary one if the government is to win support from society. For this reason, we find that the KMT has been forced to expand its welfare efforts in the face of competition from the DPP. Can improvements in state welfare relieve the pressure on the Taiwanese state? In practice, even if the KMT wished to implement social welfare measures, it would not be a simple matter.

Table 6 also shows an important feature of the Taiwanese political economy, that is, the relatively low tax burden compared with Western welfare states. Over the past decade, the per capita tax burden as a percentage of income has remained around 20%. This is part of a deliberate policy of the state to encourage investment through three measures: the establishment of an economic infrastructure, tax rebates and financial assistance (Ku, 1997b: 149-51). The expansion of state welfare could cause an increase in taxes. This would not be welcomed by the general public if it were to take the form of a tax on income and consumption. On the other hand, the capitalists would be even more opposed to the tax increase coming from profits. Moreover, improvements in state welfare accompanied by an increase in taxes would entail greater state intervention in the market, which is fundamentally in conflict with the development of deregulation at the global level, and is particularly in conflict with the economic policy of the government since the 1980s.

As early as 1982, the eighth 4-year plan for economic development adopted economic liberalization and internationalization as new guiding principles, and put greater emphasis on the functioning of market forces and price mechanisms. This policy integrated Taiwan's developing economy even further into the capitalist system at the global level. Negotiations with international organizations such as GATT and the WTO also pushed Taiwan to open up its domestic market and deregulate the economy. Under intensive economic competition, as well as the unacceptability of rigid repressive measures on production relations and wage levels because of democratization, the government turned to the task of strengthening and upgrading its basic infrastructure and developing technology-oriented industries in order to encourage more private investment and to expand production of high value-added goods for higher profits. The 6-year National Development Plan 1991-96 was therefore proposed and implemented by the government in pursuit of four goals: raising national income, obtaining more resources for continued industrial growth, promoting balanced regional development, and raising standards of living. This would be expected to have an important impact on state finances, to the extent that the government would have to increase its expenditure on economic development. We can see the expansion of total government expenditure in relation to GNP and the increasing burden of public debts in the early 1990s in Table 2. However, the development of state welfare also needs more public resources and this causes radical competition between governmental expenditures on economic growth and social welfare.

Furthermore, the liberalization policy is in accordance with the development of globalization, in which capital is allowed to flow in and out of the country, freely and rapidly. If the government cannot maintain a good rate of return for capital through improving the investment environment, investors will move to other countries with better opportunities for profit, especially those countries in Southeast Asia and China with low labor costs. This could make the unemployment rate rise and in turn increase pressure on state welfare. If the government pours more public resources into state welfare, then the shortage of money for economic development will be critical and could damage the profitability of enterprises even further. If the government chooses not to expand its welfare efforts, then it could lose its status as a ruling power in the next election. A great challenge emerges, as Ku (1997a) argues:

> In the process of globalization, local laborers are not only competing with other laborers in the country, but they are also competing with foreign laborers for limited job opportunities. Having or not having jobs, and the levels of wages will influence employees' subsistence and enterprises' profits directly. However, wage levels are very difficult to increase because of global competition. If the government wishes to raise wages through social programs and statues, they risk reducing job opportunities... Both high unemployment and low wages will greatly damage the legitimacy of the state ... [and the] economic crisis will transform into a political crisis...

Is there a way out? Can Taiwan cope with the challenges coming from, on the one hand, deregulation of the economy under globalization, and on the other, the establishment of a safety net under democratization? What role does the Taiwanese state plan to play? These issues will be considered in the next section, followed by a brief assessment of the Taiwanese welfare regime in the concluding section.

A TAIWANESE WELFARE STATE?

The 1980s was indeed a decade of conservative thought, attacking the idea of the welfare state and calling for more individualistic self-reliance. This is particularly evident if we read papers written by politicians and scholars of the New Right like David Marsland (1996: xvii). He insists:

> State welfare is causing grave damage in the United Kingdom, in the United States, and elsewhere through the free world. It is impeding the dynamism of global economic competition, and thus slowing world economic growth. Through the bureaucratic centralization and the underclass dependency which it inevitably creates, it poses a serious long-term threat to liberty and to the stability of democracy.

In Marsland's view, the welfare state is an evil which impacts negatively on human life, which is not only to be interpreted in terms of economic growth but also in terms of liberty and democracy, the longstanding values of modern politics.

The so called 'welfare state in crisis' has given some Taiwanese economic technocrats a perfect excuse to neglect state welfare over the past few decades and to voice their criticisms of it. Although some other studies find that in reality the welfare state is not dismantling at all (e.g. Pierson, 1994), this fact does not claim the attention of these economic technocrats, and welfare retrenchment is still the main theme. For example, a report published by the CEPD warns of the possible damage to the economy by state welfare, arguing that if the annual average growth rate of state welfare is 10%, the annual average growth rates of economic growth, inflation and employment will be 6.1%, 3.9% and 1.0% respectively; if the annual average growth rate of state welfare is 20%, the others will reduce to 5.9%, 3.1% and 0.4% respectively (CEPD, 1996b). These figures will be even worse if the government is forced to raise taxes to finance state welfare. Before the full report was published, the CEPD leaked some of its primary findings to a national newspaper in Taiwan, which exaggerated the results in its headline: 'Be careful of your job if welfare grows too fast' (*United Daily News*, 2 October 1995). As a result, some economic policy-makers insist that the national pension scheme should be postponed until the economy has been upgraded and is strong enough, even though the government pledged to implement it in the local elections of 1993.

The proposal of a national pension scheme remained, therefore, in draft form and its implementation date was held back by the CEPD till as late as the end of 1997. But this situation could not last, not least because the next election of local authorities was approaching and the public were expecting the government's promise of a national pension scheme to be fulfilled. In order to win the local election on 29 November 1997, President Lee Teng-hui announced that the KMT would establish a universal allowance for those aged 65 and over at the rate of NT $5,000 per month, as a supplementary measure before the national pension scheme is up and running, even though he strongly criticized the same program proposed by the DPP in the local election of 1993. This claim provoked lively political debate and many commentators thought that it was an attempt to recapture declining support for the KMT for its inability to realize the national pension system. The KMT spokesman blamed the anti-welfare attitudes of the CEPD, causing the KMT to come under critical attack by the opposition. The Premier Hsiao Wan-chang was finally forced to announce the government's full intention to implement the national pension scheme, which will finalize its planning and be realized by 2000 (*China Times*, 5 November 1997).

However, the public were no longer satisfied with the promises made by the KMT, especially its inefficiency in promoting social development, not only with respect to the pension issue but also issues of security and safety in everyday life. The KMT finally lost the local election. Out of 23 counties, the DPP won 12 seats to the KMT's 8 (3 seats went to independent candidates), and for the first time the DPP received more votes, 43.32% compared to the KMT's 42.12% (*China Times*, 30 November 1997). In fact, the KMT has lost its status as a ruling party at the local level. It seems impossible for it to run the risk of postponing the national pension scheme any longer, particularly because the year 2000 is a highly politicized date, being the year when the presidential election is also due. Following the successful implementation of the NHI in 1995, the national pension scheme seems set to happen. The Taiwanese state will inevitably have to increase its intervention through the establishment of comprehensive and institutional state welfare.

Another impact made by welfare reforms in the Western welfare states should not be overlooked. Since the publication of Norman Johnson's book on welfare pluralism (1987), the idea that social and health care may be obtained from four different sectors, namely the statutory, the voluntary, the commercial and the informal, has been widely advocated in Taiwan. So are concepts like privatization, decentralization, managerialism, mixed economy of welfare, quasi-market, non-profit organizations, community care, and so on. All of these imply a less dominant role for the state in the provision of social welfare. For example, a national conference on community development was held by the Department of Social Affairs under the Ministry of Interior Affairs in 1995, which reached the conclusion that community-based welfare services should be promoted (MIA, 1995). This is a sign that the government is attempting to adopt pluralist approaches to social welfare and to share its welfare responsibilities with other sectors, by introducing newly developed theories of social welfare in the Western welfare states.

A sizable literature and studies relating to these theories have appeared in Taiwan, particularly focusing on the privatization of social welfare. Also, official reports published by the Department of Social Affairs clearly demonstrate the government's policy preferences towards developing more welfare service providers from within the family, community and voluntary sector, and even profit organizations (W. Chen, 1996). Welfare privatization corresponds more closely to the liberal orientation of Taiwanese economic technocrats for at least three reasons. Firstly, more service providers from different sectors means that the state can be released from the burden of state welfare with its pressures on government finance. Secondly, effectiveness and efficiency should be better established in the private sector than in the public sector, and this is particularly important in view of the limited resources. Finally, more service providers imply more choices, thus empowering welfare consumers and encouraging self-reliance.

However, whether or not privatization is a unique way out of the welfare crisis is still being examined in the Western welfare states (Esping-Andersen, 1996). Some issues arising from privatization should be noted. The first concerns the state role. Privatization as a state policy entails the state actively promoting this process, mainly through subsidies, which implies a structural gap between theory and practice. Privatization in practice is not an activity that is wholly confined to the private sphere, and state intervention continues to operate as usual. The second issue concerns the defects of privatization, especially if the profit motivation is in social welfare. Although profits and competition for profits should be able to guarantee effective services and efficiency, these could exclude marginal groups of welfare consumers without sufficient money to pay for the services. Moreover, the satisfaction of needs under privatization could prove to be the most profitable services rather than the most needed. The third issue relates to the service network and integration. More service providers can expand the resources available to social welfare, but these could become too piecemeal and create gaps in welfare provision if there is no collective effort to organize these service providers into an integrated network. These reflections indicate quite clearly that the state cannot stand outside the provision of welfare. As Ku (1997a) concludes, even though the state may not be the only provider of resources, it should still be an important one and must be a positive participant in the future.

CONCLUSION

We have reviewed some important features of the welfare regime in Taiwan, focusing mainly on the development, debates and challenges in the most recent decade. Economic growth in Taiwan has been accompanied by improvements in general social conditions that have put Taiwan on a par with the developed countries. However, it is difficult to say whether the state has paid enough attention to state welfare, either in terms of government expenditure on social security, which is lagging far behind the Western welfare states, or in terms of those groups which benefit most — veterans, civil servants and military servicemen are still the biggest beneficiaries of welfare spending. Education remains the most preferred policy in the social domain. Apart from education, social insurance programs are gradually expanding to cover more of the population. The most remarkable development in social insurance has been the establishment of the NHI in 1995, which is projected to cover 98% of the population in 1997, making it nearly universally available to all residents.

Even so, due to the lack of unemployment benefit and the underdeveloped social assistance, a safety net does not yet properly exist to secure incomes in the event of economic downturn. This makes the pension issue a nationwide concern, and the implementation of a national pension scheme, following the success of the NHI, is another important welfare program to develop by the year 2000. Although some economic technocrats have expressed concern about the possible damage to the economy by expanding state welfare; and the liberalization and globalization of economic development also constrain the capacity of the state to finance and implement welfare provisions, the KMT is still compelled to increase its welfare efforts under democratization in general and in the face of competition from the DPP in particular. To balance these requirements, privatization and related theories newly developed in the Western welfare states are being introduced to share the welfare responsibilities of the state among different sectors. But the state seems unable to relinquish its role in social welfare and the degree of state intervention is expected to increase in the near future.

In the case of Taiwan's welfare regime, we see its initially conservative nature demonstrated in three traits: a focus on economic growth, education as investment in human capital, and the consolidation of existing stratification according to occupation statuses. The rapid economic growth accompanied by full employment has brought about a huge increase in national prosperity which has helped to equalize income distribution in the short term; but the relatively underdeveloped social policy is not sufficient to construct a stable production relation which can support such rapid economic growth in the long term. The existing social structure has been damaged and social problems have arisen internally, providing an opportunity for the opposition to rise with pledges of social reform. As democratization confirms, state welfare cannot be distributed according to entrenched occupational statuses as this would only exacerbate existing social inequalities. The push towards a comprehensive welfare system with consistent universal benefits is being realized, which should transform the conservative nature of the Taiwanese state in the future.

In short, we would argue that state welfare does not spontaneously grow alongside economic growth, and nor is the state always likely to improve social conditions through public means. Rather, its development is constrained by the contradictions and conflict induced by capitalist development at both domestic and global levels. In the case of Taiwan, this theme is particularly pertinent.

REFERENCES

Castles, F. G. and D. Mitchell (1992). Identifying Welfare State Regimes: The LinksBetween Politics, Instruments and Outcomes. Governance: An International Journal of Policy and Administration, 5(1): 1-26.

Chen, H. H. Nancy et al. (1996). An Evaluation of Social Welfare System in Taiwan. Taipei: Council for Economic Planning and Development. (in Chinese)

Chen, Wu-hsiung (1996). The Investigation and Prospect of Social Administration Affairs in ROC, Community Development Journal (Quarterly), No. 75: 5-15. (in Chinese)

China Times, 5 November 1997. (in Chinese)

China Times, 30 November 1997. (in Chinese)

Council for Economic Planning and Development (CEPD) (1996a). Taiwan Statistical Data Book, 1996. Taipei.

Council for Economic Planning and Development (CEPD) (1996b). Impacts of Social Welfare Expenditure on National Economic Development. Taipei. (in Chinese)

Democratic Progressive Party (1993). A Just Welfare State: White Paper ofDDP's Social Policy. Taipei.

(in Chinese)
Deyo, F. C. (1989). Beneath the Miracle: Labor Subordination in the New Asian Industrialism. Berkeley, California: University of California Press.
Deyo, F. C. (1992). The Political Economy of Social Policy Formation: East Asia's Newly Industrialized Countries, in R. P. Appelbaum and J. Henderson (eds.), States and Development in the Asian Pacific Rim, pp. 289-306. Newbury Park, California: Sage.
Directorate-General of Budget, Accounting and Statistics (DGBAS) (1996). Social Indicators in Taiwan Area of the Republic of China, 1996. Taipei.
Esping-Andersen, G. (1990). The Three Worlds of Welfare Capitalism. Cambridge: Polity.
Esping-Andersen, G.(1996). After the Golden Age? Welfare State Dilemmas in a Global Economy, in G. Esping-Andersen(ed.), Welfare States in Transition: National Adaptations in Global Economics, pp.1-31. London: Sage.
Fei, J. C. H., G. Ranis, and S. W. Y. Kuo (1979). Growth with Equity: The Taiwan Case. New York: Oxford University Press.
Johnson, N. (1987). The Welfare State in Transition: The Theory and Practice of Welfare Pluralism. Brighton: Wheatsheaf.
Korpi, W. (1993). Economists as Policy Experts and Policy Advocates: On Problems of Values and Objectivity in the Welfare State - Economic Growth Debate , paper presented at the Conference on Comparative Research on Welfare States in Transition, Oxford, September 9-12.
Ku, Y. W. (1995). The Development of State Welfare in the Asian NICs with Special Reference to Taiwan, Social Policy and Administration, 29 (4): 345-364.
Ku, Y. W. (1997a). The Welfare State under the Trend of Privatization: a Challenge, Community Development Journal (Quarterly). (in Chinese)
Ku, Y. W. (1997b). Welfare Capitalism in Taiwan: State, Economy and Social Policy. Basingstoke: Macmillan.
Lin, C. C. (1995). Economic Development and Social Welfare, in W. I. Lin (ed.), Social Welfare in Taiwan: A View from the Society, pp. 103-130. Taipei: Wu-nan. (in Chinese)
MacPherson. S. (1992). Social Policy and Economic Change in the Asia Pacific Region, Social Policy and Administration, 26(1); 55-61.
Marsland, D.(1996). Welfare or Welfare State? Contradictions and Dilemmas in Social Policy. Basingstoke: Macmillan.
Midgley, J. (1986). Industrialization and Welfare: The Case of the Four Little Tigers, Social Policy and Administration, 20(3): 225-238.
Midgley, J. (1995). Social Development: The Developmental Perspective in Social Welfare. Thousand Oaks, California: Sage.
Midgley, J. (1997). Social Welfare in Global Context. Thousand Oaks, California: Sage.
Ministry of Interior Affairs (MIA) (1995). Special Issue of the National Conference on Community Development. Taipei. (in Chinese)
Ministry of Interior Affairs (MIA) (1997). Statistical Data Book of Interior Affairs. Taipei.
Pierson, P.(1994). Dismantling the Welfare State? Reagan, Thatcher, and the Politics of Retrenchment. Cambridge: Cambridge University Press.
Social Security Administration (1997). Social security Programs Throughout the World 1997. Washington. DC.
The 21st Century Foundation (1992). A Survey of Public Opinion on Social Conditions in Taiwan, 1992. Taipei. (in Chinese)
The 21st Century Foundation (1993). A Survey of Public Opinion on Economic Conditions in Taiwan, 1992. Taipei. (in Chinese)
United Daily News, 2 October 1995. (in Chinese)

SUNWOO LEE & IN-JAE LEE

CHAPTER FOUR

SOCIAL WELFARE DEVELOPMENT IN KOREA: PAST, PRESENT, AND FUTURE

INTRODUCTION

South Korea, one of the Newly Industrialized Countries (NICs), has fallen into serious economic crisis since the second half of 1997 and is now under the control of the International Monetary Fund (IMF). The current economic troubles were unexpected by most Koreans, but the causes of the troubles seem to be rooted deep in the Korean economic structure.

The economic structure of Korea has been shaped mainly by several economic development plans through which the country has been developing rapidly since the 1960s. One of the most important factors in the successful economic development has been the close relationship between Chaebols (conglomerates in Korea) and bureaucrats. The Korean government pursued economic development through an export-drive policy in which Chaebols played the most important roles. Consequently, the government has supported the Chaebols, mainly through loans at low-interest rates. The growth of Chaebols has come to represent the growth of the Korean economy. Hyundai, Samsung, Daewoo, and other Chaebols have become internationally known corporations.

Koreans have worked very hard to rebuild the economy from the total destruction of the Korean War. On average, they worked 25.2 days a month and 51.6 hours a week in 1970. In the 1990s the time devoted to work is less, but only marginally. On average, Koreans worked 24.4 days a month (1), and 46.7 hours a week in 1997 (National Statistical Office, 1998). Thus, they still worked much longer hours than workers in the developed countries.

As a result, the GNP per capita increased rapidly during the periods of the five economic plans. It was a mere US $594 in 1975, but soared to US $2,568. In a decade it had increased four-fold. It surpassed US $10,000 in 1995 and was US $10,543 in 1996 (National Statistical Office, 1998). (2)

Over a period of 20 years, GNP per capita grew 17 times larger. Owing to this remarkable economic growth, Korea has enjoyed very low unemployment rates, ranging from 3% to 4% in the 1970s. The highest unemployment rate was only 5.2% in 1980, when General Chun became president after the military coup in 1979. In the

K.-L. Tang (ed.), Social Development in Asia, 61–82.

1990s, the unemployment rates went down even lower to under 3%.

However, the level of social welfare development in Korea has been relatively low due to the concentrated focus on economic development. The proportion of social security and welfare expenditure to GDP was a mere 0.5% in 1980 and 1.3% in 1996. The proportion of social security and welfare spending to the total government budget was 2.7% in 1980 and 6.7% in 1998 (National Statistical Office, 1997; 1998). Although Korea has introduced industrial injury insurance, health insurance, a national pension scheme, and unemployment insurance, social welfare in Korea is considered to be underdeveloped (Choi, 1995).

One of the main reasons for the underdevelopment is the weakness of labor unions. In the 1960s and 1970s, Korea was under the rule of President Park who took power after a military coup in 1961. The government was highly authoritarian and oppressive so that labor unions were very weak. After President Park was assassinated by one of his own men in 1979, the union movement quickly began to flourish, attaining a 21% union membership rate in 1980.

With the arrival of another military government headed by General Chun in 1980, labor unions were again severely oppressed. As a result, the union membership rate continued decreasing to 16.8% in 1986. However, the union movement became active with the democracy movement in 1987. More workers were organized in labor unions, and the number of labor disputes peaked to 3,749 in 1987. Consequently, the union membership rate rose again to 19.8% in 1989.

The Chun Government was followed by the Roh Government in 1988, and the new government was clearly less authoritarian than the two previous governments, though President Roh was also a former general. Korean society became more stable and wealthy. With the new mood of optimism, people became more conservative. Thus, the union membership rate dropped again to 12.2% in 1997. The number of labor disputes was only 78. (3)

The level of education attainment improved rapidly under the economic development. In 1975, only 19.7% of the population had received high school or higher education. In 1995 the proportion had increased to 57.7%. The economic development raised life expectancy from 59.8 for males and 66.7 for females in 1970 to 69.5 for males and 77.4 for females (National Statistical Office, 1997). The number of persons per hospital bed went down from 1,000 in 1980 to 271 in 1997.

The 'party' ended abruptly in November 1997. Despite the success of economic development, the economic structure led by bureaucrats and Chaebols became increasingly inefficient as the size of the Korean economy grew. The economy could no longer be maintained by inefficient management and investment by Chaebols. Moreover, economic development driven by Chaebols has concentrated national wealth on a small proportion of the people. Consequently, despite a marked improvement in living standards, rapid economic development has widened inequalities between income classes.

With the economic crisis, Korea has a new president, Dae-Jung Kim, who was once the most well-known dissident. To alleviate the crisis, the new government passed a law in 1998 allowing companies to lay off workers. Previous governments had prevented companies from laying off workers because until 1995 Korea did not have unemployment insurance. Thereafter, the unemployment rate rose to a historically unprecedented level, 7.8% in July 1998. It dropped a little to 7.1% in October 1998, but went up again to 7.8% in January 1999. The number of unemployed is estimated at over 1.5 million, excluding the underemployed (4).

Social safety nets are not well established yet in Korea even though unemployment is growing. It is expected that more people will need help from the government. In the next section we will focus on policies of income maintenance, health insurance, industrial injury insurance, unemployment insurance, and housing. We will examine the historical paths of these policies and current issues associated with them, and consider their future.

SOCIAL WELFARE POLICIES IN KOREA

A. Income Maintenance Policy

Income maintenance policy in Korea consists largely of two parts: a national pension and public assistance.

1. National Pension Plan

History

Korean pension schemes began with the Public Employee Pension Plan in 1960. Two other pension systems subsequently began to operate: the Military Personnel Pension Plan in 1963, and the Private School Teacher's Pension Plan in 1975. These three public pensions were actually fringe benefits for government employees rather than social insurance for citizens.

The National Pension Law was enacted in 1986, and the National Pension Plan (NPP) as a social insurance system was launched accordingly in 1988. The NPP provided compulsory old-age insurance benefits for all workers between the ages of 18 and 60 who were employed at firms with 5 or more employees. Farmers, fishermen, and the rural self-employed became compulsorily insured in 1995. The self-employed in urban areas could join the NPP voluntarily. (5) Persons insured by the three other public pensions are excluded from the NPP.

Types and Levels of Pension Benefits

The National Pension Plan has three types of benefits: old-age pension, disability pension, and survivor's pension. Workers employed at firms with 5 or more employees and farmers, fishermen and the rural self-employed between the ages of 18 and 59 are covered compulsorily. Workers employed in firms with less than 5 workers and the urban self-employed are covered voluntarily (Social Security Administration, 1995).

Full benefit of the old-age pension is payable at age 60 to persons with at least 20 years of contributions. Reduced benefits are available to persons with at least 15 years of contributions at the reduced rates of 72.5~92.5% of basic benefit. If a person is entitled to full benefit, but has a job with income, the pension will be reduced to 50~90% of the basic benefit. With at least 5 years of contributions, those who were between the ages of 45 to 60 at the onset of the NPP in 1988 are entitled to monthly payments at the reduced rates of 25~70% of the basic benefit.

Disability pension is available to persons who become disabled as a result of sickness or injury with at least a year of contributions and is payable according to the degree of disability at 40~60% of the basic benefit.

Survivor's pension is payable to an insured person's spouse, child (under 18 or with a 2nd degree of disability at any age), or parent (including parent of spouse) when he/she dies with at least one year of contributions. The rates of benefit are 40~60% of the basic benefit. Lump-sum death benefit is payable to a person with less than 15 years of contributions.

Levels of pension are determined in two parts: basic benefit and additional benefit. The basic benefit consists of three parts: an equal part, a part proportional to income, and a part proportional to periods of contributions. Equal part is calculated regardless of earnings. Suppose a person's average earnings for the entire period of contributions is equal to the average earnings of all the insured. If that person contributes for 20 years, the benefit will be about 40% (41% for a couple) of previous earnings under the current system. If a person contributes for 30 years, it will be 62.5%. For 40 years of contributions, it is 70% of previous earnings. The International Labor Organization (ILO) recommends that the minimum level of pension benefit be 45% (55% for a couple) of previous earnings. Developed countries generally provide pension benefits of 44~69% for one person, 50~83% for a couple (Nam and Cho, 1995). Therefore, the level of Korean pension benefits is low compared to developed countries. Additional annuity is given as family allowance. If a beneficiary has a spouse, children, or parents, he/she is entitled to additional pension at fixed rates per person.

Finance

The National Pension Plan has three sources of finance: employers, employees, and the retirement payment reserve for compulsory subscribers. Each of the three sources pays 3% of standard monthly earnings. The retirement payment reserve is drawn from wages. Hence, employees actually pay 6% while employers pay 3%. But voluntary subscribers pay the full 9% of the standard monthly earnings. Governments pay only management costs.

For farmers, fishermen, and the rural self-employed, a person's income is decided according to his/her income report. A person is classified into one of 45 standard income brackets from 220 thousand Won (6) to 3,600 thousand Won depending on the reported income. The Agricultural Special Tax Fund pays a part of insurance premiums. It is currently set for all farmers at 2,200 Won which is one-third of premiums for the lowest income bracket.

Management of the Pension Fund

The National Pension fund is managed in public, social welfare, and financial parts. The fund in the public part is used for government public works such as constructing Citizen's Housing and promoting small businesses. The fund in the financial part is used for investing in stocks. The fund in the social welfare part is spent on purchasing Citizen's Housing Fund Bonds to support housing construction for workers.

In 1994, the Law of Public Capital Management Fund was enacted. It requires that the National pension fund be deposited into the Financial Investment and Loan Special Account to be used as government finance. The Fund Management Committee was established to be an operating body of the Fund. The Committee members include the Minister of Finance and Economy, Minister of Trade and Industry, Minister of Health and Welfare, Minister of Labor, President of the Bank of Korea, and other ministers.

Issues and Future

Several issues related to the NPP have been raised. The first issue is that those who need income maintenance most urgently are not covered by the NPP. Employees at workplaces with less than 5 workers, the self-employed in urban areas, the unemployed, and those who were over 60 when the NPP was introduced, are not covered by the Pension. These are the people who need income maintenance most because they are poor.

The second issue concerns financing problems of the Pension. Two factors are threatening its solvency. First, the levels of benefits are set too high compared to the levels of contributions. Second, the Pension fund has been managed so inefficiently and loosely that the profitability of the fund is dubious. The average profit rate of the fund was 10.7% until November 1997. The government has been using 68.9% of the fund as the public fund (7), and the National Pension Management Corporation has been investing 28.0% in stocks and bonds. Compared to investment in stocks and bonds, investment in the public fund has shown lower profit rates. The profit rate of the public fund was 1.95% lower in 1988, 2.83% lower in 1990, and 3.66% lower in 1994 (Chosun Ilbo, 17 January 1998).

The government established a planning board to improve the National Pension Plan in 1997. It recommended that the levels of benefit be lowered to 40% of previous earnings from 70% (after contributions for 40 years) at the end of 1997. This suggestion was severely criticized by the public. As a result, the Ministry of Health and Welfare announced its plan to reform the Pension in January 1998. According to the reform plan, benefit levels will be 55~60% of previous earnings.

The financial crisis of Korea since the end of 1997 is expected to have a significant influence on the Pension. Its influence is already reflected in the reduction in levels of benefit. Moreover, the sudden fall of the Korean stock market has brought a big loss to the fund in the financial part. The worsening financial conditions of the Pension threatens to postpone the planned expansion of the Pension to the self-employed in urban areas in July 1998.

2. *Public Assistance: Life Care System*

History

In 1946 The American Military Government in Korea set a rule that made public protection available to those who were 65 years or older, or less than 13 years old, or who were mothers with a child of less than 6 years old, or who were chronically sick, pregnant, or disabled. Beneficiaries must be poor with no family and relatives, be unable to work, and have no other place to stay except public shelters.

The main components of the 1946 ruling were maintained when the Korean government introduced the Law on Life Care in 1961 after the military coup. In addition, the military government enacted the Law of Pension for Public Employees in 1960, the Child Welfare Law in 1961, the Law of Health Insurance in 1963, the Law of Industrial Accident Compensation Insurance in 1963, the Law of Pension for Military Personnel, and the Law of Social Security. The Law on Life Care has become the basis of public assistance in Korea though the enactment was used more as a propaganda opportunity than as a means to build an adequate welfare system.

Who Receives Life Care?

According to the Law, there are three requirements for receiving Life Care. First, a person must not have a family who can care for him/her. Second, a person must be 65 or older, or less than 18, (8) a prospective mother, disabled, unemployed, or low-waged. Third, a person must not have wealth and earnings in excess of a yearly standard set by the Minister of Health and Welfare (Ministry of Health and Social Affairs, 1994, p. 232). The total number of Life Care beneficiaries was 1,414 thousand in 1997, which was 3.1% of the total population. Life Care benefits consist of Residential Care, Institutional Care, and Self-Help Care. In 1997 the proportions of their beneficiaries were 21.0%, 5.4%, and 73.6% respectively (National Statistical Office, 1998). Residential care beneficiaries are provided with public assistance at their own residence. Institutional care beneficiaries stay at residential facilities because they do not have their own residence or because their own residence is not adequate to live in. Self-help care is provided to those who are able to work. The government set up Temporary Life Care for the low-income unemployed.

Types and Levels of Benefit

Life Care Beneficiaries are entitled to medical aid, assistance with living expenses, education costs, job training, and loans for petty businesses and community work. The living expense allowance pays for food, heating, and clothing. It used to be provided in-kind, but has been provided as cash since 1995. The average monthly cash benefit in 1998 per person was 167,000 Won, which provided 90% of the minimum living expenses. (9)

This amount includes living expense care, educational care, and health care. Educational care is provided to life care beneficiaries who are in the school age bracket. It is also given to medical aid beneficiaries whose income is lower than the standard set by the Ministry of Health and Welfare. Educational care only covers the expenses (entrance fee and tuition only) of middle schools and high schools (Chung,

1998).

Job training is provided to the unemployed or the under-employed whose income is lower than the standard income. Those who receive job training may also be entitled to allowances (100 thousand Won for a household head), living expenses for family members (30 thousand Won for each family member), and travel expenses (30 thousand Won). The number of job trainees was 12,327 in 1992. Among them, 48% succeeded in finding jobs.

Loans for petty businesses are given to encourage people on low incomes to start their own businesses. However, the amount of the loan is only 12 million Won, which is considered too little to set up a stable business. Moreover, only 5,500 households benefited from the loans in 1993.

Medical aid is provided to life care beneficiaries and those whose income is lower than the standard income. Beneficiaries of residential care and institutional care are able to receive type 1 medical aid. This pays full expenses for outpatients and inpatients. Beneficiaries of self-help care are entitled to type 2 medical aid. Type 2 pays medical expenses for outpatients with a deductible of 1,500 Won for each visit, and 80% of medical expenses for inpatients. If the expenses for inpatients exceed 100,000 Won, type 2 pays the excess, but beneficiaries must pay it back within three years. Low income women who give birth are eligible for medical aid and/or living expense care for sixty days. If beneficiaries of residential care and institutional care die, 250,000 Won is provided for their funeral.

Delivery of Benefit

Life care benefits are delivered by officials at offices of Eup, Myon, and Dong, which are the end of the public bureaucratic hierarchy. They used to be general public employees. However, the government began to hire social welfare experts since 1987 who are social workers and who passed an exam. There are about 3,000 social welfare experts working at the end of 1995 (Chung, 1998).

Issues and Future

Life care in Korea has been criticized for two aspects of the qualifications for beneficiaries: first, a person may not receive life care if he/she has parent(s), a spouse, or a child who are able to support him/her. Even though they may not be willing to provide support, he/she may not be a beneficiary. Second, there is no explicit standard income to decide beneficiaries of life care. Therefore, it is possible for the government to set the standard income based on the budget, not on the needs of people. Moreover, arbitrary decisions on the qualifications are frequent.

In addition, the level of benefits for life care is too low for the poor to maintain a minimum standard of living. Since the intention of the welfare system is to encourage the poor to support themselves, the level of benefits is so low that they cannot guarantee minimum living expenses. The Korea Institute for Health and Social Affairs found in 1994 that the minimum living expense for a 4-person household in big cities was 712 thousand Won. Therefore, 167 thousand Won per person is far less than the minimum.

The types of benefits are very limited, too. Some people have shown needs for social work services as well as cash benefits. But the current personnel at local government level are not able to provide social work services. Their backgrounds do not permit them to provide services that require professional knowledge and skills. Moreover, their average caseload is over 300 households. It is almost impossible for them to use professional knowledge and skills.

As a result, more resources are needed to reduce the problems of life care. However, it is very unlikely that the Korean government will allocate more of its budget to life care. Since the recent economic crisis is producing very large numbers of unemployed people, the government is being forced to focus on the unemployment issue. Therefore, those who need public assistance for living seem to be suffering the most in recent years.

B. Health Insurance System

History

The Korean Health Insurance Act was passed in 1963, and twelve voluntary health insurance programs have been organized since 1965. The history of voluntary health insurance shows that it was hardly capable of achieving the goal of universal health coverage. In fact, only 0.2% of the Koreans were covered by the scheme after twelve year's operation despite substantial amounts of government subsidization (Shin & Lee, 1996).

A compulsory health insurance system was introduced in 1977 with the Medical Aid program (a public assistance program for the poor). Since 1977, its coverage has been gradually extended from larger firms to smaller firms. Finally, Korea established universal health insurance coverage in 1989.

The health insurance act required firms with 500 or more workers to organize health insurance associations, which were guided by the National Federation of Health Insurance (NFHI). The rationale behind this policy was to expand them gradually, taking the financial conditions of firms into account. This was followed by the implementation of the Public and Private School Employees Health Insurance Act in 1979, administered by the Korea Medical Insurance Cooperation (KMIC). Thus, the employee health insurance program was divided into two different entities: NFHI and KMIC. KMIC expanded its coverage to include the families of soldiers and primary school administrators and their dependents in 1980.

NFHI gradually expanded its coverage to smaller firms, to firms with 300 or more workers in 1979, to firms with 100 or more workers in 1981, to firms with 16 or more workers in 1983. Firms with as few as five workers could join the program on a voluntary basis.

In 1986, a special task force was formed to blueprint the universal health insurance coverage. The task force proposed to expand health insurance to the rural self-employed prior to the urban, and to use a modified formula for levying contributions. The formula consisted of four factors - income, assets and properties, family members, and household size. By January 1988, 134 regional health insurance associations were organized to cover the entire rural population. In July 1989, compulsory coverage was extended to the self-employed in urban areas. In addition, the coverage was extended to firms with five or less workers, and to those who were voluntarily enrolled. Pharmacists, physicians, crop dealers, and taxi drivers were also brought into the compulsory regional health insurance scheme (Shin & Lee, 1996).

Current Policies

Coverage

The health security program is categorized into two systems: medical insurance and medical aid. Table 1 shows the number of beneficiaries of the health security system in 1996.

Medical Insurance

Medical insurance has three types of beneficiaries. First, wage-earners and their dependents who accounted for 36.6% of the population in 1996. Second, public and private school employees and their dependents who accounted for 10.5% of the population. Third, non-wage-earners (the self-employed) and their dependents who accounted for 49.1% of the population (Table 1).

Table 1: Number of Beneficiaries of Health Security

Classification		Total Population (ten thousand)	Proportion (%)
Total		4,582	100.0
Medical Insurance	Total	4,408	96.2 (100.0)
	Industrial workers	1,675	36.6 (38.0)
	Public & Private school employee	481	10.5 (10.9)
	Self-employed	2,252	49.1 (51.1)
Medical Aid	Total	174	3.8

Source: Ministry of Health and Welfare, *Yearbook of Health and Welfare Statistics*, 1997.

Medical Aid

Medical Aid provides health care for the poor, and the beneficiaries are divided into two categories: people living in public residential facilities and the unemployed, who rely on family support for their living costs. The proportion of the population eligible for this assistance was about 3.6% in 1997.

Benefits

Cash benefits are nominally provided in cases of nursing care, maternity, and funeral/burial. For example, maternity or delivery expenses are given to cover medical expenses incurred at non-designated facilities, including home delivery.

In-kind benefits are the main type of medical aid. There are statutory benefits that include medical care benefits, maternity benefits, and pharmaceutical benefits. Sometimes additional benefits may be available in accordance with the level of financial conditions set by health insurance associations. They may include funeral expenses, maternity allowances, and refund of the deductibles that the insured paid to health institutions (Moon, 1994).

Management

Each insurance program has its own insurance associations. In the case of employees, large firms have their own insurance associations, while smaller companies are grouped together to form sizable associations. By 1995 there were 145 medical insurance associations (63 single associations, 82 grouped associations) for employees. For non-wage-earners (the self-employed), there are 130 associations in urban areas and 97 associations in rural areas. These associations are financially independent and may accumulate surplus. Every association is required to join NFHI (Y. Kim et. al, 1996). For the public employee and private school employee program, only one association, KMIC, exists.

Finance

The financial resources of the insurance system consist mainly of contributions paid by the insured and employers, and of government subsidies. For wage-earners and public employees, contributions are based on the wages of the insured. Every employee pays the same percentage of his/her wage in the same association. Employers pay half of the contributions. As for private school employees, the insured pay 50% of the contributions, while the school board pays 30% and the government pays 20%.

The insurance program for the self-employed is financed by contributions from the insured and by the government subsidy. The contributions from the insured are determined on the basis of personal income, property, and family size. The government subsidizes a part of the contributions, including the program's administrative cost. It is supposed to subsidize 50% of the total expenditure of the program, but it actually pays less than this.

Issues

Since providing universal health care for the whole population in 1989, the efficient utilization of health resources, the equitable distribution of health services, and good quality health care have remained the primary objectives of the health care service. The main issues for the health insurance system are: strengthening social solidarity, improving efficiency, and integrating different systems.

Strengthening Social Solidarity

The Korean health care system is equitable in the sense that everybody has health insurance. However, there are several issues concerning distributional equity. To strengthen social solidarity the government tries to improve the equity of the health care system by extending the range of benefits that are reimbursed by the insurance, and by reducing financial imbalances and premium differences among different insurance associations.

In 1994, the government launched a plan to develop new policies for redirecting or changing the present health care system. The plan recommended that the government change its formula for subsidizing. If the change is made, insurance associations in rural areas with higher percentages of members whose expected health care costs are high would receive more government subsidies. The plan also recommended that the proportion of risk adjustment funds (10) among insurance associations, which is currently approximately 7%, increase to 19% by 1997. The funds will be used for compensating benefits for elderly patients over 65 years and for preventive and health promotion services (Y. Shin et. al., 1996).

Improving Efficiency

Efforts to promote the efficiency of the health care system concentrate on developing the providers' cost consciousness, inducing consumers' rational utilization of health services, and improving the insurers' administrative efficiency. Physicians and hospitals are paid through a fee-for-service schedule which is determined by the government. The fee-for-service reimbursement system in Korea provides inappropriate incentives for health care providers and they have no economic incentive for cost-control. The plan recommended that the government gradually replace the current fee-for-service schedule with a prospective payment system (PPS) using DRGs (Diagnosis Related Groups) (11) for inpatients and an RBRVS (resource based relative value system) for ambulatory care services. The new payment system is expected to reduce problems of health care services. The PPS began in 1995 with extensive preparation (Y. Shin, 1997).

There is a lack of dynamic adjustment towards the changing health care environment. The health care system has not been able to respond adequately to the rapidly increasing need for health services. Long-term care, ambulatory surgery, group practices, home care services, nursing homes for the elderly, and facilities for the mentally disabled are clearly needed but not well developed yet.

Integrating Different Systems

The Kim Dae-Jung Administration decided to integrate the health insurance systems. As mentioned above, each insurance program has different types of insurance associations. Integrating the different systems means that the 275 associations of the NFHI and the single association of the KMIC will be integrated into one society. In 1989, the National Health Insurance Act which required the different systems to integrate, was passed by Congress, but then President Roh Tae-Woo rejected the bill. Integrating the systems is expected to strengthen social solidarity and to improve efficiency.

Due to the current economic crisis, many Koreans are experiencing economic difficulties. Some cannot pay their medical expenses. In light of this the government decided that the unemployed should pay only 50% of their medical insurance contributions.

C. *Industrial Accident Compensation Insurance*

History

The Industrial Accident Compensation Insurance (IACI) was established in 1963. Initially, it covered only employees of firms in mining or manufacturing industries with 500 or more employees. An 'accident' was defined as an injury that needed 11 or more days of treatment. As the economy grew, its coverage continuously widened. The IACI extended its coverage to firms with 100 or more workers in 1967, to firms with 16 or more workers in 1973, and to firms with 10 or more workers in 1982. Coverage was extended to workplaces with 5 or more employees in 1994. It also covers firms in construction, electricity, gas and water, transportation, storage and communication, and other industries. Moreover, the definition of an 'accident' has extended to include injury needing 4 or more days of treatment since 1981.

The number of injured workers has gradually decreased since the 1980s. The accident rate was lowered from 3.15% in 1985 to 1.76% in 1990 and to 0.99% in 1995. But, the severity rate does not show a stable trend. The severity rate (number of lost working days per 1,000 working hours) was 2.7% in 1985, 2.7% in 1993, and 2.2% in 1996. Table 2 shows trends of industrial accidents.

Table 2: Trends of Industrial Accidents

	Firms Covered by IACI	Workers Covered by IACI	Injured Persons				Rate of Accident
			Total	Death	Injury	Occupational Disease	
1985	66,803	4,495,185	141,809	1,718	138,533	1,558	3.15
1990	129,687	7,542,752	132,893	2,236	129,019	1,638	1.76
1991	146,284	7,922,704	128,169	2,299	124,333	1,537	1.62
1992	154,820	7,058,704	107,435	2,429	103,678	1,328	1.52
1993	163,152	6,942,527	90,288	2,210	86,665	1,413	1.30
1994	172,871	7,273,132	85,948	2,678	82,352	918	1.18
1995	186,021	7,893,727	78,034	2,662	74,252	1,120	0.99

Note: Rate of Accident = Injured Persons/Workers Covered by IACI 100.
Source: Korea Labor Institute, *The Profile of Korean Human Assets: Labor Statistics 1997*, May 1997.

Current Systems

Coverage

The number of employees covered by the IACI was 8,156,894 in 1996 which included employees at workplaces with 5 or more workers. Financial institutions are not covered by the IACI. Table 3 shows the number of workers covered by the IACI by industry and year.

Table 3: Number of Workers Covered by the IACI by Industry and Year

Industry	Workers (1992)	Workers (1993)	Workers (1994)	Workers (1995)
Total	7,058,704	6,942,527	7,273,132	7,893,727
Forestry	3,931	4,958	6,519	9,501
Fishing	2,804	3,611	3,752	3,730
Agriculture	12,060	11,558	12,107	13,828
Mining	54,556	45,344	40,308	35,291
Manufacturing	3,225,717	3,066,846	3,084,827	3,066,431
Electricity, Gas, & Water	43,255	53,250	53,674	49,419
Transport, Storage & Communication	579,983	603,882	641,032	715,058
Construction	1,911,378	1,816,892	1,978,629	2,240,990
Others	1,225,020	1,336,186	1,452,284	1,759,479

Source: Ministry of Labor, *1996 Yearbook of Labor Statistics.*

Provision

Injured workers may receive six types of benefits: Medical Care Benefits, Sick Leave Benefits, Disability Benefits, Survivors Benefits, Funeral Benefits, and Disabled Survivor Benefits. Table 4 shows expenditure by the types of benefits in 1996.

Table 4: Expenditure by the Types of Benefits

Units: Million Won, %

	Total	Medical Care Benefits	Sick Leave Benefits	Disability Benefits	Survivors Benefits	Disabled Survivor	Funeral Benefits
Finance Level	1,355,337	342,974	435,729	347,751	179,502	32,782	16,598
(%)	100	25.3	32.1	25.7	13.2	2.4	1.2

Source: Ministry of Labor, Yearbook of Industrial Accident Compensation.

Finance and management

The IACI is financed solely by employers. The government may pay the administrative costs of the insurance. It is under the control of the Ministry of Labor, but it is the Labor Welfare Cooperation that actually manages it.

Issues

The main issue with the IACI concerns the proposed privatization of the insurance. Government bureaucrats in economy related departments and financial institutions support privatization. They argue that it has three advantages: First, the main principle guiding the IACI is similar to that of private insurance, which is the beneficiary burden principle. Second, private insurance companies have direct knowledge of industrial accident insurance since they have managed private employee injury insurance. Third, privatization of insurance would prevent bureaucracy and rigidity within the IACI (J. Kim, 1998).

But scholars and researchers in social welfare argue that privatization of the insurance has these disadvantages: First, to privatize the insurance, the inefficiency of the IACI's management must be proved (Seok, 1998). Its administrative costs are only 4% of the contributions. But the costs are 22.8% in private care insurance, 18.2% in private life insurance, and 18.4% in private non-life insurance. In fact, its management is more efficient than that of private insurers. Second, a private insurance company is a for-profit organization. It may accept firms with low risks, but may not accept firms with high risks. Consequently, firms with high risks may have to join public insurance schemes, which would lead to higher administrative costs of public insurance. Third, in the IACI, there are additional labor welfare programs. Additional welfare programs are medical and occupational rehabilitation services and industrial health services. They may be scaled down if the insurance is privatized.

D. Employment Insurance (EI)

History

The Employment Insurance Act was passed in 1995, and the EI system began to operate on 1 July 1995. The purpose of the system is twofold. One is to provide unemployed workers with unemployment benefits. The other is to enhance employment stability and the job ability of workers through active labor market policy measures within the framework of the EI. This is the reason why the system is called ‘employment insurance’ rather than ‘unemployment insurance’. The unemployment insurance system is a form of social insurance to alleviate workers’ hardship while unemployed by paying cash benefits to the insured.

The experience of other countries shows that simply paying unemployment benefit is not sufficient protection for unemployed workers. The best program for workers is to prevent unemployment by improving their job stability and job capacity. Therefore, in many developed countries, the traditional unemployment insurance system has adopted active labor market policies such as job placement services, vocational training, employment promotion programs, and so forth.

There is a widespread negative image of unemployment insurance in Korea because of fears that it may increase unemployment spells and thereby increase the unemployment rate. Therefore, the EI was introduced in Korea. The EI includes not only unemployment benefit schemes, but also active labor market schemes such as active job placement through a public employment office network, job security schemes for workers, and job ability development schemes throughout a worker's lifetime (K. Yoo, 1992).

Current Policies

The purposes of the EI are: to strengthen job placement services provided by public authorities in order to enhance job matches and the efficiency of the labor market; to prevent unemployment by promoting employment adjustment and by improving workers' job capacities; and to maintain workers' standards of living by providing cash benefits while involuntarily unemployed.

The EI has three major elements: Employment Stabilization Schemes, Job Ability Development Schemes and Unemployment Insurance Schemes. The Employment Stabilization Schemes are designed to prevent unemployment, to promote employment adjustment, to improve employment conditions, and to increase employment opportunities. The Job Ability Development Schemes are designed to encourage vocational training in the private sector and to enable workers to develop and improve their skills required in their jobs throughout their working lives. The Unemployment Insurance Schemes are designed to alleviate financial hardships that result from the loss of wage income during unemployment (K. Yoo, 1993).

Coverage

The three elements of the EI have different coverage. By 1998, the Unemployment Insurance Schemes cover all the workers including the self-employed except workers employed on a seasonal basis. The Employment Stabilization Schemes and Job Ability Development Schemes cover full-time workers of firms with 70 or more workers. The number of employees covered by the EI was 4,325,940 in 1997. The EI covers 32.5% of the total employees, 13,319,000 (J. Kim and Y. Yeu, 1998).

Workers employed on a seasonal basis, or whose employment is semi-illegal, are excluded from the EI's coverage because it is very difficult to identify their employment status and wages. Public employees and teachers are not covered by the EI because they have their own insurance systems and are not at risk from involuntary unemployment.

Finance and Management

Unemployment insurance is financed by contributions from workers and/or their employers. In many countries governments also finance a part of unemployment insurance costs. The insured get direct unemployment benefits directly from the EI and have to pay half of the contributions to the Unemployment Benefit Schemes. Employers are responsible for unemployment and get benefits from the Employment Stabilization Schemes and Job Ability Development Schemes. Therefore, employers pay half of the contributions to the Unemployment Benefit Schemes, and pay the entire costs of the Employment Stabilization Schemes and Job Ability Development Schemes. The government may pay the administrative costs of the system. The EI is directly managed by the Ministry of Labor.

Issues

Due to the economic crisis initiated by the foreign-currency crisis in 1997, the unemployment rate is expected to be the highest in modern Korean history in the near future. At the end of 1998, the number of unemployed had reached 1.5 million. An important issue related to this problem is how the government provides the unemployed with job opportunities and meets their basic needs. Since 1998, the Unemployment Insurance Schemes have provided cover for all workers except those employed on a seasonal basis. They are the first victims of the current economic difficulties. Presently, a key issue is to finance the expansion of the Unemployment Insurance Fund. On March 1998, the government decided that it would increase the fund to 5.8 trillion Won.

E. Housing Policies

History

Housing problems in Korea may be defined as a housing shortage, soaring housing prices, unfair distribution of housing, and poor housing quality. Housing quality has improved remarkably due to economic development. But a chronic housing shortage persists due to a sharp rise in demand caused by the continuous population increase, the trend toward nuclear families, and rapid urbanization. This was followed by soaring housing prices. The overall housing supply ratio, which indicates the level of housing shortage, had been decreasing until it was 69.2% in 1987. However, the housing shortage was much more serious in urban areas where the ratio was only 48% in 1987 (Korea National Housing Corporation, 1997).

The government has continually implemented various housing policies as part of its economic development plans to deal with housing shortages and soaring housing prices. The Housing Construction Promotion Law in 1972 encouraged housing construction by the public sector. Consequently, in the period 1972~1976, the number of housing units constructed by the private sector remained at the same level as in 1967~1971, but that by the public sector increased rapidly, accounting for 30.1% of all housing construction. In the public sector, the Korea National Housing Corporation (KNHC) and Seoul Metropolitan Government played the main role until the mid-1980s. Since the mid-1980s, the KNHC has been the most important public constructor, accounting for 11.2% and 11.1% of the periods 1987~1991 and 1992~1996, respectively. The government used the public sector to construct low-cost housing for low and moderate income classes. For example, during the 1962~1988 period, 10.89% of all the housing construction in the city of Seoul was rental housing, which was intended for the low- income class (Korea National Housing Corporation, 1989). But, its housing policies have been market-centered from the 1960s to the 1990s. The public sector focused on constructing housing for sale. As a result, low income households who were mostly tenants had difficulty finding suitable and affordable housing.

Table 5: Housing Construction by Builders, 1962~1996

Builders	Public			Private	Total
Year	Central Government	Local Government	KNHC		
1962~1966	16,301 5.0%	-	4,603 1.4%	305,031 93.6%	325,935 100.0%
1967~1971	16,527 3.1%	-	7,739 1.4%	516,072 95.5%	540,338 100.0%
1972~1976	174,346 22.9%		54,420 7.2%	531,825 69.9%	760,591 100.0%
1977~1981	27,219 2.4%	192,031 17.2%	158,731 14.2%	737,093 66.1%	1,115,074 100.0%
1982~1986	12,903 1.1%	173,696 15.0%	180,621 15.6%	787,851 68.2%	1,155,071 100.0%
1987~1991	7,155 0.3%	168,141 7.0%	268,435 11.2%	1,942,760 81.4%	2,386,491 100.0%
1992~1996	-	92,726 3.0%	346,126 11.1%	2,665,982 85.9%	3,104,854 100.0%

Source: Korea National Housing Corporation, Housing Handbook 1997.

For the first time, in the fourth 5 Year Economic and Social Development Plan of 1977~1981, the government expressed its willingness to implement housing policies to reduce the gap among income classes. Nevertheless, the policies were not significantly different from the previous ones.

As a housing shortage and extremely high housing prices became a serious social problem, the government introduced an ambitious housing program in 1988. The program aimed at building 2 million units of housing over a 5-year period from 1988~1992. Consequently, the number of new housing units over this period was about 2.7 million, improving the housing supply ratio to 77.5% in 1992 (Korea National Housing Corporation, 1997). The program also contributed somewhat to stabilizing rising housing prices. Even so, housing prices in urban Korea have still been increasing twice as fast as average income. The average housing price was 9.38 times that of the average annual income in 1991. An average rent was 35% of the average monthly income. The program was successful in that it achieved its goal of housing construction, but it was criticized on the grounds that it widened the housing gap between the middle-income and low income classes.

While the program focused on massive construction of housing for sale, it included an important sub-program, construction of public housing for permanent rental. The government planned to build 250 thousand units for rental, but actually built 190 thousand units during the same period. It was the first and last program to provide permanent public rental housing. In that sense, it was a housing program that had the characteristic of a social welfare program.

Public permanent rental housing (social housing) was available only to the poor designated by law. Moreover, selection of residents for the housing was based on current housing conditions, household heads' ages, and types of households, in other words, based on their needs rather than their ability to pay. It was the only housing program that selected beneficiaries by means-test.

It was considered as a housing program that benefited low-income households, but the program ended when the Kim Young-Sam Administration came in. Even the social housing had problems. It did not consider social and economic conditions of beneficiaries and the housing conditions of the community in which social housing was constructed (Ha, 1997). A small number of apartments were built for rental before and after housing for permanent rental. These were called long-term rental housing or short-term rental housing. They were not really rental housing because they were sold after 1~5 years. Moreover, they were illegally sold even within 1~5 years. Therefore, low-income non-homeowners, target population of long-term and short-term rental housing, could not benefit from the rental housing program (Lee, 1995).

Unfair distribution of housing

Through the several economic plans, Koreans had been enjoying their wealth until the 1997 economic crisis. However, the economic growth also increased the gap among income classes. Housing was one of the areas that the gap was extremely evident. High-income households enjoyed life in 4~5 bedroom luxurious apartments in southern Seoul by the Han river, while low-income households lived in shanty houses of Seoul's hillside. Despite the poor quality of the shanty houses, they could provide low-income households with low-cost housing near jobs. However, the government has been continuously eradicating the shanty houses by urban redevelopment, thereby depriving low-income households of their home.

Urban redevelopment since the end of 1980s is different from redevelopment in the 1970s and the early 1980s. The recent redevelopment aims at building apartments while the past redevelopment usually aimed at constructing business areas. Since the end of the 1980s, land for housing has been exhausted in Seoul. Consequently, apartment constructors tried to get land for new apartments by redeveloping the remaining slum areas in Seoul. Original residents of the redeveloped areas were not the main beneficiaries of the redevelopment. Middle-income households purchased newly constructed apartments in the areas, while only 10% of the new residents in the areas were the original residents (Ha, 1997). Housing has been unfairly distributed among income classes.

Housing Policies

Despite enormous housing construction since 1988, housing shortage has not been resolved yet. The housing supply ratio was 89.2% in 1996 (Korea National Housing Corporation, 1997). There were at least 1,222 thousand households who had to share space with others because of housing shortage. Housing shortage in Seoul was more serious in that the housing supply ratio was 70%.

In this section, two aspects of housing policies will be examined: housing construction and housing distribution.

Housing Construction

Housing construction by the public sector tends to decrease in recent years. The government intervened into the housing market since the 1970s because of serious housing shortage, but it slowed down its intervention since the end of the 1980s. Instead, the market has become the major player in housing construction.

The government has focused on housing construction for sale. Construction of rental housing increased from 6.7% of all housing construction in the period 1982~1986, to 15.8% in 1987~1991. But, it decreased to 10.7% in 1992~1996. The emphasis on housing for sale was an effort to encourage home-ownership. Moreover, the government does not have resources enough to build rental housing for low-income households. Therefore, even public housing is constructed to meet the demands of middle-income households. Consequently, low-income households have difficulty in finding affordable housing. The Kim Young-Sam Administration launched the New Economy 5 Year Plan in 1993. According to the Plan, the public sector supports housing for low-income households, while the private sector's role is expanded.

In 1995, housing construction by the public sector accounted for 36.8% of 619 thousand units. Rental housing construction in the public sector was 34.2%. Total housing construction decreased to 592 thousand units in 1996, but housing construction by the public sector increased from 228 thousand units to 232 thousand units. Especially, rental housing construction in the public sector increased to 45.2%.

However, the public sector planned to construct only 200 thousand unit of housing, and only 75 thousand rental housing (37.5% of housing construction in the public sector) in 1997. Among them, long-term (50 years) rental housing units are only 5 thousand. The remaining rental housing will be short-term (5 years) (Korea National Housing Corporation, 1997).

Housing distribution

One of the most interesting aspects of Korean housing is its distribution system. Soaring housing prices has been a serious social problem since the 1970s. This problem has led to overheating of the housing market and to induced speculation on housing. Since 1976, housing prices were escalating due to increasing housing demand and speculation.

Consequently, the government has controlled prices of new apartments in the private sector as well as in the public sector to stabilize housing prices since 1977. Price regulations were criticized for many reasons. Price regulations, private housing constructors argued, forced them to reduce housing construction and/or insolvent construction. In addition, price regulations set the price of new housing much lower than the price of existing housing. This has led to speculation on new housing. To deal with this problem, the government added the housing bond bidding system to the existing price regulations for privately-built housing.

Price regulations of new apartments in the private except in Seoul and its metropolitan areas were abolished in 1996. The abolition was expanded to Seoul in February 1998 because housing construction was badly damaged by the economic crisis of 1997. The economic crisis caused by the foreign currency market rocketed interest rates of funds for housing purchase. This abolition does not apply to new apartments in the public sector and Citizen's housing (less than 60 m2) financed by the Citizen's Housing Fund (CHF). In addition, the housing distribution system in Korea specifies the eligibility for new apartments in the public sector and the private sector. To be eligible for Citizen's housing financed by the CHF, an applicant must a renter and household head for more than one year. Moreover, he/she must save by installments on the Housing Installment Savings Deposit Plan. If he/she gets a Citizen's housing, he/she will not be eligible for another housing within 10 years.

To be eligible for privately-built housing, an applicant must be a household head and must have deposited an amount based on the size of the housing to an Apartment Application Deposit. If he/she gets a privately-built housing, he/she will not be eligible for another housing within five years.

Issues and the future

Recently, the government is going to amend the system May 1998: it will reduce non-eligibility period for Citizen's housing from 10 years to 5 years, and abolish for privately-built housing. The amendment is expected to help housing builders to survive the serious recession.

The economic crisis of Korea has seriously damaged private housing builders. Several big builders are already bankrupted. Private housing builders expect that they will construct 200 thousand units of housing, only 40% of 1997 (Chosun Ilbo, 3.16. 1998). Moreover, housing builders in the public sector are expected to reduce their housing construction because of government budget. The IMF asked the Korean government to reduce its budget. The reduction of housing construction might explode housing prices in the public sector as well as in the private sector in the near future since Korea still has a housing shortage.

CONCLUSION

Since the mid 1980s, the income gap among income classes in Korea had been decreased until the economic crisis. Gini's coefficient, which is an index of income concentration, shows that unequal income distribution improved from 0.3449 in 1985 to 0.2954 in 1996. However, the lower income classes are more severely influenced by the economic crisis than the upper income classes are. When working households are classfied into five group by income with equal proportions, the highest income class (20%) lost 8.0% in the third quarter of 1998 compared to the second quarter, while the lowest income class (20%) lost 24.4%. The lower income classes are more likely to suffer from the unemployment.

Korea has not established her social safety nets to help the lower income families to overcome this crisis. Thus, needs for expanding social welfare systems are greater than before. Experiences of other countries have shown that a societal crisis could be an impetus for expanding social welfare systems. The United Kingdom drafted her social security system during the World War II, and the United States during the Great Depression.

How will Korea respond to her economic crisis? Korean people say the current economic situation controlled by the IMF is the most serious hardship since the

Korean War that Korea has dealt with. The number of the unemployed is expected to go over 1.5~2 million. Considering that the Korean government counts a person employed if he/she works for even an hour per week, it must be recognized that the unemployment rate of Korea has been under-estimated. Therefore, the current economic crisis may be much more damaging to the life of Korean people. But, the Kim Dae-Jung Administration has been focusing on economic problems rather than on social welfare needs of the people. It seems that the current crisis is reducing Korean social welfare systems rather than expanding them.

It is not sure yet when the IMF control and the economic crisis will end in Korea. But, it is likely that the life of Korean people is getting much worse than before. Massive unemployment is coming on the way, but the government is not willing to expand its efforts for social welfare.

ENDNOTES

1. The average work days a month is for 1996.
2. The Bank of Korea announced that per capita GNP in 1997 was US $ 9,511 due to the depreciation of Korean Won. It also expected that per capita GNP would be reduced to US $ 7,000 in 1998 (Chosun Ilbo, 3.17.1998).
3. It was 1, 616 in 1989 (National Statistical Office, 1998).
4. These are mainly construction workers who work on daily-bases.
5. They are scheduled to become compulsorily insured since April 1999.
6. Before the current economic crisis, US $1 used to be about 800 Won. The rate went up rapidly to over 2,000 Won at the end of 1997. The rate is about 1,180 Won in January 1999.
7. The government promised to limit using the Pension Fund as the public fund.
8. The age limit is no longer required from 1999 onward.
9. It was estimated as 186 thousand Won in 1997.
10. Risk Adjustment Funds represent financial risk pooling in order to reduce financial inequality among health insurance associations because of corporatist health insurance.
11. DRG means common disease or patient may take equal payment in spite of multiple level of medical care.

REFERENCES

Choi, Kyun (1995). Evaluation and Issues of Social Welfare Policies in Korea. In Korea Social Science Institute (Ed.), Understanding Korean Social Welfare (pp. 13-31). Seoul: Dong-Poong.

Chung, Won-Oh (1998). Guarantee on Minimum Living and Public Assistance. In Korea Social Science Institute (Ed.), The Present Situation and Issues of Social Welfare Policy in Korea (pp. 248-267). Seoul: Ingan-kwa Bokji.

Ha, Sungkyu (1997). A Prospect on Housing Problems and Housing Policies in Korea. Http:\\www.interpia.net\~chhg\genjung\jumun.htm.

Kim, Jingu and Yeu, Yujin (1998). Issues and Prospect of Employment Insurance in Korea. In Korea Social Science Institute (Ed.), The Present Situation and Issues of Social Welfare Policy in Korea (pp. 221-247). Seoul: Ingan-kwa Bokji.

Kim, Jinsoo (1998). A Study on the Problem of Privatization of the Work Injury Insurance. Korean Journal of Social Welfare Studies vol 10.

Kim, Yongha, Seok, Jaeeun, and Yoon, Sekhwan (1996). Proposal for Efficiency of social insurance administration in Korea. Seoul: Korea Institute for Health and Social Affairs.

Korea Labor Institute (1997). The Profile of Korean Human Assets: Labor Statistics. Seoul: Korea Labor Institute.

Korea National Housing Corporation (1997). Housing Handbook 1997. Seoul: Korea National Housing Corporation.

Korea National Housing Corporation (1989). Housing Handbook 1989. Seoul: Korea National Housing Corporation.

Kwon, Soonwon (1993). Social Policy in Korea: Challenges and Responses. Seoul: Korea Development Institute.

Lee, Young-Hwan (1995). A Trend and Issues of Public Rental Housing. In Korea Social Science Institute (Ed.), Understanding Korean Social Welfare (pp. 143-163). Seoul: Dong-Poong.

Ministry of Health and Social Affairs (1994). White paper on Health and Social Affairs. Seoul: Ministry of Health and Social Affairs.

Ministry of Health and Welfare (1997). 1997 Yearbook of Health and Welfare Statistics. Seoul: Ministry of Health and Welfare.

Ministry of Labor (1996). 1996 Yearbook of Labor Statistics. Seoul: Ministry of Labor.

Ministry of Labor (1996). 1996 Yearbook of Industrial Accident Compensation Insurance. Seoul: Ministry of Labor.

Moon, Okryun (1994). Development of the health insuranceprogramme in Korea. A paper presented at the joint seminar between the Korean Medical Association and the Russian Academy of Medical Sciences. Seoul, South Korea.

Nam, Sejin and Cho, Heungsik (1995). Social Welfare in Korea. Seoul: Nanam.

National Statistical Office (1997). Social Indicators of Korea 1997, National Statistical Office.

National Statistical Office (1998). Social Indicators of Korea 1998, National Statistical Office.

Park, Myungsoo (1993). Industrial Accidents and Occupational Safety. Youngbum Park (Ed.). Labour in Korea. Seoul: Korea Labor Institute.

Seok, Jaeeun (1998). Issues and Prospect of Industrial Accident Compensation Insurance in Korea. In Korea Social Science Institute (Ed.), The Present Situation and Issues of Social Welfare Policy in Korea (pp. 176-220). Seoul: Ingan-kwa Bokji.

Shin, Youngsoo (1997). Health Care Systems in Transition: Korea. The Journal of Public Health Medicine.

Shin, Youngsoo and Lee, Kyusik (1996). The Health Insurance System in Korea. The Journal of Public Health Medicine.

Shin, Youngsoo, Moon, Okryun, Kim, Konghyun, & Kim, Changyup (1996). Evolution of Health Care Policy and Programme in Korea. Paper presented at the 47th session of the WHO Regional Committee for the Western Pacific.

Social Security Administration (1995). Social Security Programs throughout the world—1995. Washington DC: Author.

Yoo, Kilsang (1992). Employment Insurance Schemes of Korea: Proposals and Policy Options. Seoul: Korea Labor Institute.

Yoo, Kilsang (1993). A Proposed Employment Insurance System for Korea.In Kilasng Yoo & Manfred Ziemek (eds.), Unemployment Insurance system in selected countries. Seoul: Korea Labor Institute.

KWONG-LEUNG TANG

CHAPTER FIVE

ECONOMIC GROWTH, PATERNALISM AND NATION BUILDING: SOCIAL DEVELOPMENT IN SINGAPORE

INTRODUCTION

Singapore is an affluent city-state. Though it just has a small population of 3 million, it has enjoyed very successful economic development in the last twenty years. Along with Hong Kong, Taiwan and South Korea, it has contributed to the East Asian miracle. Since 1960s, its growth has been "staggering" (Berger, 1986), consistently averaging 8% in the last three decades. In terms of per capita income, it is the second in Asia, after Japan. Its per capita was US$26,400 on a nominal basis and US$23,400 on a purchasing-power-parity basis in 1995. According to the United Nations Development Programme (UNDP) (1997), Singapore is ranked high in the Per Capita Index: 15 out of 175 countries. Because of such impressive growth record, its social development has often been taken for granted. Often, it is difficult to gauge the actual extent of social development claim since most developed Asian countries either lack (or refuse to publish) reliable statistics. Based on statistics from international organizations and estimates from local scholars, this chapter will look at some indicators of social development and pose the questions what are the level of social development in Singapore and whether social development in this city-state has synchronized with its rapid economic development? It will look at several areas of rising concern: poverty, inequality, and gender equality. The role of the state in enhancing social development will be discussed at the end.

SOCIAL DEVELOPMENT MEASURES

Recently, Singapore has been rated as a free, competitive and economically developed city-nation. This city-state has received some highly positive comments from the world organizations. The economy of Singapore was rated the second most competitive in the 1997 IMD World Competitiveness Yearbook and the second freest economy by the conservative Heritage Foundation based in Washington DC. As of 1996, Singapore has formally achieved 'developed country' status according to the Organization for Economic Cooperation and Development (Enricht et al., 1997).

K.-L. Tang (ed.), Social Development in Asia, 83–97.

Social scientists, on the other hand, have argued improved material quality of life ensues from its rapid economic development.

It would be necessary to look at some objective social indicators of development (Table 1). It can be seen that Singapore compares rather well with other developed societies in terms of mean years of schooling, enrolment rate and adult literacy rate. It also has low unemployment, low inflation, and huge foreign reserves. Its foreign debt is zero.

Table 1: Social Indicators for Singpore and Other East Asian NIC's

	GNP per Capita ($US) 1991	Mean years of Schooling 1992	Enrolment Ratio for All Levels 1990-91	Adult Literacy Rate (%) 1992	Population Per Doctor 1990	Government Spending (% of GDP) 1990
Hong Kong	18520	7.2	69	90	1080	14.4
South Korea	6670	9.3	74	96.8	1370	17
Singapore	14734	11.0	68	92	920	22.7
Taiwan*	10599	---	---	89.8	913	22.7
Canada	20510	12.2	89	99	450	21.8
Japan	26840	10.8	73	99	630	15.8
Sweden	25180	11.4	70	99	370	47.5

*Data come from Asian Development Bank (1994-95).
Sources: Asian Development Bank (1994); United Nations Development Programme (1994)

Another way to measure quality of life is the human development index (HDI) which is created and developed by the UNDP. It is based on three indicators of well-being at the national level -- longevity, knowledge, and standard of living. Longevity is measured by life expectancy. Knowledge is measured by a combination of adult literacy and mean years of school. Standard of living is measured by purchasing power, based on real GDP per capita adjusted for the local cost of living. The latest estimate of HDI for Singapore can be seen from Table 2. In 1994, Singapore reached 0.900. It is ranked 26, after Hong Kong (22). Hence it is classified as high human development country. It can be seen that, using this measure, Singapore has come close to the industrial countries. It far outpaces other less developed Asian countries (e.g. China and Thailand).

A trend analysis of human development index from 1960 to 1994 indicates a continual improvement (Table 2). The index was 0.519 in 1960, improved to 0.682 in 1970 and 0.780 in 1980. In 1992, it reached 0.836 which was considerably lowered than the mean (0.918) for the industrial countries. Its latest measure in 1994 was 0.900, which enabled Singapore to rank 26 in the world.

Table 2: Human Development Index for Singapore and Selected Countries (1960-94)

	1960	1970	1990	1992	1994	HDI Rank 1994	Per Capita Rank 1994
Singapore	0.519	0.682	0.780	0.836	0.900	26	11
Hong Kong	0.561	0.737	0.830	0.875	0.914	22	5
South Korea	0.398	0.523	0.666	0.859	0.890	32	37
China	0.248	0.372	0.475	0.664	0.626	108	111
Thailand	0.737	0.465	0.551	0.798	0.833	59	51
Canada	0.865	0.887	0.911	0.932	0.960	1	8
USA	0.865	0.881	0.905	0.925	0.942	4	3

For 1994, HDI and Per Capita Rank: Highest rank is "1". Lowest rank is "176".
Sources: United Nations Development Project (1994-97)

It would be interesting to compare HDI ranking with its GDP per capita ranking since their congruence would signify an equal emphasis. In 1994, its per capita rank is much higher than the HDI rank (11). As a result, the gap between human development rank and per capita rank is negative 17. Such a wide margin reflects the fact that Singapore still has considerable potential for translating its income into improved well-being for the people.

SOCIAL SERVICES AND ANTI-WELFARISM

Economic growth, meritocracy, work ethic, and a general sense of pragmatism are the key ethos in Singapore. There has been a strong antipathy against social spending in order to bring about higher standard of living. The conviction that fruits from rapid economic development would spread through the population is so strong that the government should not intervene and undermine the working of the market. Not surprisingly, the rising quality of life is attributed wholly to improved economic performance by the government. In particular, welfare state development has been frowned upon by the ruling party, People's Action Party (PAP) which has ruled Singapore since its independence. In fact, the ruling party has taken every opportunity to belittle the institution of welfare state and use Great Britain, its former colonial master, as an example where welfare state has proven untenable. In this regard, the PAP government in its 1998 budget reaffirms its anti-welfare ideology and the importance of voluntarism:

> The absence of large scale public assistance programmes reflects the Government's stand on state welfarism. We believe that extensive welfare programmes damage the fabric of our society as they discourage individual responsibility, self reliance, community support and the work ethic. Even in the UK, the Government has realised that welfarism is not the right way to go, and is trying to roll back many of the welfare programmes and policies introduced after the Second World War.

The government continues to identify its own style of social policy: "Our approach is one of many helping hands, with co-funding from Government and public donations and services rendered by volunteers and members of the community."

Looking at the history of social welfare development in Singapore, one can find ample instances when this anti-welfare position was empirically validated. First and foremost, Singapore has not established an elaborate social safety for its disadvantaged. The public assistance program has been small and ungenerous. Unemployment insurance, one of the mainstays of welfare state, is absent. Even though discussion of this institution has been raised or recently implemented in other tigers like Hong Kong and South Korea, countries which are also known for its anti-welfare stance, there has been a total lack of debate on unemployment insurance. However, if social policy should be defined more broadly to include social security, education, housing and health and if one looks closely at the reality, the ruling PAP has engaged actively in various aspects of social policy, in particularly central provident fund, public housing and education. Arguably, had the government not intervened in these areas, the quality of life enjoyed by the people would not have occurred. But a caution is needed. It is argued here that the government does intervene in providing social programs but there is a limit when the government is not willing to cross and it continually and actively belittles its role in social intervention. It is important to look at some of the major social institutions and programs set up by the government.

Central Provident Fund (CPF): Singapore is rather unique in implementing a large-scale central provident fund for its citizens. Academics have argued that social forms of social intervention is indispensable in advanced industrial countries. Thus it is contended by some scholars that the provision of social security is functional to the survival of any capitalist society (Offe, 1983). Singapore is no exception to this analysis. Arguing from a neo-Marxist perspective, Castells (1992) notes that Singapore has successfully used welfare expenditures and public housing to facilitate the reproduction of labour. Prior to its independence, social needs were massive but social services in Singapore were underdeveloped. This situation is conducive to public discontent. An analyst comments that in the face of poverty, extreme inequality, and lack of social services, the colony was open to agitation and Communist subversion, which shook Singapore in 1947-50 and again in 1954-55 (Regnier, 1991). In this respect, the institution of CPF represents the approach the government has adopted to ensure social stability, as a means to attract foreign capital investment and avert social crisis (Sherradan, 1997).

Established by the British colonial government in 1955, the CPF is an attempt by the government of Singapore to use earmarked forced savings to finance merit goods such as provision for old age, housing and medical care (Asher, 1985). This program is an embodiment of individual responsibility, allowing working people to save their earnings and invest them in a wide range of programs (buying public housing, investment, insurance, hospital expenses, and retirement etc.). Though contributions from employees and employers constitute the key source of savings for this program, it is centrally administered. While social insurance (with contributions from state, employers and employees) is the model of choice for many other developed nations which has led to some degrees of income redistribution, Singapore has steadfastly held on to this kind of provident fund. With the rise of neoliberal ideas in the last two decades for private provision of welfare, in many advanced industrial countries including the United States, there has been discussion of turning their present social insurance scheme into provident fund-like program in order to instil an element of individual responsibility.

There are some positive aspects with this program. In the short history of CPF, the government of Singapore has brought about a very high rate of national savings, which has been used for development purposes. Moreover, for the individuals, the purchase of public housing is made possible when the government allows people to withdraw money from the CPF. This results in extremely high home ownership rate (90%) which in turn contributes to social stability of the Singaporean society.

On the down side, there are a number of outstanding issues: adequacy, access, and redistribution. First and foremost is the question of adequacy. When the program is linked not just to retirement but to a number of other contingencies (insurance, health etc..), its level of accumulation has always been problematic. Recent studies from local scholars have found that balances of a vast majority of contributors are low, making it necessary for them to look for other sources of income for social security purposes. According to statistics on CPF contributors, 45.6% of wage earners earned less than S$1,000 per month. This increases to 80.3% if a wage level of S$2,000 is used (Asher, 1993). This includes many of those who are close to retirement. This concern is partially validated by a recent study conducted by Singapore Press Holdings (7 April, 1998, *The Straits Times*) when 30% of the respondents felt that they might not have enough savings for their retirement and there will be no one to look after them. The extent of concern was the same between the two main groups -- those aged 20 to 34 and those aged 35 years and above. For those who are not worried, only 28% feel that the government would take care of their retirement needs.

The extent of coverage is always an issue. The very nature of provident fund, centralized or otherwise, means only those who are working will benefit while those who are not in workforce (housewives, disabled, unemployed. self-employed etc..) would be excluded. It is estimated that only 75% of workforce is under the protection of CPF.

From a social policy perspective, this form of social security can be problematic in that its redistributive impact is inherently weak (Midgley, 1984). Worse still, the government of Singapore exacerbates inequality by making CPF contributions non-taxable (Asher, 1991; 1993). Obviously, those who contribute more will reap the greater benefits from this tax policy. In early 1998, there have been much talks of privatizing the whole system, which, if implemented, will further make it a powerless tool for income distribution.

Social Services: Most notable of all the social services is housing. Singapore's investments in public housing are unequal in the developing societies. The home ownership rate now stands at 90%, the highest in the world (General Household

Survey, 1995). The political connotation of public housing cannot be missed by anyone. Prime Minister Goh has indicated that "public housing is where the centre of gravity of (Singapore) society will always be." The symbolic power of public housing is crucial to the government. As noted by Chua (1995: 139), "the overwhelming presence of more than half a million completed dwelling units is a constant reminder to the population of the PAP government's achievement."

Additionally, the small city-state has extensive public education and health services. Education receives the top priority from the government. According to the 1998 budget, 4% of GDP is devoted to education. The PAP government has always seen education as an investment in human capital (Deyo, 1992; Chua, 1995; Republic of Singapore, 1997). With a strong emphasis on economic growth, an educated workforce is always deemed to be indispensable by the ruling party.

In the recent budget of 1998, the government announces 3% of the GDP is given to health services. This level of funding is at best modest and it has been subject to some criticism. Financing for health services, according to social scientists in Singapore (Asher, 1991), has been decreasing. Toh and Low (quoted in Asher, 1991) estimate that health spending has been diminishing over the years: 3.9% of GDP in 1960, 3.5% in 1970 and 3% in 1988. Needless to say, such level of health spending is considerably lowered than other industrial countries which have the same level of GDP per capita. Both the United States and Canada, for instance, had spent over 7% of their Gross National Product on health services as early as in 1970s. To counterbalance governmental retreat, several changes (i.e. the introduction of Medisave and MediShield) have been made to the CPF so that people can withdraw money from their accounts to pay for their own health and hospital expenses. With impending aging population and the escalating costs of health services, it seems that reliance on the CPF is almost impossible to meet all the health needs. The example of health spending demonstrates the unwillingness of the government to commit more than what has been expended. The will of the party not to increase social spending and its emphasis on private savings as a means to solve social needs cannot be overemphasized.

POVERTY, INCOME INEQUALITY, AND GENDER EQUITY

With a limited budget for social and community services, it is expected that the government of Singapore has a rather restrictive role in social services. Thus, like other industrial countries, the presence of massive social needs can be discerned in a few areas.

Poverty: Any assessment of poverty rate can be elusive in most societies. There are some major reasons for this. The poor are politically invisible and they are atomized. A sizeable proportion of the people in the poverty pool may change from year to year. More importantly, the permanently poor are often isolated. In East Asia, many governments, consciously or unconsciously, tend to wish away the problem of poverty in order to showcase their vibrant economies to the rest of the world.

Like many other Asian countries, the government of Singapore has not developed any official definition and measurement of poverty. Hence, reliable estimates are lacking. However, there is constant official optimism about the complete eradication of poverty. This position is backed by the international organizations as, for instance, the United Nations (1993) which claims that poverty is no longer an issue in the four Asian tigers. However, time line analysis only shows a drastic improvement (Table 3), but not the total elimination of poverty. The trend in poverty is based on the Amalgamated Union of Public Employees (AUPE) poverty line (Lim et al., 1988). The reduction of poverty is rapid, from over 30 % in 1973 to about 15% in 1978 and 7.2% in 1983. But it would be far from the truth to argue that absolute poverty is eliminated altogether, particularly when there was a substantial number of poor people in early 1980s.

Table 3: Poverty Rate in Singapore: 1966-1983

Year	Households in Poverty (%)
1966	37
1973	31.9
1978	15
1983	0.3/72*

*From Lim et al (1988). Two poverty lines are used in this study: an extreme absolute poverty line of S$60 per month per capita and a moderate poverty line.
Sources: Bautista (1990); Lim et al. (1988)

Because of rapid and continuing economic growth, some assessment of poverty rate in Singapore has been extremely optimistic. For instance, Lim and her associates (1993) comment that rapid economic growth has almost removed absolute poverty which is largely confined to elderly and disabled. However, Prime Minister Goh indicated in 1996 that some 6 % of households were not able to own public housing, which would be an indirect indicator of relative poverty. Also, there is no lack of anecdotal accounts which shows the presence of poverty (3 April, 1997, *The Straits Times*). Comparatively, poverty in all the other tigers is still a major social problem. A case in point is Hong Kong which has attained the same level of economic development as Singapore. Lately, it has "rediscovered" poverty; one study gives an estimate of 10% poverty rate (Oxfam, 1996). In view of the fact that poverty continues to be a persistent and difficult problem in other advanced industrial countries, this claim on the extent of poverty may be difficult to accept. Instead, it stands to reason that some forms of poverty remain latent. This conclusion is made more credible when the full impact of Asian economic turmoil on Singapore gradually unfolds. According to official estimate, the unemployment rate is set to rise and there will be some 20,000 people being retrenched. Seven out of 10 workers are from the manufacturing industries (4 June, 1998 *The Straits Times*). As expected, the older workers would find it difficult to get new jobs. As a result, the government is now spending some S$50 million on the Skill Redevelopment Programme in order to retrain some 20,000 older workers.

Human Poverty Index: Another way to look at the extent of poverty in Singapore is the human poverty index which is developed by the United Nations (UNDP, 1997). Looking at this poverty index, Singapore is ranked very high, fourth out of 78 countries (Table 4). A breakdown of the measure, however, shows some areas which deserve some attention. Survival deprivation (measuring the percentage of people not expected to survive to age 40) is 3.2 for Singapore, which is much lowered than other Asian countries under examination. Likewise, Singapore does well in two other measures of human poverty (population without access to safe water and health services). However, its adult illiteracy rate is 9%, which is much higher than those of Philippines (5.6%) and Thailand (6.5%). The percentage of underweight children under five is 14 for Singapore, which does not compare well with Cuba (2), Chile (3) and Trinidad and Tobago (1), countries which are relatively much poorer than Singapore.

Table 4: Human Poverty Index: Singapore and Selected Countries

HPI Rank	HPI Value	Survival Depriva-tion (1990)	Adult Illiteracy (1994)	Pop without Access to Safe Water (1990-96)	Pop Without Access to Health Services (1990-95)	Underweight children under age 5 (%) (1990-96)
1. Trinidad & Tobago	4.1	5.4	2.1	3	0	7
2. Cuba	5.1	6.2	4.6	11	0	1
3. Chile	5.4	4.6	5.0	15	3	1
4. Singapore	6.6	3.2	9.0	0	0	14
5. Costa Rica	6.6	4.1	5.3	4	20	2
18. China	17.5	9.1	19.1	33	12	16
19. Philippines	17.7	12.8	5.6	14	29	30

Note: Survival deprivation is measured by "people not expected to survive to age 40(%) in 1990." The last 3 measures (population without access to safe water, population without access to health services, and underweight children under age 5) contributes to "the deprivation in economic provisioning."
Source: United Nations Development Project (1997), p.126.

Income Distribution: Another improvement measure of social development is income equality. In the last decade, income distribution has been worsening in many industrial countries (Atkinson et al., 1995). The same is true for most of the four tigers. Along with Hong Kong, Singapore is the East Asian country with greatest income disparity. This is seen from the latest estimates of Gini Coefficient (Table 5). In 1994, it stands at 0.44. In the last thirty years, this measure has hovered around this level for Singapore. The coefficient in 1966 was measured at 0.50 but declined to 0.45 in 1975 (Rao, 1990; Tan, 1997). By the middle to late 1980s, Singapore was able to shift its labour-intensive industries to other less developed countries in the region and developed capital-intensive, high-technology industries. Hence, economists attribute to the worsening income distribution to this industrial restructuring. In contrast, both Taiwan and South Korea, having very high rates of economic development, have managed to bring the Gini Coefficient down to 0.30. Even Hong Kong, for a short period in the 1970s, has lowered its Gini Coefficient to 0.39.

Table 5: Gini Coefficient for Household Income in the East Asian NICs 1966-1996

Year	Korea	Taiwan	Singapore	Hong Kong
1966	0.342	0.358	0.498	0.467
1968	0.305	0.362		
1970	0.332	0.321	0.470	
1971	0.360		0.430	0.409
1972		0.318	0.430	
1973			0.430	
1974		0.319	0.430	0.398
1975			0.440	
1976	0.391	0.307	0.440	0.409
1977			0.440	
1978	0.400	0.306	0.440	
1979			0.424	0.373
1980	0.389	0.303	0.420	
1981			0.443	0.453
1982	0.357	0.308	0.465	
1983			0.440	
1984		0.312	0.460	
1985	0.356	0.317	0.460	
1986				0.458
1988	0.340			
1991				0.480
1994			0.440	
1996				0.510

Sources: Fields (1984; 1991); Lim et al (1988); Haggard (1990); Sundrum (1990); Tsang (1991)

This worsening problem of income disparity can be seen from another measure: the ratio of income for the top 20% against the bottom 20% (Table 6). This income ratio stands at 9.6 for the period 1985-89. Comparatively, this is the highest among the 4 tigers (Hong Kong 8.7, South Korea, 7.5 and Taiwan, 8.3), indicating the a very high degree of inequality. Assessing it on a longer time span (1980-94), it can be seen from Table 6 that per capita income is US$4,934 for the poorest 20% while that for the richest 20% is US$47,311. Thus, the income ratio stands at 9.58, which is the highest compared to all other Asian countries under examination.

Table 6: Singapore's Income Ratio (In US Dollars) (1980-94)

Country	Top 20% Per Capita	Bottom 10% Per Capita	Income Ratio* Per Capita
Singapore	4934	47311	9.58
USA	5800	51705	8.91
Japan	8987	38738	4.31
Sweden	7160	33206	4.61
Canada	5971	42110	7.05
Hong Kong	5821	50666	8.70
China	722	5114	7.08

*Income Ratio (Per Capita) is the ratio of top 20% to lowest 20% in terms of per capita income.
** The average income ratio (per capita) for advanced industrial countries is 6.98.
Sources: World Bank (1980-95); UNDP (1997).

Gender Measures: Feminists have recently alert us to the role of women in the development process of the Asian tigers. Family support to the industrialization process has been found important in most studies (McLaughlin, 1993). Essentially, the family "puts into place an economy that draws on female wage labour" (Salaff, 1992). Despite the positive role of women, their status remains inferior in the society. One can get some confirmation from data collected by international organization.

Most recently, the UNDP (1997) generates two objective indicators to assess gender development: Gender-related Development Index (GDI) and Gender Empowerment Index (GEI). The first measure uses the same variables as the HDI. The difference is that the GDI adjusts the average achievement of each country in life expectancy, educational attainment and income in accordance with the disparity in achievement between women and men. The other measure, gender empowerment index, looks at the relative empowerment of women and men in political and economic spheres of society. The following variables are factored into the equation: women's and men's percentage share of administrative and managerial positions and their percentage shares of professional and technical jobs. A third variable, women's and men's percentage shares of parliamentary seats, is chosen to reflect political participation and decision-making power.

While Singapore has fared well in the Gender-related Development Index (27) which is close to its HDI ranking (26) in 1994, its Gender Empowerment Index raises cause for concern (Table 7). Singapore's ranking is 47, with a low earned income share at 31. Its GEM is 0.423, considerably lowered than most other industrial countries. In short, there is a lot of room for Singapore to improve the status of women in its society.

Table 7: Gender Empowerment Measure (GEM): Singapore and Selected Countries

	GEM Value	GEM Rank	Seats held in Parlaiment (% women)	Administrators & Managers (% women)	Professional & Technical Workers (% women)	Earned Income Share (% to women)
Singapore	0.423	47	2.5	34.3	16.1	31
Korea	0.302	73	3.0	4.2	45.0	28
Canada	0.700	6	19.3	42.2	56.1	38
USA	0.671	7	11.2	42.0	52.7	41
High Human Development	0.549	--	12.6	25.3	47.2	40

Source: United Nations Development Project (1997), p. 152

LABOUR MOVEMENT

As noted, Singapore is unique in having developed a comprehensive national pension plan (CPF) which give some protection to the workers against several contingencies. There is yet no unemployment insurance in this city-state. Severance pay and worker compensation programs are required of employers (Deyo, 1992). The ingredient of labour welfare, wage determination, is heavily influenced by the government. The formulation of wage is done through the National Wages Council which comprises of representatives from the government, the National Trade Union Congress (NTUC) and employers' associations. It has the sole duty of formulating annual wage guidelines for the economy.

Because of the strong state presence, wage determination is almost guided by the government. For instance, in the current austere economic contraction, the National Wage Council has suggested wage restraint as the prime solution to the problem so that companies could moderate their business costs and remain viable (27 May 1998, *The Straits Times*). The government quickly backed this stand and encouraged: "(the) workers must also lower their expectation and accept the wage restraint recommended by the NWC."

Generally, labour movement has been rather weak in Singapore. Union membership reached a peak of nearly 250,000 or about a quarter of the workforce in 1979, but since then has fallen. More than 90% of total union membership is affiliated with the National Trade Union Congress, a government-led body. In fact, since 1959, the union movement has come under government control (Murray & Pereia, 1996). When labour movements in many industrial societies have been an important force to reckon with as far as social welfare and labour welfare are concerned, this variable has been missing in its entirety in Singapore.

The weak labour movement is also a reflection of how ineffective civil society is in Singapore. Ironically, Prime Minister Goh Chok Tong had said recently that there was a need to promote a civil society in Singapore. To him, civil society should be striped of all political connotation; it only comprises non-governmental organizations and bodies that reflect people's views and needs (*Straits Times*, 14 April, 1998). In sum, over the years, the PAP government has successfully depoliticized the labour movement, established de facto government control over unions, transferred bargaining power from workers to employers and ushered in an era of labour peace that persists to this day (Murray & Pereia, 1996). This is necessary to attract foreign investment which is crucial to the economic development of Singapore.

THE PATERNAL STATE

From the foregoing, it is noted that the PAP government has played a key role in orchestrating economic development of Singapore. Often, what brings to mind about Singapore to many people is the existence of a paternal state (or 'hard state' after Mirza, 1986). Since its independence in 1959, the government of Singapore has been controlled by a single political party, the PAP. Singapore has been noted for having great control in economy and strong restrictions on individual activities (Tan, 1995; Enricht et al., 1997). It has managed its economy with a firm hand and has relied on overseas multinationals to build the economy. This is reflected in the scale of state spending, the activities of state-owned enterprises, and even in the rate of national savings (Mirza, 1986).

Such intrusive role could also be reflected in social policy reforms which target at restrictive state involvement (Deyo, 1992): "Large industry-wide unions were decentralized and house unions were encouraged. Some social insurance programs were partially decentralized to firms... while educational and welfare programs, and later, medical coverage, devolved to firms...."

If the state had played a major role in the economic and social development of Singapore in the past (Wilson, 1978; Chris & Drakakis-Smith, 1993), it has not changed its position, as exemplified in the recent budget speech of the government:

> ...A deliberate policy to keep the public sector lean and trim, avoidingwelfarism and confining Government's role to one of providing basic public goods and services, thus freeing more manpower and financial resources to the private sector as the engine of growth....

Socially and politically, the down side for a paternal state has been well documented: much regulation, less freedom of expression and information, more state paternalism, and more favouritism for state companies (UNDP, 1991; Enricht et al., 1997). The PAP government has defended its authoritarian rule by relating political control to economic growth and argued that the former is a prerequisite for capitalist development and attracting foreign investments. Lee Kuan Yew, the former Prime Minister, has once remarked: authoritarian arrangements are essential to economic success (Hitchcock, 1998).

To the government, a second necessary condition for economic growth is the restriction of state intervention in social welfare. Essentially, social welfare is seen an inhibitor of economic growth. The small budget on public assistance and the absence of other social programs like unemployment insurance coupled with the strong economic growth in Singapore has given the government some ammunition to justify its position. However, as noted above, this official argument is rather deceptive, considering the massive investments of the government in social policy (i.e.

education, health, and housing) between 1960 and 1990 which had minimal impact on the growth of the economy. Government investment in low cost public housing, education, and medical care has kept the cost of living down and pre-empted demands for wage increases in spite of the long hours of work which most workers had to endure (Castells, 1992; Tan, 1995). Socially, the government could afford to do more but it refrains from doing so. Hence, the uplifting of standard of living has to await for improved economic performance. The upshot of these has been the presence of social problems in this small but advanced economy.

Ideologically, welfare state, covering such institutions as the full employment policy, the provision of public assistance, and unemployment benefits etc., is considered as an evil by the state which has to be shunned at all costs. As a mature capitalist society, there is utmost respect for private ownership and property rights. The market would remain the ultimate arbiter of economic outcomes. The world-wide trend toward marketization appeals to the PAP party. Not surprisingly, the government is pursuing a privatization strategy and tries to privatize some government-owned enterprises. Most notably is its action in cutting back health spending and encourage people to fend for any medical contingency and the efforts toward the liberalization of the CPF.

CONCLUSION

From the foregoing, it is noted that there are social needs and problems in Singapore which demand increased state activities. Potentially, the state is very powerful and able to exert influence which would have been substantial. Its huge financial reserves is another asset. If the state has much latitude in economic and social planning, its primary objective is to promote economic growth. Social objectives become secondary and they are only important when the state runs into some great difficulties. In reality, the government has not taken the society further as far as social provision is concerned.

Are there factors which might prod the paternal state into expanding its social welfare in the near term? There are a few possibilities. First, the continuation of Asian financial turmoil which began in late 1997 and the prospect of a dwindling economy might render it necessary for the government to intervene on behalf of those who are badly affected. If the economic crisis lingers, then unemployment and relative poverty would rise quickly, stabilizing the status quo and worsening the present social problems such as income inequities. The lowering of quality of life from the crisis would entail a far larger effort on the part of the government.

In this regard, the example of Hong Kong is illustrative. Like Singapore, the new government has steadfastly refused to expand social programs under any circumstances. But the worsening economic crisis has prodded some political parties to demand for the introduction of unemployment insurance which is to be funded only from employees' contribution. In other words, the challenge of the Asian crisis changes from economic to social in nature. It is likely that demands for this kind of protection would increase further if the crisis deepens. In other words, crisis may trigger social reforms even in Singapore which is under the rule of an anti-welfare government.

A second factor relates to the aging population and its needs, which would require substantial governmental intervention. But , like other Asian countries, the aged group in Singapore is not a strong political force vis-a-vis the government. Moreover, the government has not neglected this group entirely, as evidenced from the 1997-98 budget which awards some S$85 million to the 300,000 old people (12 July 1997, *The Straits Times*).

A third possibility comes from the growing middle class. Bullard (1997) observes that the Asian middle class have begun demanding for democratic reforms, greater political freedoms and more equitable distribution of the gains of economic development. Middle class in South Korea and Hong Kong have become more and more visible, as a result of the Asian crisis and growing urgent needs, which exerts some pressure on their governments to modify their social policy. But civil society in Singapore is weakly developed, even though the middle class do express their needs and show some degrees of discontent with the existing situations. This can be seen from a survey which reveals a considerable percentage of citizens (9% in 1997) who opted for emigration to other countries.

Against these, there is a strong ideology of social non-interventionism and a commitment to self reliance in Singapore. The ruling PAP has successfully tried to cultivate this ideology among the masses. Perhaps, to some extent, this "self-help" ideology can be traced to or it is fuelled by the Confucian ideology of family support and mutual aid for one another. It remains to be seen if economic and political crises, increased globalization, and greater exchanges between nations will spur the ruling party to social action.

REFERENCES

Asher, Mukul G. (1985). Forced Saving to Finance Merit Goods: An Economic Analysis of the Central Provident Scheme of Singapore. Working paper No 36, Australian National University Centre for Research on Federal Financial Relations.

Asher, Mukul G. (1991). Social Adequacy and Equity of the Social Security Arrangements in Singapore. Singapore: Times Academic Press.

Asher, Mukul G. (1993). Planning for the Future: The Welfare State in a New Phase of Development.In Garry Rodan (ed.) Singapore Changes Guard (pp. 153-167). New York: St Martin's Press.

Atkinson, A. B., L. Rainwater & T. Smeeding (1995). Income Distribution in Industrial Countries. Paris: OECD.

Berger, Peter (1986). The Capitalist Revolution: Fifty Propositions about Prosperity, Equality, and Liberty. New York: Basic Books.

Bullard, Nicola (1997). The Nation-State Confronted with Globalization: Asian Perspectives. Development, 40(4): 31-35.

Castells, Manuel (1992). Four Asian Tigers With A Dragon Head: A Comparative Analysis of the State, Economy and Society in the Asian Pacific Rim. In R.Appelbaum and J. Henderson (eds.) State and Development in the Asian Pacific Rim (pp. 33-70). Newbury Park: Sage.

Chua, Beng-huat (1995). Communitarian Ideology and Democracy in Singapore. London: Routledge.

Deyo, Frederic (1992). The Political Economy of Social Policy Formation: East Asia's Newly Industrialized Countries. In R. Appelbaum and J. Henderson (eds.) State and Development int he Asian Pacific Rim (pp. 289-306). Newbury Park: Sage.

Dixon, Chris & Drakakis-Smith, David (1993). Economic and Social Development in Pacific Asia. London: Routledge.
Enricht, Michael J., Scott, Edith E., & Dodwell, David (1997). The Hong Kong Advantage. Hong Kong: Oxford University Press.
Henderson, Jeffrey (1993). The Role of the State in the Economic Transformation of East Asia. In C. Dixon and D. Drakakis-Smith (eds.) Economic and Social Development in Pacific Asia (pp. 85-114). London: Routledge.
Hirschman, A. O. (1990). A Rebuttal to Critics of Social Welfare. Dialogue, No. 87, pp. 48-53.
Hitchcock, David (1998). Cultural Side of the Asian Crisis. The Straits Times, Perspective, April 15.
Lim, Chong-Yah et al. (1988). Policy Options for the Singapore Economy. Singapore: McGraw-Hill.
Lim, Linda, E. F. Pang and R. Findlay (1993). Singapore. In R. Findlay and S. Wellisz (eds.) Five Small Open Economies (pp. 93-139). New York: Oxford University Press.
Low, Linda (1993). The Public Sector in Contemporary Singapore: In Retreat? In Garry Rodan (ed.) Singapore Changes Guard (pp. 168-183). New York: St Martin's Press.
Midgley, James (1984). Social Security, Inequality and the Third World. New York: John Wiley & Sons.
Midgley, James (1986). Industrialization and Welfare: The Case of the Four Little Tigers. Social Policy and Administration, 20(3): 225-237.
Midgley, James (1992). Development Theory, the State, and Social Development in Asia. Social Development Issues, 14(1): 22-36.
Mirza, H. (1986). Multinationals and the Growth of the Singapore Economy. London: Croom Helm.
Murray, Geoffrey & Pereia, Audrey (1996). Singapore: The Global City-State. New York: St Martin's Press.
Ramesh, M. (1996). Social Security in ASEAN: Trends and Directions. Toronto: University of Toronto-York University Joint Centre for Asian Pacific Studies.
Rao, B. (1990). Income Distribution in Singapore: Trends and Prospects. Singapore Economic Review, 35(1): 143-160.
Regnier, Philippe (1991). Singapore: City-State in South-East Asia. Honolulu: University of Hawaii Press.
Republic of Singapore (1997). Singapore 1997. Singapore: Ministry of Information and the Arts.
Rodan, Garry (ed.) (1993). Singapore Changes Guard: Social, Political and Economic Directions in the 1990s. New York: St Martin's Press.
Salaff, Janet W. (1992). Women, The Family, and the State in Hong Kong, Taiwan and Singapore. In R. Appelbaum & J. Henderson (eds.) States and Development in the Asian Pacific Rim (pp. 267-288). Newbury Park, CA: Sage.
Sherradan, Michael (1997). Provident Funds and Social Protection: The Case of Singapore. In James Midgley and Michael Sherradan (eds.) Alternatives to Social Security: An International Inquiry (pp. 33-60). Westport, CT: Auburn House.
The Straits Times, 12 July 1997, $85 Helping Hand to Over 300,000 Older Singaporeans
7 April 1998, Young Prepare Early for Old Age
Tan, Gerald (1995). The Newly Industrializing Countries of Asia. Singapore: Times Academic Press.
Tan, Gerald (1997). The Economic Transformation of Asia. Singapore: Times Academic Press.
Tan, Kevin Y.L. & Lam Peng Er (eds.) (1997). Managing Political Change in Singapore. London: Routledge.
Tang, Kwong-Leung (1998). East Asian Newly Industrializing Countries: Economic Growth and Quality of Life. Social Indicators Research, 43(1-2): 69-96, February.
United Nations Development Project (1997). Human Development Report 1997. New York: Oxford University Press.
Wilson, H. E. (1978). Social Engineering in Singapore. Singapore: National University of Singapore Press.
Yeo, Lay Hwee (1995). Singapore: The Year in Review 1995. Singapore: Times Academic Press.

VORAVIDH CHAROENLOET

CHAPTER SIX

INDUSTRIALIZATION AND LABOUR FRAGMENTATION IN THAILAND

Thailand's economy is presently undergoing a structural crisis, which is a result of a bubble economy -- the divergence between speculative investment and the "real" economy. In 1987, the Thai economy went into a boom, and Thailand was in line to be the fifth "Asian Tiger" (as South Korea, Taiwan, Singapore, and Hong Kong were dubbed). The only question was when it would happen. A Time magazine story even trumpeted Thailand as the up-and-coming "Tiger," and the International Monetary Fund (IMF) predicted that Thailand would be one of the next newly industrializing countries (NIC) by the year 2000. Ten years later, in 1997, the boom became a bust. Now, speculation centres on how long the crisis will last. The IMF predicts that the crisis may last 2 to 3 years if a Structural Adjustment Program (SAP) is strictly implemented. The Thai government sees a return to prosperity around the corner, and it has already launched big publicity campaigns to promote this idea. My impression is that Thailand's economic crisis is here to stay. We are not yet at the depths of the crisis -- it is only the beginning, and we are rolling down the hill. The crisis is structural. I may be pessimistic, but we have to wake up from the dream of the "Asian miracles" and trace our own destiny. We cannot let the market do that.

It was not difficult for Thailand to reproduce the "Asian miracles," the growth of the Tigers and the Dragons; the important question is how to sustain this growth. The period of economic boom between 1988 and 1992 came about with the process of internationalizing the Thai economy. During the export-led growth of this period, the Thai economy enjoyed a double-digit growth rate. For the first time, the growth rate exceeded 13% in 1988. In 1989 and 1990, the rates were 12.3% and 11.5%, respectively, and it was the fastest-growing economy in Asia. The formula for growth was quite simple: in 1987, the currency was devalued to kick off export growth, the interest rate was kept high to attract foreign capital, a fixed exchange rate was adopted to protect investors against risk, the financial sector was progressively deregulated, trade was liberalised to promote a free in-and-out flow of capital (Bello, 1998), and labour relations were stable as the unions became progressively institutionalized in the tripartite system. These factors produced a huge inflow of foreign investment into the country beginning in 1987. Between 1985 and 1990, some $15 billion worth of Japanese direct investment flowed into Southeast Asia.

K.-L. Tang (ed.), Social Development in Asia, 99–125.

That which flowed into Thailand in 1987 exceeded the cumulative Japanese investment (Bello, 1998, p. 10). Some new investment also came from the NICs, which were shifting the labour-intensive industries in search of cheaper production sites. The period also saw a boom in tourism, with five to six million tourists arriving in the country each year.

It can be concluded that the economic boom of the 1980s and early 1990s (Table One) resulted from three factors: foreign investment, foreign markets, and foreign tourists. To many Thais, especially the newly rich, economic prosperity meant the booming stock market. As a result of the economic boom, the SET stock index shot up to more than 1,500 points, land prices increased tenfold, and construction of high-rise office buildings and condominiums, many of them still empty even now, turned Bangkok into a concrete jungle with the world's worst traffic problem. Questions were often posed as to who would really benefit from this rapid economic growth.

EXPORT-ORIENTED INDUSTRIALIZATION AND NONWAGE WORKERS

Since the early 1980s, the Thai government has carried out different policies to liberalise Thailand's economy. An attempt has been made to address the serious problems that arose during industrialization in the era of import substitution: the trade deficit, inflation, wealth and income disparities, high tariff barriers, an inward-looking industrialization, the lack of a domestic market, stagnation of the agricultural sector, high unemployment, and restrictive foreign exchange controls. To overcome this situation, a number of SAPs were implemented to restructure the economy along the path of export-led growth. Measures taken included increased production of foods for export, reduced levels of protection, currency devaluation, a reduced role of the state, large-scale privatization, and liberalization of foreign exchange controls.

Table 1: Growth Rate of GDP by Sector: 1960-1996

								Average %	
	1960-1965	1965-1970	1970-1975	1975-1980	1980-1985	1985-1990	1990-1995	1960-1995	1995-1996*
GDP Growth	7.20	8.60	5.60	7.90	5.60	9.90	8.27	7.57	6.70
Agriculture	4.80	6.00	3.80	4.00	4.90	2.92	3.29	4.24	3.30
Industry	11.50	10.40	7.30	10.60	5.00	13.93	11.17	9.95	7.70
Services	7.20	9.50	5.60	8.20	6.30	9.74	7.15	7.66	6.60
Real Per Capita GDP	4.20	5.60	3.00	5.50	3.60	8.20	6.99	5.29	--
Population	3.00	3.00	2.60	2.40	2.00	1.70	1.28	2.28	--

Source: Between 1960-90, NESDB National Accounts and Population of Thailand. For 1960-95, TDRI Projections.

At the end of the 1980s, the Thai economy rapidly integrated into the world economy as a result of this industrial restructuring. The 1987-1990 economic boom was mainly supported by a combination of foreign trade, foreign capital, and foreign tourists (Charoenloet, 1991). Foreign investment increased by more than 400% in 1988 compared to the previous year (Table 2). Furthermore, the 1977 code of investment was amended in 1991 to make guarantees and grant privileges to foreign investors in the export sector. Special economic zones, such as the industrial estates, were set up to attract foreign direct investment (FDI) from the NICs searching for a cheaper production base for exports. Thus, the Thai economy was carried along by an impressive increase in exports. The average annual growth rate of exports between 1980 and 1993 was 15.5%, according to 1995 World Bank statistics.

Table 2: International Trade

	1961	1971	1981	1996
Share of International Trade to GDP (%)	37.3	38	54	89.4
Share of Exports by Sector (%)				
Agriculture	86.4	67.9	52.1	12.3
Industry	2.4	10.5	35.8	83.2

Source: Board of Trade, Thailand.

During the period of high growth, the Thai economy became rapidly internationalized. The share of trade in the country's gross domestic product (GDP) rose from 23.8% to 43.6% from 1950 to 1986, then increased from 43.6% to 65.5% in just 3 years, from 1986 to 1989. In 1996, it was 89.4% (Table 3). This shows that Thailand has a very open economy. Much of its dynamism comes from its contact with the world market through trade and investment, but future economic growth will be subjected to external constraints, market fluctuation, and the international norm of competition.

Table 3: Share of Employed Persons by Industry (%)

Employed Persons	1960	1980	1986	1991	1997
Agriculture	82.3	7.8	63.7	60.6	54.1
Industry	3.6	8.1	9.3	11.0	13.5
Constructio n	0.5	1.9	2.6	3.8	5.6
Commerce	5.7	8.5	10.6	10.9	11.5
Services & Others	7.9	10.6	13.8	13.7	15.3
Total	100.0	100.0	100.0	100.0	100.0

Source: NSO Labour Force Survey, Thailand.

Because of the trend toward economic liberalization, market opening, and intensified global competition, the private sector was inclined to take short-term solutions (i.e., adopting cut-cost strategies). The search for "downward flexibility" has, in fact, led to segmentation of the labour market.

THE CONCEPT OF NONWAGE LABOUR

According to the classical definition, a wage worker or wage labourer refers to a person who is employed for a fixed number of hours a day or week and receives a regular wage but also has the status of "permanent worker" -- that is, entitled to social welfare, bonuses, and annual promotions. Job security is often used as a demarcation line between "permanent" and "nonpermanent" work.

Thailand's population at the end of 1997 reached about 60.3 million, with a labour force of more than 32.0 million. The number of employed persons was about 30.0 million (NSO, Labour Force Survey, Round 1, February 1994-1998), of which the majority, 54.1%, was still in agriculture. The manufacturing sector's share in total employment has increased steadily, from 3% in 1960 to 10% in 1988 and 13.5% in 1997. The share of commerce and services in total employment also rose considerably during the 1980s. It accounted for 26.8% of total employment (Table 4). Although the share of agriculture in the GDP has been declining successively from 39% in 1961 to 10.4% in 1996, it is still the biggest generator of employment (Table 5).

Table 4: Shares of Real GDP by Economic Sector (%)

Sector	1961	1971	1981	1992	1996
Agriculture	39.4	26.8	20.0	12.3	10.4
Industry	12.4	16.9	32.2	29.1	32.6
Services	48.2	56.3	57.2	58.6	57.0

Source: NESDB, Thailand.

Table 5: Structure of Trade Unions and Employer's Organization in Thailand, 1997

Organizations	Bangkok	Provinces	Total
Trade Unions	302	679	981
Labour Federation	7	10	17
Labour Congress	7	1	8
Employers' Association	120	26	146
Employers' Federation	2	1	3
Employers' Council	7	--	7

Source: Registration Office, Thailand.

What can be deduced from these statistics? First, the evolution of different components of the labour force in Thailand confirms that the country is in the process of modernization, although industrialization in Thailand did not set in motion massive rural-to-urban migration as experienced in many developed countries. More than 50% of the labour force is still employed in the agricultural sector.

Second, although the manufacturing sector has been the most dynamic, it employs only 13% of the labour force. Thailand has not had a rapid expansion of wage labour. In 1993, the total number of employees (e.g., wage workers) was 4.5 million (nonfarm). The figures can be broken down into four components: stable wage workers in medium- and large-scale industries (2 million), small-scale industries (1 million), casual workers (1 million), and seasonal labour (500,000). Thus, we see that wage labour employment in medium- and large-scale modern industries is only a small part of the labour force (Oudin, 1995, p. 9).

Third, under global competition, firms tend to compete by externalizing the production cost. This leads to the "casualisation of labour" and the extensive use of the subcontracting system. It creates job insecurity and hinders development of a complete wage-labour relationship: unstable and unprotected workers. During the export drive, women were successively integrated into the exporting industries as assembly-line workers (Charoenloet & Soonthorndhada, 1988). The feminisation of the labour force[1] in the period of export-led growth has developed hand in hand with the process of labour fragmentation.

The labour movement in Thailand has become progressively fragmented in the process of its institutionalization. The weakness of the labour movement is due to low union membership -- of 9 million wage earners in the industrial establishments, only 270,000 workers are unionized (i.e., only 2-3%). In the past, trade unions overcame this limitation by becoming a part of the social movement, such as during the student uprising of October 1974 against the military dictatorship. Currently, trade unions work closely with nongovernmental organizations (NGOs), women's groups, and other democratic movements in the country.

There are a number of explanations for the low rate of unionization in Thailand. Because three-fourths of industrial establishments are small- and medium-sized factories that are widely dispersed, the Thai labour culture tends to be paternalistic, and workers lack their own organization. Moreover, neither labour laws nor the enforcement efforts of the government provide effective barriers to the unfair dismissal of union leaders. Management often employs this technique to bust unions. In the absence of a trade union, Thai workers prefer to take individual action. When dissatisfied, they will leave and take another job. Employers often complain about the high rate of labour turnover that, in turn, hinders the creation of strong trade unions. Also, the government constantly tries to weaken the trade unions because of its interest in having a policy of cheap labour. As the trade union became institutionalized, it became separated from the social movements, and its role became economic and confined within the legal framework. The Labour Disputes Act of 1965 provided provisions for dispute settlement, which empowered the Ministry of Interior to make decisions on cases. Representatives of both parties (employers and employees) were allowed to submit claim notifications to the other party and participate in any negotiation, conciliation, and voluntary arbitration. If disagreement remained unresolved after all necessary procedures, the parties could resort to strike or lockout (Ogena, 1997, p. 63). In 1979, the labour court system was established. It has tripartite composition and is empowered to consider, decide, and issue orders on disputes over rights and obligations under the labour protection law.

With the introduction of a tripartite system, for example, conducting centralized bargaining and fixing the minimum wage have lifted the poorest-paid workers out of poverty, but it has also been used by the state as an instrument of labour control. Representatives are elected to the tripartite committee under a system of one union, one vote. Because the existing law requires a minimum of only 10 workers in the same workplace to organize and apply for the registration of a labour union (Thanachaisethavut, 1998, p. 40), it is not difficult to set up trade unions to vote for representatives on the committee. However, this practise leads to a proliferation of small and inactive trade unions and creates factionalism and disunity inside the trade union movement. Presently, there are 8 Labour Congresses, 17 Labour Federations, and 981 trade unions for 270,000 union members. There are also 7 employers' councils (see Table 6). Thus, in decision making, the government always dominates as the others are left to fight among themselves for representation.

Table 6: Labour Intensity in Thailand's Manufactured Exports

	1989	1991	1993	1995
Labour-intensive	50.13	40.45	34.50	26.26
Medium-high	25.46	31.87	37.40	45.94
Other	24.41	27.68	28.11	27.80
	100.0	100.0	100.0	100.0

Source: M. Kkrongkaew, Thailand's Internationalization and its Rural Sector, ASEAN Economic Bulletin, November, 1995.

The State Enterprise Labour Relations Act, enacted on April 19, 1991, is another example of how state intervention weakened the labour movement. This ruling allows state enterprise trade unions to function as associations but not to have trade union rights or collective bargaining power. This effective abolition of state enterprise unions weakened the labour movement as an organized social force, as the following statistics illustrate: As of July 1, 1992, 707 trade unions were registered with the Labour Department, but only 250,000 workers (or 5.6%) in the private sector held union membership, and 57.3% of the 700,000 state enterprise workers were unionized. The act also prohibits state enterprise workers from forming labour congresses with private-sector labour and from engaging in work stoppages or slowdowns.

The weak trade union movement has been the major cause of poor working conditions and the degradation of work in Thailand, especially in the period of export-led growth. In Thailand,

- Workers have the longest working hours in Asia (i.e., 55 to 60 hours a week, or even up to 77 hours a week in some small undertakings).
- Since 1976, the minimum wage has been determined on the basis of an individual worker's needs, without reference to the worker's family situation.
- The minimum wage is not always set at a level that will alleviate poverty. In a 1991 survey covering 700 workers in four industries, the minimum wage was 100 bahts a day, and the daily expense of a worker was 112 bahts a day (Heron, 1995, p. 13). Workers in such a situation have to cover their daily expenses by taking on a second job, borrowing money, or lowering their standard of living below the level of basic needs. Working overtime to supplement family income has been a common practise. In addition, many workers have to send part of their earnings to their rural-based families to enable them to survive. The Arom Pongpangan Foundation Thailand Labour Resource Centre (1997) conducted a survey on work intensity and found a preponderant use of amphetamines among workers in the garment sector.
- Surveys by the Division of Labour Protection showed that the enforcement rate is not very encouraging. In 1990, 44% of the sample workers who should have received the minimum wage received less. In 1992, the figure was 55% (34% in 1994), but in some provinces, it was as high as 74% (Heron, 1995, p.12). Thailand does not have an effective labour inspection system. Labour inspectorates lack resources, and in many cases, visits to enterprises are infrequent. No inspectors are well trained in wage enforcement techniques, and no legal powers exist for applying heavy sanctions in cases of noncompliance.
- In 1990, the social security system for Thai workers was approved. The Social Security Act applies to all employers with 10 or more employees but covers only four types of benefits: death, sickness, accident or disability occurring outside the workplace, and maternity leave. There are no unemployment insurance or old-age pension or retirement benefits; it is not yet a welfare system.
- Many workers face job insecurity, being employed casually or on short-term contracts.
- Workers face union busting -- once a union is set up, the employers lay off the leaders and the organization fails.

EMPLOYMENT FLEXIBILITY

One can distinguish two phases of economic growth during this period of export-oriented industrialization. Prior to 1985, agricultural exports (including fisheries) were always greater than manufactured exports. Then, in 1985, the value of manufactured exports surpassed the value of agricultural exports for the first time. And by 1990, the value of manufactured exports was more than three times that of agricultural exports (TDRI, 1994), indicating that the source of growth had shifted to the urban-led industries

During the first phase of export-oriented growth, the bulk of Thailand's manufactured exports consisted of labour-intensive products such as garments, sports shoes, artificial flowers, gems, and jewelry. The increased export of these products was directly related to the shift of the production base from the Asian NICs to countries such as Thailand. However, by the early 1990s, there were indications that these labour-intensive industries were quickly losing their competitiveness, especially in labour costs. With the appearance of low-labour cost countries such as China, Indonesia, and Vietnam, Thailand's competitive advantage in the export of labour-intensive manufactured products is and will be eroded. Because labour productivity has been lagging behind money wage increases, this has led to rising labour costs of production in manufacturing (Pitayanon, 1998, p. 5). In the second half of the 1980s, Thailand's labour-intensive manufactured exports were growing at 30% to 40% per annum; currently, the growth rates of these products are about 10% per annum or less (TDRI, 1994) (Table 7). After 1989, the share of labour-intensive product exports of Thailand declined sharply to 40.45% in 1991 and dropped to 26.26% in 1995 (Table 8).

Table 7: Labour Force Share by Educational Level

Educational Level	1981	1986	1988	1990	1995	2000
Primary and Below	88.0	85.1	83.9	83.0	79.5	72.8
Lower Secondary	4.0	5.2	5.9	6.4	7.9	11.4
Upper Secondary	0.9	1.6	2.2	2.5	3.2	4.2
Vocational	1.5	2.3	2.7	2.8	3.1	3.9
Technical	0.4	1.1	1.5	1.3	1.6	2.2
University	0.9	1.6	1.9	4.1	4.6	5.4
Total	100.0	100.0	100.0	100.0	100.0	100.0

Source: NSO Labour Force Survey, Thailand.

Table 8: Rate of employment in formal and informal sectors classified by regional urban centres in August 1988

Region	Formal Sector	Informal Sector	Total
Total	100.0%	100.0%	100.0%
Bangkok and periphery	70.1%	61.4%	64.7%
Central	8.4%	11.0%	10.0%
Northeast	5.8%	8.7%	7.6%
North	8.4%	9.7%	9.2%
South	7.3%	9.2%	8.5%

Source: TDRI (1990:12), quoted in Phongpaichit, 1992.

As Thailand begins to lose its initial comparative advantage in low-cost labour, policy initiatives undertaken at this stage will be vital in configuring the economy for the future. This must be done in such a way as to reduce the Thai economy's dependence on low labour costs for export growth, increase skill-intensive and technologically sophisticated economic activities, and develop new, less fleeting sources of comparative advantage that should be based more on innovation and quality production. Since 1990, there has been a persistent trend toward high export growth in items such as computers and parts, electrical appliances, electrical circuits, and vehicle parts. Some observers may classify these products as medium-high technology industries. But a major portion of this group consists of computers and their components, which are still produced on assembly lines by young women workers who do not have any skills (Charoenloet & Soonthorndhada, 1988). Thailand will face difficulties in upgrading its industries because it has never taken human resources development seriously or has seized the opportunity to upgrade skills during the boom years. Currently, about 80% of the country's workforce possess only primary education or less (Table 9).

Table 9: Income Shares of Population by Quintiles

	1975 1976	1980 1981	1985 1986	1988 1989	1990 1991	1991 1992	1993 1994	1996 1997
Richest 20%	49.26	51.47	55.63	55.01	56.48	59.04	57.52	55.38
Next Richest 20%	20.97	20.64	19.86	20.30	20.11	18.95	19.60	20.14
Middle 20%	14.00	13.38	12.20	12.20	11.92	11.06	11.60	12.10
Next Poorest 20%	9.37	9.10	7.87	7.98	7.44	7.01	7.29	7.89
Poorest 20%	6.05	5.41	4.55	4.51	4.05	3.94	3.99	4.49
Richest 40%	70.22	72.11	75.49	75.31	76.59	77.99	77.12	75.52
Poorest 60%	29.78	27.89	24.51	24.69	23.41	21.01	22.88	24.48
Gini coefficient	0.426	0.479	0.481	0.485	0.522	0.536	0.525	0.497

Source: Estimates derived from the NSO Socioeconomic Survey, TDRI 1994) and Kakwani and Krongkaew (1996).

With growing international competition from low-cost labour countries, some firms are looking for short-term cost-cutting strategies. In the search for flexible employment, firms have resorted to employing casual labour. Many firms also rely on externalizing production to cope with market uncertainties and to reduce production costs, which leads to widespread subcontracting and the "informalization" of the economy, with work divided into formal and informal categories. This has led to a segmented labour market, with protected and unprotected labour, and it is why cheap labour is being produced and reproduced in Thailand.

THE EMPLOYMENT OF TEMPORARY WORKERS

Short-term employment is widespread in Thailand's textile, hotel, and food and beverage industries. A survey of the employment situation in 1988 showed that 18.5% of the 32,062 employed persons in the Prapradaeng area were temporary employees. In 6 of the 46 establishments surveyed, 40% or more of those employed are temporary employees. The short-term employment situations in the Omnoi and Omyai areas were the most serious: of 9,377 employees in 31 establishments, 60% were employed on a temporary basis. In Rangsit and nearby areas, about 15% of the total employees were temporary (Limskul, 1994, p. 117).

The past government accommodated workers' demands that temporary work be abolished. However, in one of the government's Interior Ministry announcements, the difference between permanent and temporary employees was eliminated by making the term "employee" refer to all workers, whether or not they work for wages. Employers usually get around the law by employing workers on short-term contracts. The employment is terminated before the contract expires, and the workers are rehired under new contracts.

SUBCONTRACTORS IN GARMENT MANUFACTURING: THE ROW SHOP-HOUSE IN THE INFORMAL SECTOR

Rapid economic growth in Thailand over the past 10 years has led to the emergence of many activities that generally fall in the categories of the small-scale and self-employment. These activities are generally known as the informal sector or as microenterprises or shop-house manufacturing. The growth of the informal sector is directly related to the subcontracting organised by trading firms or factories in the formal sector.

Owners of garment shop-houses do not need much initial investment. Most of the shops start with two or three sewing machines, a rented two-storey building in a low-cost housing area, and young workers recruited from the villages. The problem is in the informal sectors -- that is, in tailor shops, where they learned not only to make clothes but also to conduct business. They got their orders or contracts from traders they knew during that time. They had networks of friends in the same business who often came from the same villages and had similar backgrounds. They relied on one another in their business dealings (i.e., getting orders, sharing work during rush periods, or borrowing money). A shop-house owner skilled at making patterns could also get a contract by offering his own design.

That all happened in the "old days," when competition was not too great. Nowadays, shop-house owners face a process of "de-skilling." As the garment business is exposed to intense international competition to increase production and lower production costs, factories or trading firms do the designing and pattern cutting while small subcontractors in the informal sector perform only the sewing or assembling of parts. This simplification of works has led not only to a proliferation of small subcontractors in the garment business but also to an increasing role of intermediaries or middlemen.

Typically, the middleman receives a contract order from a trading company and spreads the work among several subcontractors.[1] The middleman thus acts as an intermediary between the market and producers, taking his share of the profit from the producer. To avoid involving too many intermediaries, a subcontractor will try to get a contract directly from a trading firm or may try to market the products himself but without much success because he lacks marketing skills or outlets. Obtaining raw materials can also be a problem: some patterns of cloth cannot be bought on the open market because trading firms have arranged with textile factories to supply them directly.

In the garment production chain, those who control the market take a large share of the profit. The price of labour per piece is divided by a factor of two between the owner of the shop-house and his workers, while the largest share of income is taken by the trading firm (Commission on Justice and Peace, 1993). However, high competition among the increasing numbers of shop-house operators tends to depress the price per piece, and trading firms and middlemen have bargaining power over the dispersed, unorganised, small-scale subcontractors. Thus, while the shop-house owners' income has contracted in recent years, this decrease cannot be passed on to the workers by reducing the piece wage rate because the workers could then return home or find a job elsewhere. The shop-house owner often finds himself in a similar situation to his workers in that he too is a "piece-rate worker."

Because income is directly related to the number of orders contracted, all means are used to get as many contracts as possible. This creates an atmosphere of suspicion and distrust. Firsthand subcontractors do not inform others about the source or terms of contracts for fear that the others may undercut them. Price-cutting competition is one obstacle to a more united and constructive action by small producers vis-a-vis the trading firms.

To keep his income from declining, a shop owner tries to increase orders and increase his production and also tries to avoid or save on certain expenses that he deems unnecessary. These cuts generally have an adverse effect on the health and safety of workers in the workplace; the degradation of working conditions in small shop-houses is apparent. There is a hyperconcentration of small subcontractors in low-cost housing areas where basic hygiene is barely maintained. Many workplaces have poor lighting and bad ventilation. Workers toil for long hours in uncomfortable positions; they often complain about ill health, most commonly headache, cramps, and backache. No assessment has been made so far of the long-term impact on health, such as lung disease or chemical poisoning[1] because the informal sector is not supposed to be "visible" to the authorities. Working conditions are unsafe: workers work, eat, and sleep in proximity to bundles of cloth, yet there is usually no firefighting equipment or alarm system installed. In some reported cases of fatal fires, victims' families have not been compensated by the shop-house owner because informal workers are not covered by the protection laws, and the owner of shop-house has no savings.

As competition among the many subcontractors has become intense, working conditions in the shop-houses have regressed. Workers are urged to work long hours to complete the orders on time, sometimes from morning until midnight. In the past, workers paired up and more or less completed an entire garment. But now, in the interest of speed, each worker does only one part of the work required to make a garment. Thus, workers not only work long hours, but their work is more intense and less skilled. A continuing stream of labour is needed to feed this large-volume production. When a labour shortage begins to develop in an urban area, especially Bangkok, shop-house owners are forced to invest in more productive sewing machines, they are confronted with rising production costs even as they face a declining rate per piece.

THE "PUTTING-OUT" SYSTEM IN THE COUNTRYSID

The growth of the informal sector in Thailand has tended to be high in the urban centre because of urbanization, the availability of markets, and industrial concentration. For example, Bangkok and the periphery have the highest rate (about 61%) of employment in the informal sector, as Table 10 illustrates. But as competition becomes more intense, firms have begun to search for lower-cost locations. The extension of the subcontracting system into rural areas has led to the diffusion of small, decentralized production units or “home-based workers.” The middleman receives the contract and organizes production through a “putting-out” system, with the middleman supplying the raw materials and buying the finished product. In the countryside, the labour force’s production cost is lower, with much of this cost having been socialized by rural families and the existence of a large subsistence economy.

Firms frequently keep some production going inside the factory, especially for the more stable part of the market, while contracting out production for a more unpredictable market. Thus, home-based workers constitute small and diffuse production units that create flexibility for the firm in the formal sector. The contacting out of garment making, especially in the north, generally proceeds as follows: a dress is divided into several pieces, which are in turn spread among several villages, each of which sews only a part of the dress. Final assembly is done by a subcontractor located in the town or nearby village. In this kind of arrangement, the middleman has a big role in setting up the production chain. In the formal or big factories, there is no problem of child labour, but child labour is prevalent in the small subcontracting units. In this currently practised strategy of “defensive flexibility,” home-based workers are subjected to the process of “dequalification” as well as low wages and a lack of welfare benefits.

CHILD LABOUR IN MANUFACTURING

A study on “Child Labour in the Manufacturing Industries in Thailand” (Charoenloet & Yodkamonsart, 1997) revealed that children between 13 and 16 years old were working in deplorable conditions and earning low wages. Children from poor families often have to drop out of school after a very basic education and enter the labour market unprotected. In the past, the dropout rate was as high as 60%. Currently, the government's policy is to extend compulsory education to 9 years of age, but persistent poverty continues to push children out of school, as well as out of their villages, to earn income at a very young age.

One leather factory that produced ladies' handbags was quite successful in its drive to export. The company twice received awards for the best-quality product meeting international standards. Ten years ago, it was a small row-house shop that employed a few workers. Now, the company is located in a four-storey building and employs about 800 regular workers. But the company also employs children as subcontracted workers to do the production work (sewing and gluing), and the regular workers handle quality control and supporting work. Subcontracted workers work in teams of two to seven. Each team has a leader, who may be either an adult working with his wife or a worker who began as a child worker and gained sufficient experience and skill in leather goods to become a team leader. It is the team leader who subcontracts work from the company, normally in the following way: the company asks the subcontractor (team leader) to reproduce a sample product. Once the reproduction is made and approved, the company places an order, stipulating the quantity to be produced and the collection date. The subcontractor is paid for the entire lot, and it is up to him to subdivide the work among his team, organize the production, and pay his workers. A subcontractor normally gets between 20 and 40 bahts per piece, depending on whether it is a small purse or a large handbag. He earns between 10,000 and 20,000 bahts a month, depending on the size of his team.

By comparison, a child worker usually earns between 1,000 and 1,500 bahts a month at first, but after working for a year and becoming more skilled, he can earn up to 4,000 bahts a month. The company does not interfere with the organization of the work, just the supply and the quality control. Once the model is divided into pieces, the subcontractor and his workers do the assembling and sewing. The company sets rules and regulations, especially working hours, normally from 8 a.m. to 11 p.m. The subcontractor and workers get every other Sunday off. The company provides machines and materials, and all production is one on the fourth floor of the building. Children are lodged together, with four or five to a small room. Team workers usually live, work, and eat together. Usually, they also come from the same village as the team leader. Workers do not usually change teams. Young workers aspire to become team leaders to earn more money, independence, and prestige.

The problem with subcontractors and children in this factory is that they are not considered as regular company workers, even though they live and work there. Therefore, these workers fall outside the labour protection law and have no access to the social security and welfare system. The company can avoid applying the law because there is no trade union in the factory. The factory is an export firm. The products made by these workers do not have the brand name attached -- that is done by regular workers, as is packaging and transportation. The finished leather goods are shipped to different parts of Europe such as Germany, Holland, Italy, France, and the United Kingdom.

In this factory, each production team has one or two children younger than 15 years old. There are 50 to 60 workers between 13 and 17 years old. Once children are old enough and skilled enough, the company encourages them to open small shop-houses in the vicinity. The factory then gives contracts to these shop-houses, supplying them with materials and renting out special sewing machines. The work has to be finished on time and approved by the quality control officers. Shop-house owners feel more independent in terms of their working arrangements but are still subordinated to the company in getting the order. The shop-houses adopt the same working hours as the company, and they do not try to bargain up the piece rate. When contracts slow down, the shop-house owner has to bear full responsibility for maintaining his workers. In this way, such a production arrangement can be considered as contract labour. The shop-houses are simply labour recruiters or suppliers to the contracting firms. This disguised employment of labour has been very popular among exporting firms because it permits them to recruit cheap labour without being seen as a direct employer.

SUBCONTRACTING AND THE DEGRADATION OF WORK IN THAILAND

In the past, Thailand was able to develop labour-intensive exporting industries quite rapidly. But under intensified global competition and the emergence of new centres of production, the life cycle of these industries has been considerably shortened, so some factories try to compete by shifting up the production ladder. New and more efficient machines are being employed, and workers are downsized. Some factories shift their production base to the border to employ cheap, migrant labour. Others have adopted subcontracting as a means to cut costs. Subcontracting has been very popular in many sectors such as garment, footwear, artificial flowers, and precious stones. Usually, subcontractors are small- and medium-scaled firms both in the formal and informal sectors. Large factories employing more than 3,000 workers also can be subcontractors in the international commodity chain. Some firms have produced garments for export under known brand names such as American Wear, Mickey Mouse, Bugs Bunny, Club Vogue, Sindy, and so on.

Eden and the "Triangle Manufacturing"

In 1978, at the time of its establishment, Eden was one of the largest garment businesses in Thailand. In 1991, Eden employed about 4,000 workers, but in mid-1996, only 700 were employed. The Eden group was an Austrian-owned multinational corporation with its main operation in Bangkok, Thailand, and sales offices in Europe. To profit from low-cost suppliers, the tactic used by the TNC was to organize "triangle manufacturing" (Geriffi, 1997). U.S. corporations with known brand names placed their orders with Eden, the big distributor in Europe that, in turn, shifted the production to low-wages countries (Thailand, China, India, and Bangladesh). Eden's products were marketed in Australia, Hong Kong, Italy, France, Germany, Spain, Britain, and the United States. The firm exported more than 12 million pieces each year (Kokit, 1997).

In 1991, Eden began to adopt the cut-cost strategy by doing the following:

- By implementing one-shift and overtime work and transferring posts, many workers were made redundant and had to be dismissed. In 1994, the number of workers was reduced to 2,000.
- The company then employed 200 casual and temporary workers to work on the production line. Because these workers did not have the status of regular workers, they were not entitled to welfare benefits and could be discharged anytime without being paid the legal compensation.
- Fifty-two workers were dispatched to work in a sweatshop, but the move was unsuccessful because of the trade union's resistance.
- The company subcontracted some parts of its operation. Some printing (or dyeing) work was distributed to approximately 15 agents around Bangkok and Samut Sakorn. The other part of work (i.e., sewing) was distributed to 30 other informal agents around the same area.

On February 24, 1995, the company announced the layoffs of 1,400 workers with 3 months of wage compensation. Later, with the agreement from the union, voluntary resignation was urged with 6 months of wage compensation. From the profile of 319 workers with employment termination, we found that 84% received a daily wage of 150 to 152 bahts (the minimum wage was 145 bahts a day). Seventy percent of the workers had been employed between 6 and 15 years with the company, and more than half were older than age 30. About 40% had only primary school education, and the majority of workers were women. More than half were or had been married, and two-thirds lived in rented rooms. Because many of the women workers were elderly and had less education, once unemployed, they had a slim chance of finding new jobs. The unions and workers organized protests, demanding an end to subcontracting and more compensation[1] for workers who had been laid off. On March 1, 1996, the rest of the 800 workers, including union officials, were given letters terminating their employment, but no compensation was given. Workers went to occupy the factory but found out that the owner of Eden had fled the country. With the absence of the owner, workers were informed that no legal action could be taken against him.

Workers in Thailand are not only cheap because of low wages, but their lives are also considered cheap. On May 10, 1993, the worst-ever factory fire in the world occurred at the Kader toy factory in Nakhon Pathom province near Bangkok, Thailand. The company employed more than 3,000 workers; 174 women and 14 men died in the incident, 469 workers were injured, and most of the remaining workers remain jobless. A government inquiry concluded that improper building designs, inadequate fire exits and stairways, and no fire alarm at Kader were the major contributing factors that prevented victims from escaping in time. Survivors reported that locked doors and barred windows prevented many of the victims from escaping (ICFTU, 1995). Kader was set up as a foreign joint venture from Hong Kong with the Thai business group (Charoenloet, Ponkapand CP), a large conglomerate in the agrobusiness. It received contracts from U.S. toy companies such as Toys 'R Us, Hasbro, Mattel, Tyco, J. C. Penney, and Acro, employing cheap, migrant workers from the countryside to minimize production costs and saving on investing in building and safety equipment. Many of its toys sold in the European and U.S. markets on Christmas Eve.

OCCUPATIONAL HEALTH AND SAFETY

During 40 years of industrialization, the Thai workers have made many sacrifices. They have sacrificed not only by working for low wages, but their lives have been considered very cheap. Since the initiation of export-led economic growth in 1985, occupational health and safety have been crucial issues for Thai workers. According to data gathered in 1993-1995 by the Workmen's Compensation Fund on injuries in the workplace, there were 156,548 injured workers in 1993, 186,053 in 1994, and 216,335 in 1995. The injury rate increased by 23.8% between 1990 and 1996 (Ministry of Labour), while the GDP growth rate during the same period was 7% to 8%. This underlies the fragile situation of the Thai health system, which has had to shoulder increasing costs with fewer resources.

Compared with other countries in the region, Thailand's industrial injury rate is hopelessly high. From 1988 to 1992, when the GDP growth rate was in double digits (10%-12% per year), the rate of job-related injuries in Thailand was much higher than in Malaysia (with the same level of industrialization) and in South Korea. In 1988, the injury rate in Thailand was 36 per 1,000 workers, a figure that rose to 43 per 1,000 in 1992. Meanwhile, in Malaysia, the injury rate decreased from 23 to 22 per 1,000 workers in the same period. In South Korea, the rate was 24 per 1,000 workers in 1988 and declined to 15 per 1,000 in 1992.

Among the serious injuries, fatalities appear to be very high. The highest fatality rates in 1984 were registered in the construction industry (142.3 per 100,000 workers), transport and communication (105.6), and mining and quarrying (64.2). The figure for construction workers is more than 10 times that in advanced countries such as Britain (9.9) and Holland (13.1). Factory fires are frequent and cause numerous sudden deaths. The 1993 Kader incident, which killed 188 workers and injured 350, was one of the worst factory fires in history. Not long after this tragedy occurred, another fire broke out in a row-house garment shop employing more than 100 workers, killing 11 workers who had been trapped behind barred windows. Six months after Kader, the collapse of a three-star hotel in the provincial town of Korat killed 137 people and injured 330. A recent fire in a five-star hotel at a beach resort killed 91. These tragedies have a similar cause -- that is, the owners, in their pursuit of greater profits, did not invest in proper firefighting and fire prevention equipment. When the fires broke out, there were no alarms, not enough emergency exits, and doors were found locked (in the Kader factory, doors were locked to prevent workers from leaving the building before day's end; in the hotels, it was to prevent guests from leaving without paying their bills). In all these cases, it was found that the building materials were substandard or that the structure had been altered to provide more space. In the case of the factory, most government investigations concluded that the factory owner was responsible, but the workers who were accused of starting the fire ended up in jail. They were the victims; they were the accused. It appears that

Thai workers are cheap because of low wages and because their lives are considered cheap.

These tragedies could have been avoided had there been an effective inspection system and if the government had been more open to worker participation in health reform. Thailand cannot afford any more tragic incidents involving massive deaths of workers. Kader raised many questions, such as inefficiency of the government bureaucracy, the lack of coordination among government departments dealing with health and safety, the corruption of government inspectors, and employers' preoccupation with profit rather than a safe working system. It took 3 months of continuous pressure before the owner of the Kader factory yielded to give the families of the victims compensation, in the form of 300,000 baht and the provision of educational fees and expenses for the victims' children, which were standard enough.

In early 1997, the Arom Pongpangan Foundation (Ativanichayapong, 1997) conducted a survey of 30 families of victims (both dead and injured) and found that this compensation did not cover the serious, lasting consequences of the fire: children left without mothers; misuse of the money put aside for children's education, with much of it used to pay for funerals; disabled workers unable to reintegrate into new employment and becoming poorer; some workers still not fully recovered; and many workers facing deteriorating health. It appears that once the compensation was paid, there was no follow-up. The government was pleased that the conflict had been resolved, and the owner of the factory felt that its brand name had not been tarnished. But the workers and their families still have to live with the situation every day.

One of the unresolved conflicts among workers, management, and government that has emerged in recent years concerns work-related illness. When workers have viewed an illness as work related, the government, as manager of the compensation fund, usually has been more conservative in its judgment. In the struggle for social justice, victims of work-related illness have raised a number of problems that have not been resolved, such as the reliability of government medical doctors, the diagnosis procedure, and the fact that Thailand's present criteria for work-related illness do not meet international standards. Cases of illness related to work have been fought out in the labour court, which usually seeks medical verification from the specialists appointed by the government. In many cases, workers have lost out.

In Thailand, the Workmen's Compensation Fund compensates about 100 cases of work-related injuries per year. This number is very small, considering the level of economic development and rapid industrialization in Thailand. This may indicate that workers are being abused or are unaware of their rights. Consider the following, for example:

- The management failed to post a list of workers who were in the factory at the time of the Kader fire.
- The government was too slow in providing relief, and a lack of coordination among government agencies meant workers had to go from place to place to get assistance.

- Victims' families felt that the legally required compensation was too little. Compensation is calculated by using the last wage payment as a point of reference. Because workers get only a minimum wage, which is strictly minimum, the amount of compensation is thus very little.
- The Kader trade union was too small, with only 300 members. After the fire, the union broke up and the members dispersed.

Two years after the fire, a working group was set up to support the Kader workers' demands. It comprised 22 organizations such as the labour councils and federations and NGOs. This was the first time that the labour movement took interest in the issues of health and safety. The working group demanded that the government set up a centre at the site of the fire where negotiation, assistance, and information gathering and dissemination would be carried out. After 3 months of continuous pressure, negotiation, and demonstration, the Kader management yielded to a demand to pay 300,000 baht in extra payment to each victim's family.

The Kader tragedy demonstrated that multinational companies that relocate to Thailand are not always the country's best employers because many of them shift their investment around in search of low-cost labour and cheap production sites. Laws on health and safety exist, but they are not strictly enforced. The Kader workers felt that it was legitimate to demand for just compensation beyond what was required by the existing law. From the point of view of the workers' struggle, certain lessons can be drawn.

First, the centre set up at the site proved to be very effective. It was a positive experience for the government, labour, and NGOs to work out a solution together and to provide a framework for negotiation. Moreover, an alliance of workers, government officials, and the mass media is important, as is international networking. Kader workers went to Hong Kong, where the labour NGOs organised a mass demonstration at Kader headquarters, while Thai workers rallied in front of the CP building in Bangkok. These moves were very effective in getting management to the negotiation table, as was the threat to organise a consumer boycott of the company's products outside the country.

After the immediate demand for extra compensation had been met, the Campaigning Committee for Health and Safety of Workers was set up to push for institutional reform. The committee is composed of labour organizations, NGOs, and academicians working together closely as an advocacy group. Its first demand was to press the government to declare May 10th National Safety Day, in memory of the Kader fire victims but also as a reminder to those who survived to carry on the fight for improving health and safe working conditions for workers. The committee also demanded the setting up of a safety committee at the factory level, as well as a national and provincial tripartite health and safety committee, in order to push the government to incorporate workers' participation in the concept of occupational health and safety in the workplace.

The campaigning committee also set up a short-lived hotline to receive calls from workers seeking advice on health and safety and also to gather information to pass on to management and government officials to solve immediate problems and formulate an effective long-term policy on health and safety. The hotline was soon discontinued because it lacked resources and experienced counselors. Nevertheless, attempts had been made to go beyond the immediate problem, and health reform has become a crucial issue. The degradation of working conditions in many factories; the government's unresponsiveness to workers' demands, especially for compensation for work-related illness; and the trade unions' incapacity to respond to these challenges led victims of occupational disease to form an informal association called the Council of Work and Environmental-Related Patients' Network. This association and the labour-NGO campaign committee came up with blueprints for health reform that were eventually merged into a single blueprint. The 3-month demonstration by the Assembly of the Poor led to the setting up of a committee of equal numbers of government representatives and the poor (including workers, NGOs, and academics) to draft a bill on setting up an independent organization on health and safety in the workplace.

The idea is to transfer management of the worker's compensation fund to the new institute so the fund can play a more preventive role. Although the new body is under the supervision of the Ministry of Labour, it will be managed independently under a five-partite system: workers, employers, government, victims of occupational disease, and specialists/academicians. The board and council will be elected by all sides equally. The new independent organization (Occupational Health, Safety, and Environmental Protection in the Workplace) will empower workers by institutionalising their participation in decision making. Its scope of work will deal not only with occupational health and safety in the workplace but also with communities affected by industrial pollution.

The draft bill was completed in June 1997 after 7 months of drafting. The Ministry of Labour has to forward the bill to the cabinet awaiting consideration before being voted in the parliament. But in doing so, the Ministry of Labour, which participated throughout the drafting period, replaced the drafted bill with its own version (i.e., to consolidate the existing social security, worker's compensation fund, and the National Institute for Improvement of Working Conditions and Environment [NICE] under a new department within the Ministry of Labour).

At present, the government has enacted a law in which a safety committee must be established in a factory with more than 50 workers. After 4 years of campaigning, the cabinet recently agreed to adopt May 10th as National Safety Day. However, government bureaucrats have not been ready to push for health reform as proposed by the workers. The Labour Congress of Thailand has taken up the issue to negotiate with the government.

On March 15, after the meeting to review the situation of the new bill, a number of decisions were made by the Labour organization:

1. To collect 50,000 signatures of eligible voters to support the new bill. According to article 170 of the new constitution, one channel open to the public allowed the bill to proceed to parliament for consideration.

2. To demand government to support the move because the drafting committee of the new bill was appointed by the Ministry of Labour under the resolution of the cabinet.
3. To meet with the leaders of political parties to hand in the drafted bill.
4. To demand support from members of parliament to pass the bill.
5. To put the new bill as the top agenda of the 'May Day' demand and call for signatures.

THE INSTITUTE FOR PROTECTION OF OCCUPATIONAL HEALTH & SAFETY AND WORKING ENVIRONMENT

The committee to draft the bill on setting up the Institute for Protection of Occupational Health & Safety and Working Environment was appointed by the Ministry of Labour and Social Welfare (MOLSW) under the resolution of the cabinet. It consists of 32 members comprising representatives from the government, employers and employees' organizations, and academics. The drafted bill was completed on June 27, 1997. The new institute is invested with the following objcctives: to act as an independent organization (although the new institute is under the supervision of MOLSW); to engage in health promotion, prevention, research and development, and compensation and rehabilitation; and to encourage participatory management through representatives from the employees, employers, government, victims' organization of work-related illness, and specialists/academics.

NICE and the worker's compensation fund are transferred to the new institute in order to implement comprehensive measures on compensation, rehabilitation, and prevention. The institute will be composed of the Occupational Heath & Safety Council and an administrative board.

The Occupational Health & Safety Council is a five-partite body, each with 10 representatives comprising representatives from the workers, employers, government, victim's organization on work-related illness, and academics. These representatives are elected, and the duration of the council's post is 2 years. Its functions include setting policies, approving work plans, and setting rules and regulations. The administrative board has five parties, each with 3 representatives. The total number should not exceed 15 persons. The director is the secretariat of the board. The post of director is 2 years but can be reappointed. The institute is empowered to do the following: conduct surveys, research, and development as a base for setting objectives and target planning; develop and upgrade the occupational health and safety standards in the workplace; carry out factory inspection; enter the factory's premises to investigate, inspect, and make inquiries or demand the company's documents to promote a safe working environment; issue warnings or warrants to the factory to prevent damages; certify and give license to agencies for factory inspection and conduct training in occupational health and safety; promote delivery of medical and standard services; and administer the worker's compensation fund.

The new institute has a number of strengths. It carries out comprehensive work on compensation, rehabilitation, and prevention as to achieving the highest efficiency with the lowest costs. Its emphasis is on the prevention of occupational accidents. It develops and upgrades the occupational health and safety standards in the workplace. It also empowers the workers through equal representation and participation in the decision-making process. More important, it presents a reform of the government structure by promoting participatory democracy, which is in line with the new constitution.

The Paradox of Thailand

Economic liberalization brought about a huge inflow of foreign investment into the country. But about 40% of this inflow was speculative capital seeking short-term profit. So, first we had a proliferation of private financial institutions and banks that were profiting from the high interest rates. They borrowed cheaply abroad, at interest rates of 5% to 6%, and loaned the money domestically at 16%. They used the profit only to finance speculative investments -- 80% of the present debt is held by the private sector.

Second, political parties raised funds by manipulating the stock market. Some used personal connections in the banks to get overdrafts, which they then used to buy land from peasants to develop golf courses, resorts, and other real estate projects.

Third, the government enjoyed the overspending spree, making new investments, receiving commissions, and expanding the ministries in its empire rather than seizing the opportunity to invest in human resources development or worker training in industries that needed upgrading. This is at the root of some of the factors that caused the worsening condition of workers in Thailand.

1. *Migrant Workers*

With economic globalization and intensified global competition beginning in 1990, investors competed with each other at the lower end of the economy. The number of illegal workers in Thailand is more than 1 million, of which 80% are from Myanmar (IPSR, 1997). Migrant workers are cheap for employers since employers do not have to pay them benefits. Starting in 1990, some factories, including garment and sports shoe manufacturers, began relocating to the border region to take advantage of inexpensive migrant workers from Myanmar. The government later adopted a policy that legalized the use of illegal migrant workers, estimated at 1 million, in 43 provinces. They may work in three sectors: agriculture, especially rubber plantations and fruit production; fisheries and related industries; and construction. Illegal workers may register with the government and receive a 2-year work permit.

The advantages to employers of hiring migrant workers are the following: they are prepared to work for a third of what a Thai would receive in wages; the employer is not required to pay them social security benefits; they will do dirty, difficult, or dangerous jobs that Thais refuse; and they are voiceless. Meanwhile, Thais go abroad and receive wages that are 10 times what they would earn at home.

During the economic boom, the government wanted migrant workers to ease the tight labour market, and the private sector welcomed them as cheap labour and wanted to make it even easier for them to enter the country. Trade unions regarded them with caution, however, and local people feared that they brought crime with them. Still, migrant workers were not a problem in the prosperous times, but when the economy goes bust, such as now, they bear the brunt of the blame. The government now paints them as a threat to national security (a television advertisement by the Military High Command says, "Do not hire migrant workers if you do not want any crimes"), and trade unions view them as competitors for domestic jobs.

Migrant workers in the ASEAN region are seen as a factor of production. In prosperous times, borders will be open and migrant workers brought in to satisfy the economic need, but when there is a recession, these workers are pushed out, and the borders are closed. The influx and outflow of migrant workers are thus regulated by the economic cycle. Migrant workers, viewed in these economic terms, are not seen as human beings with certain rights. Migrant workers have problems similar to those of women workers because they are subjected to unequal treatment in wages and welfare benefits, but they also have their own specific problems. Once they cross the border, they become stateless. They are not visible, and their status is that of nonpeople. Migrant workers are thus vulnerable to oppression -- they may be used as forced labour in plantations or on fishing boats, or corrupt officials may extort money from them.

ASEAN often holds regional meetings to develop trade and investment cooperation, but what is missing is the social dimension, such as migrant workers' rights. It is becoming clear that the issue of migrant workers can cause conflict between states, such as the case of the hanging of a Filipino maid. Tackling the issue on a bilateral basis will not resolve the problem because migrant workers are a transnational phenomenon. Capital moves freely across borders, but the movement of labour is still regulated within a nation-state framework. In this way, the protection of the labour market leads to the unequal treatment of labour. Basic rights such as equal pay and social security need to be extended to cover migrant workers. They must be allowed to form associations to have a dialogue with the authorities and to assist each other, or they should be allowed to join trade unions.

2. *Economic Crisis and Layoffs*

The first signs of the economic crisis appeared in early 1990, when economic globalization showed that the labour-intensive industries were less competitive than the new low-wage countries (China, Vietnam, and Indonesia) and urgently needed restructuring. It was clear that the traditional export industries were facing a decline in exports. The textiles sector was hit first, and it began importing new machines and laying off workers. This led to the well-known case of labour unrest in 1992, when women workers at the Thai Durable Textile Company occupied the building for nearly a month, and the situation escalated into a national demonstration. Agreement was finally reached on conditions for the layoffs: advanced notice of employment termination had to be given, the unions had to be consulted in the case of massive dismissals, post transfers had to be explored as an alternative to layoffs, union leaders had to be reemployed, and more compensation had to be given once a layoff became unavoidable.

As the crisis deepens, so does the problem of layoffs. It is estimated that unemployment may reach 3 million by the end of 1998 or the rate of unemployment about 10%. The devaluation of the baht and an increase in value-added tax are expected to cause double-digit inflation. Workers will see their wages pinched by inflation. If they lose their jobs, they will swell the ranks of the new poor and the excluded. With no proper investment in training, there will be more serious poverty, especially among low-wage earners.

3. *Economic Integration Under Export-led Growth on Income Disparities*

During the period of rapid internationalization and high growth of the Thai economy, much of its dynamic came from its contact with the outside world through trade and investment. However, the strategy of export-led growth leading to economic integration did not reduce the gap in income but aggravated it. The government policy aimed at attracting foreign investments into the country to generate growth is based on the "trickle-down" theory -- that is, let the rich become richer first, and the poor will in turn become rich as development is diffused or trickles down.

For Thailand, however, the consequence of growth has already been an increased polarization of Thai society. There is a growing concentration of wealth in the hands of a few "rich" at the expense of the majority. Many studies on income distribution in Thailand come to the conclusion that the gap between the wealthiest 20% of the population and the poorest 20% is ever widening. The share of wealth of the most affluent 20% rose from 49.3% in the past decade to 54.9% in 1988 and to 6% in 1996. By contrast, the share of the poorest 20% dropped from 6% to 4.5%, then to 3% during the same period (see Table 10).

In a high-growth period, one expects to see some improvement in income distribution. This has not materialized, however. Income distribution worsened even during the period of export-led growth. At present, Thailand ranks seventh among countries with the widest income disparities (see Table 11). Poverty is a structural phenomenon in Thailand -- the source of dynamism lies in this growing inequality, but so does structural violence.

Poverty leads to a situation in which work is an economic necessity, with people working to live rather than living to work. Poverty is one of the major factors that pushes people to migrate in search of a job. In 1992, it was estimated that 3.5 million people, or 9.8% of all people living in rural villages, had to migrate seasonally. Villages lose young women and men who move to towns or out of the country to find work. Once these migrations become more or less permanent, village communities -- the foundation of Thailand's social cohesion and democracy today -- can disintegrate. Poverty induces workers to work longer hours, leaving them no time for personal development or to participate in trade union activities. Poverty also tends to generate a segmented labour market at the expense of strong unions.

It has become clear to Thailand's workers that all they can do is bear the consequences of a decision about economic growth that was taken in their name but in which they really had no part. They see the economic problem as a political problem. Workers now are being asked to postpone their demand for a wage increase. In times of economic crisis, workers are asked to make sacrifices, but in the boom times, they were also asked not to demand a wage increase, so they would not frighten away foreign capital. Workers have had to make sacrifices in the interest of Thailand's export-led economic development.

Decision making in Thailand has always been monopolized by the state or political parties; democracy is but a question of the decentralization of power. Still, workers see the new constitution, which was written by direct representatives of the people and recently passed by the parliament after being supported at mass rallies, as a means to achieve workers' rights such as decent wages, employment, and social welfare. This is in addition to its stated support for the right to human dignity, the creation of a human rights commission, and a mechanism for monitoring politicians to make them accountable to the public.

Development has made the world rich, but rich alongside the poor. In 1995, the Forum of the Poor was founded in Thailand. It consists of a broad range of people at the lower end of society: small farmers who were marginalized by land depossession, rural people affected by development projects funded by the World Bank (displaced by dam construction), slum-dwellers in Bangkok, and workers affected by occupational disease who had already organized informally into the Council of Victims of Industrial Discasc. Thc forum's last demonstration was in early 1997, when 20,000 people camped outside government buildings for 3 months. The demonstrators gained experience in negotiating -- 128 problems were negotiated, with 56 of them resolved as of this writing.

Thailand's future lies in a movement from the grassroots and trade union and workers' movements, as well as the Forum of the Poor and the civil society, toward reform of the state. At present, there is a linkage between the workers and the poor in at least one area: the push for social reform and workers' participation in the health and safety system.

Reflections

The recent changes in the regional division of labour suggest that Thailand may soon have to phase out traditional labour-intensive industries such as textiles, garments, and leather goods as it loses its comparative advantage in labour costs to Asian newcomers such as Vietnam, Indonesia, and China (Charoenloet, 1997). Thailand has three options: to shift production out of the country, to introduce new technology that would facilitate the production of higher quality and higher value-added products, or continue the downward pressure on labour "flexibility" to maintain its initial comparative advantage.

At present, there is a persistent trend toward the third option. Firms tend to cut costs by contracting out production. Both the private sector and the government are contemplating liberalising the importation of foreign migrant workers. Such a policy would only lead to welfare reduction, underinvestment in worker training, and declining quality of employment.

Creating a social context for development could be an interesting way to reverse the present trend. In a process of globalisation, where capital movements have no national boundaries and where production is organized globally under the auspices of transnational corporations, social change can be brought about through social movements and international networking. The aftermath of the Kader factory fire showed how international pressure can push a company to comply with workers' demands, make the government more responsive to workplace safety and health issues, and encourage trade unions to become more active in social change. Another example is a recent workers' campaign in a toy factory owned by Dynamic Corporation against the use of short-term contract work and unsafe working conditions. Coordinated international efforts have pushed the company headquarters to put pressure on the local subcontractor to adopt better working conditions. The struggle of workers against unjust layoffs is also a revolt against globalization and leads us to consider the following policy tools:

1. When the economy is globalized, international cooperation is needed to set up a code of conduct for foreign investors to prevent "social dumping." Labour rights are the extension of human rights to cover social and economic aspects of the workplace.

2. When capital becomes borderless and when state authority ends at national boundaries, the problem arises of how legal action can be brought against employers who flee the country without fulfilling their responsibilities. Workers should be able to file such cases in the international court.

3. Thailand is in a transitional period, during which labour-intensive industries will be progressively phased out. Skills development will be key to a smooth transition. General skills that are appropriate to the level of economic development are needed. The government needs to have a comprehensive training program. Tax incentives could be given to enterprises that train their workers. Training needs to be reformed and gender based. Because the current strategy of externalising costs to employ cheap foreign labour is a disincentive for firms to invest in training, the subcontracting system needs to be closely regulated.

4. A fund must be set up to assist workers facing immediate layoffs to pursue the matter in court. Laws should be revised to penalize employers who break the law. The law on wage compensation for employment termination must be revised to reflect the hardship of being unemployed and also the length of time required for workers to find new employment.

5. Firms' reliance on subcontracting to reduce production costs has weakened the trade unions and has also led to deterioration in the quality of employment. The role that the trade unions can play in organizing workers in the unorganized sector may be very limited because of the widely dispersed nature of the sector and the high labour turnover. What the trade unions can do to protect the rights and improve the working

conditions of workers in the informal sector is to demand in their negotiations with management that certain labour standards should be adopted when work is contracted out.

6. In the age of globalization, the government must intervene more, especially in welfare. Industrialization in Thailand has not led to wage labour in the classical sense, but rather to the proliferation of home-based workers and piece-rate workers. At present, about 13% of the labour force in the manufacturing sector is protected by labour laws and the social security system. A large portion of workers in the small or unregistered economy has been deprived of these benefits but is contributing a lot to economic growth. Social welfare and protection need to reach these workers as well.

7. Information on subcontractors needs to be collected to assist in the formulation of policies to fix a limit on subcontracting, to set up a wage structure for piece-rate work, to set working hours, and to regulate health and safety conditions in the workplace.

8. The occupational safety and health system must be reformed. The creation of a new, independent institute of safety and health is one way to empower workers and victims of industrial disease.

ENDNOTES

1. The labour force participation rate in Thailand has been very high at about 73, 78 and % in 1986, 1991 and 1996 respectively. Thai women's labour force participation rate ranks second in the world next to China (TDRI 1994).

REFERENCES

Arom Pongpangan Foundation (1997). Survey on the Use of Amphetemin in the Manufacturing Establishment, Bangkok.

Ativanichayapong, Napaporn (1997). Lives and Families of the Workers after the Kader's Tragedy. Bangkok: Arom Pongpangan Foundation.

Bello, Walden (1998). The Rise and Fall of South-East Asia's Economy, The Ecologist, Vol. 28, No. 1, January/February.

Charoenloet, Voravidh (1991). Thailand in the Process of Becoming a NIC: Myth or Reality? Journal of Contemporary Asia, 21(1): 31-41.

Charoenloet, Voravidh (1997). Thailand in the Regional Divisional ofLabour. In Campbell, Duncan (ed.) Regionalization and Labour Market Interdependence in East and Southeast Asia. Geneva: International Institute for Labour Studies.

Charoenloet, v. And Soonthorndhada, A. (1988). Factory Mangement, Skill Formation and Attitudes of Women workers in Thailand : A comparison between an American and a Japanese Factory. In Noeleen Heyzer (ed.) Daughter in Industry: Works, Skills and Consciousness of Women Workers in Asia. Kuala Lumpur: Asia and Pacific Development Centre.

Charoenloet, V. And Yodkamonsat, S. (1995). Child Labour in Southeast Asian Manufacturing Industries: A case Study of the Garments, Leather and Gem Polishing Industries in Thailand. Bangkok: IPEC/EASTMAT/SEAPAT.

Center for Labour Information, Service and Training (CLIST) (1996). Non-formal Employment: Row House Garment Manufacturing. Clist Newsletter. No.5. Commission on Justice and Peace, 1993 (Unpublished paper).

Gereffi, Gary (1997). The Reorganization of Production on a World Scale: States, Markets and Networks in the Apparel and Electronics Commodity Chains. In Duncan Campbell (ed), Reorganization and Labour Market Independence in East and Southeast Asia. Geneva: International Institute for Labour Studies.

Heron, L.R. (1995). Minimum Wages and Wage Administration. Thailand. Bangkok: ILO/EASTMAT.

International Confedations of Trade Union (ICFTU) (1993). From the Ashes: A Toy Factory Fire in Thailand. Brussels.

Institute for Population and Social Research (IPSR) (1997). Cross-Border Migration into Thailand. Thailand: Mahidol University, Nakon Pathom.

Kokit, Nukoo (1996). Subcontracting System and Impacts to Trade Union: A Case Study on Eden Group Company." Labour Review 10(12), Arom Pongpangan Foundation, Bangkok.

Limskul, Kitti (1994). Towards a Sustainable Development by a Human Resources Development with Labour Market Information System. In Thai Economy Towards the Year 2000. Tokyo: Institute of Developing Economies.

Mounier, A., Kaewthep, K. And Charoenloet, V. (1995). Form and Phase of Thai Industrialization in a Historical Perspective. In Economies et Societes, Serie Development, croissance et priogress, No. 34, Ogena.

Nimfa, B. (1997). Globalization with Equity: Policies for Growth in Thailand. Institute for Population and Social Research, Mahidol University.

Oudin, Xavier (1995). Development and Changes in the Labour Force in Thailand. Bangkok: Chulalongkorn University Social Research Institute.

Phongpaichit, Pasuk (1992). The Urban Informal Sector in Bangkok. In Phongpaichit and Itoga (eds.) The Informal Sector in Thai Economic Development. Tokyo: Institute of Developing Economies.

Pitayanon, Sumalee (1988). Changes in Thailand Labour Force Structure and Government Policy Responses. Graduate School of International Development, Nagoya University, forum of International Development Studies No. 9.

Thailand Development Research Institute (TDRI) (1994). The Thai Economy: First Step in a New Direction. Bangkok: Thailand. Development Institute Foundation.

Thanachaisethavit, Bundit (1998). Trade Union structure and Tripartite Systems in Thailand. Bangkok: Friedrich Ebert Stiftung.

PRADEEP AGRAWAL & P. V. SRINIVASAN

CHAPTER SEVEN

SOCIAL DEVELOPMENT IN INDIA: PERFORMANCE AND CAUSES

INTRODUCTION

Indian policy-makers have traditionally emphasized poverty alleviation and social development, though the strategies used have changed over the years. And indeed, there have been significant improvements in income, education and health standards since independence in 1947. However, while there has been some progress on the social front, much more remains to be achieved. India's progress has been slow compared to what has been achieved by many other Asian countries — especially those of East and Southeast Asia — in the same period. For example, India still ranks among the poorest thirty countries in the world. Although the percentage of poor declined from around 55% in the 1970s to 36% in the 1990s, more than 300 million people are still considered to be below the poverty line and more than 50% of children under four remain undernourished. Although literacy has almost tripled since 1951, nearly 50% of the population is still illiterate and more than 45% of children do not reach grade five. There is thus great scope for reducing the number of the poor and improving the living conditions of the people. The current debate on economic reforms and its impact on social sectors has brought into focus, once again, the issues of how different economic variables and policies affect social development in general and poverty in particular.

During the 1950s and 1960s, greater emphasis was given to increasing economic growth in the hope that the benefits would be distributed to the poor through increased employment etc. However, this did not fully materialize, perhaps because under the Import Substitution strategy adopted by India, the GDP growth rate remained low and did not create employment to the extent needed. Consequently, the emphasis of the government shifted to poverty alleviation programs. Beginning in 1980, programs such as the Integrated Rural Development Programme (IRDP) and the National Rural Employment Programme (NREP) were launched to deal directly with poverty. In addition to these, increased expenditures were incurred on several social services, such as sanitation, water supply, housing, education and health, under the Minimum Needs Programme (MNP). These programs, combined with the higher growth rates experienced over the 1980s and 1990s, have led to somewhat better

K.-L. Tang (ed.), Social Development in Asia, 127–165.

results in social development and poverty alleviation over this period.

In this chapter, we analyse India's performance in poverty reduction and in other aspects of social development, such as the level of education and health facilities available to its people. For this purpose, we make use of several indicators, such as poverty rates, literacy rate, infant mortality rate, percent of population with access to safe drinking water and sanitation facilities etc. The population, education and health indicators are interlinked and are related to other variables affecting the economic well being of the nation. We analyse various factors that affect poverty and social development, such as GDP growth, public spending on social development, and growth in employment and real wages, in an effort to understand the causes of India's slow progress towards poverty alleviation and social development.

In the next section, we begin by looking at the latest nationwide trends in poverty in India. We then discuss the nature of poverty in terms of the distribution of the poor among different economic, social and demographic groups and analyse the regional and geographic dimensions of poverty. Following this, we examine the trends in various social indicators relating to education and health (including access to basic services such as safe drinking water, sanitation etc.) and consider their links with poverty levels. The variations in achievements in these areas across states are also discussed. We also compare the progress made by India vis-à-vis the East Asian countries, with respect to both poverty alleviation and social development. In the third section we look into the causes of India's relatively poor performance in poverty alleviation and in providing education and health amenities to its population. For this purpose, we analyse the trends discussed in the preceding section in terms of economic factors, such as economic growth and public development expenditure, growth in employment and real wage rates. In the final section we summarize the main findings and make some concluding remarks.

INDIA'S PERFORMANCE IN SOCIAL DEVELOPMENT

Trends in Poverty

India's National Sample Surveys, conducted every five years, provide detailed data on consumption expenditure, which yield reliable estimates of poverty. Table 1 provides data on the percentage of the population below the poverty line for the period 1973-74 to 1993-94. It can be seen that there has been a marked reduction in poverty from the early 1970s till the late 1980s as measured by the head-count index. However, the latest (1993-94) survey data, still shows the proportion of poor to be 37.3% in rural areas and 32.4% in urban areas, with the overall poverty concentration at 36%.(1) Due to rapid population growth, there has been no reduction in the absolute number of the poor and estimates reveal that it remains above the 300 million mark. The absolute number of poor in the country increased from 307 million in 1987-88 to 320 million in 1993-94. More than 75% of the poor live in rural areas and this proportion has been decreasing at a slow rate. In recent years the rate of reduction in poverty appears to have slowed down compared to earlier years. This is particularly the case in rural India. Finally, as is clear from Table 2, the poverty level in India remains significantly higher than in East Asian countries.

Table 1: Percentage of population below poverty line

Period	Expert Group estimates			Datt estimates		
	Rural	Urban	Combined	Rural	Urban	Combined
Oct 73-Jun 74	56.4 (261.3)	49.0 (60.0)	54.9 (321.3)	55.72	47.96	54.10
Jul 77-Jun 78	53.0 (264.3)	45.2 (64.6)	51.3 (328.9)	50.60	40.50	48.36
Jan 83-Dec 83	45.7 (252.0)	40.8 (70.9)	44.5 (332.9)	45.31	35.65	43.00
Jul 87-Jun 88	39.1 (231.9)	38.2 (75.2)	38.9 (307.1)	39.23	36.20	38.47
Jul 93-Jun 94	37.3 (244.0)	32.4 (76.3)	36.0 (320.3)	36.66	30.51	35.04

Note: Figures in parentheses are absolute number of the poor in millions
Source: Hashim (1998) and World Bank (1997)

Table 2: Poverty and Inequality: India and East Asia

	Population below poverty line (Per cent) 1989-94	Gini Index
India	53	33.8 (1992)
Indonesia	15	31.7 (1993)
Korea	N.A.	22.4 (1990)
Malaysia	6	48.4 (1989)
Singapore	N.A.	11.5 (1987)
China	29	41.5 (1995)
Thailand	N.A.	46.2 (1992)

Note: Poverty line is PPP$ 1 a day per person. Figures in brackets indicate year of data.

Sources: *Human Development Report, 1997, UNDP and World Development Report*, 1997, The World Bank

At the national level, rural poverty has always been higher than urban poverty, though the gap between rural and urban head count indices has reduced significantly in recent years. Since the early 1970s, poverty appears to have fallen more rapidly in rural areas. Between 1973-74 and 1987-88 rural poverty declined by 17% whereas urban poverty went down by only 8.6%, thus reducing considerably the gap between the rural and urban poverty concentrations. However, between 1987-88 and 1993-94 we find that rural poverty decreased at a slower rate (less than 2%) than urban poverty (more than 6%).

Inequality in income distribution has remained fairly stable in India (Hashim, 1998). The Gini coefficient of income inequality shows limited variability over time and no trend movement (Table 3). Since economic growth has not been accompanied by any adverse impact on income inequality (unlike, say, China where growth was concentrated in a few coastal regions) it led to a gradual reduction in poverty levels. Thus, India's income inequality is significantly lower than that of Malaysia and even China (Table 2). On the other hand, income inequality is lower in Korea and Singapore, while in Indonesia it is comparable to India's levels. Overall, income inequality in India is comparable to the average in East Asia, but the poverty levels are significantly higher because of lower income levels.

Table 3: Consumption expenditure distribution (Lorenz Ratio)

NSS round	Period	Rural	Urban
28	73-74	.2758	.3013
32	77-78	.3386	.3448
38	83	.2976	.3303
43	87-88	.2983	.3537
50	93-94	.2819	.3394

Source: Government of India (1995)

Social and Economic Dimensions of Poverty

For policy purposes it is not enough simply to know how many are poor. It is important to know who the poor are, their economic, occupational, educational and social backgrounds, and regions or areas where there is a greater concentration of the poor etc.

In general, there is a greater concentration of the poor in larger sized households. One of the reasons for this could be lack of education and awareness regarding birth control practices among poorer households. Another reason is that limited access to healthcare among the poor leads to higher infant mortality rates, which in turn lead to higher fertility rates, resulting in larger household sizes. Also, poor households tend to have a high dependency ratio, which means that the number of income earners per dependent is low (Table 4). It is also found that poor households have more females than males as compared to the richer households. Households belonging to the lowest expenditure group in both rural and urban areas have similar demographic characteristics. By contrast, the 5% of the urban population with the highest expenditure has a lower average household size and a lower sex ratio than the corresponding group in rural areas.

Table 4: Demographic characteristics of the poor relative to the rich 1993-94

	Rural India		Urban India	
	Bottom 5% of the population	top 5% of the population	bottom 5% of the population	Top 5% of the population
Average household size	5.7	3.7	5.6	2.9
Average no. of adults per household	2.7	2.8	2.9	2.3
Average female to male ratio	1.07	0.85	1.02	0.79

Source: Government of India, May 1996.

The poverty concentration (percentage of poor in the total population belonging to a particular category) is higher among agricultural labourers than other labourers and the self-employed (Table 5). Agricultural labourers also constitute a large proportion of the total number of the poor. Since real wages have been increasing in recent years without any rise in unemployment rates, one can conclude that for this section of Indian society the standard of living is improving. Poverty levels in each of the categories considered have declined between 1987-88 and 1993-94. However, the distribution of poor people among different occupational, educational and social categories has not changed much over these years. Within the labour categories, people who are employed on a casual basis are the most susceptible to poverty. Their dependence on non-agricultural employment increases during bad crop years. Non-agricultural employment becomes very important during such periods.

Table 5: Economic and social characteristics of the poor: 1987-88 and 1993-94

	Rural				Urban			
	Head-count index (per cent)		Per cent of total poor		head-count index (per cent)		Per cent of total poor	
	1987-88	1993-94	1987-88	1993-94	1987-88	1993-94	1987-88	1993-94
Self employed (agriculture)	37.28	30.04	31.36	28.46	-	-	-	-
Self employed (non agriculture)	38.72	33.31	10.67	10.50	36.34	30.34	38.36	37.4
Agricultural labor	61.80	55.21	42.36	43.44	-	-	-	-
Other labor	47.90	41.81	9.59	8.43	-	-	-	-
Employed with regular wages or salaries	-	-	-	-	20.99	16.53	29.45	26.16
Casual labor	-	-	-	-	61.24	55.12	24.59	26.40
Illiterate	52.86	46.38	67.18	64.41	53.85	49.14	40.73	41.02
Literate- up to primary/middle	39.76	34.63	24.89	24.46	38.92	34.97	37.28	33.57
Literate- up to secondary level	25.08	24.91	7.38	10.10	18.38	16.95	20.07	23.72
Higher Education	9.92	8.31	0.33	0.41	4.65	2.91	1.59	1.50
Scheduled castes	55.22	49.04	24.72	28.24	47.07	42.35	17.63	21.65
Scheduled tribes	59.92	50.07	14.62	14.40	44.69	35.67	5.67	4.43
All categories (All India)	44.86	38.46	-	-	31.62	26.89	-	-

Source: Dubey and Gangopadhyay (1998).

In the urban context, we find that poverty is least among those employed with regular wages and salaries and is highest among casual labourers. A high percentage of the poor belong to the self-employed category. The self-employed in urban areas can vary from those occupied in highly paid professions, such as doctors, lawyers etc., to those occupied in low paying activities in the informal sector. For both the casual labourer and the self-employed in low paying activities, the random and insecure nature of incomes is a major cause of poverty.(2) Increased female labour force participation has been identified as an important urban survival strategy. However, women are paid lower wages than their male counterparts and a disproportionately high number of women workers are casual labourers without job security.

In terms of social groups, the concentration of poverty is much higher than the national average among the scheduled castes and tribes, who have been underprivileged historically. The scheduled castes and tribes in rural areas together constitute around 40% of the rural poor and those in urban areas constitute around 25% of the urban poor (while their share in the national population is only about 22%). If we categorize households according to the level of education of the household head, it is found that poverty is highest among those who are illiterate and least among those with higher education.

Regional Dimensions of Poverty

The reduction in aggregate poverty that took place between the early 1970s and late 1980s was fairly broad-based. Nevertheless, the rates of reduction in poverty did vary across states, and between rural and urban areas within each state. These variations can be attributed to differences in growth rates of state domestic products, agricultural productivity and initial differences in the levels of infrastructure and human resource development (see, for example, Datt and Ravallion, 1996; Drèze and Srinivasan, 1996).

Poverty in any region, rural or urban, is affected directly by changes taking place in that region and indirectly by cross-sector spillover effects. For example, in rural regions, most of the poor are smallholder farmers and agricultural labourers. Rising agricultural productivity has a direct impact on them. However, urban growth can have an indirect impact by providing more employment for migrant labour from rural areas. Increasing productivity and real wage growth in urban centres will have a favourable impact on rural real wages assuming there is labour mobility. Growth in rural areas can also have beneficial impacts on urban centres. For example, increased agricultural output can lead to a decrease in food prices for urban consumers. Higher poverty or low growth in rural areas induces greater migration, creating greater pressure for employment in urban areas and thereby reducing urban real wages. Empirical investigations have revealed that rural to urban linkages are stronger than the linkages in the opposite direction (Ravallion and Datt, 1996b).

Distribution of Poverty Across States

Estimates reveal that rural poverty has decreased dramatically between 1973-74 and

1993-94 in all states except Himachal Pradesh (Table 6). Urban poverty declined in all the states during this period. Combined rural-urban poverty also declined in all states except Himachal Pradesh. The incidence of poverty in rural areas relative to that in urban areas varies across states and over time. Estimates for 1993-94 show that in all the southern states of India the incidence of poverty is much lower in rural areas compared to urban areas. Gujarat, Madhya Pradesh and Rajasthan are the other states that have a lower concentration of poverty in rural areas compared to urban areas.

Table 6: State-wise estimates of poverty- Head-count index (per cent)

	Rural		Urban		Combined	
	73-74	93-94	73-74	93-94	73-74	93-94
All India	56.4	37.3	49.2	33.7	54.9	36.3
Andhra Pradesh	48.4	15.9	52.6	41.5	49.3	23.1
Assam	52.7	45.0	37.2	13.2	51.2	41.5
Bihar	63.0	58.2	51.8	45.3	61.8	56.4
Gujarat	46.4	22.2	49.3	27.1	47.2	23.9
Haryana	34.2	28.0	39.6	13.1	35.2	24.2
Himachal Pradesh	27.4	30.3	13.2	8.6	26.4	28.4
Jammu & Kashmir	45.5	30.3	30.4	8.6	42.6	25.0
Karnataka	55.1	29.9	52.0	40.2	54.3	33.2
Kerala	59.2	25.8	62.2	29.6	59.7	26.8
Maharashtra	57.7	37.9	43.0	34.0	52.9	36.4
Madhya Pradesh	62.7	40.6	58.3	48.7	61.9	42.6
Orissa	67.3	49.7	56.3	40.6	66.2	48.4
Punjab	28.2	12.0	27.7	9.1	28.1	11.1
Rajasthan	44.8	26.5	53.2	31.6	46.3	22.7
Tamil Nadu	57.4	32.5	54.5	44.3	56.5	36.6
Uttar Pradesh	56.5	42.3	59.5	36.1	57.0	41.0
West Bengal	73.2	40.8	34.5	22.5	63.4	35.7
Mean	52.0	33.6	45.8	29.3	50.8	33.0
CV	24.3	34.6	28.4	46.8	22.8	33.1
Minimum	27.4	12.0	13.2	8.6	26.4	11.1
Maximum	73.2	58.2	62.2	48.7	66.2	56.4

Source: Expert Group estimates

The trends between 1973-74 and 1993-94 suggest that the disparities across states have not decreased in terms of the coefficient of variation in the head-count index of poverty across states, nor in terms of the difference between the maximum and minimum values of the poverty index across states. This divergent trend is visible even in the coefficient of variation of real per capita state domestic product, which increases over time (Nagraj et al., 1997). The relative ranking of different states in terms of poverty levels has been stable over time with few exceptions (Table 7). Assam and Haryana are states in which the relative ranking worsened and West Bengal and Kerala are among those whose relative ranking improved. Punjab remained at the forefront in terms of having the least poverty and bringing about the maximum reduction in poverty over time.

Table 7: Achievement and progress in poverty across states

	Head-count Index of Poverty, 73-74	Rank	Head count Index of Poverty, 93-94	Rank	Percentage Decrease	Rank
Andhra Pradesh	49.3	5	23.10	3	53.14	3
Assam	51.2	6	41.50	12	18.95	14
Bihar	61.8	12	56.40	15	8.74	15
Gujarat	47.2	4	23.90	4	49.36	5
Haryana	35.2	2	24.20	5	31.25	9
Karnataka	54.3	8	33.20	7	38.86	7
Kerala	59.7	11	26.80	6	55.11	2
Madhya Pradesh	61.9	13	42.60	13	31.18	11
Maharashtra	52.9	7	36.40	9	31.19	10
Orissa	66.2	15	48.40	14	26.89	13
Punjab	28.1	1	11.10	1	60.50	1
Rajasthan	46.3	3	22.70	2	50.97	4
Tamil Nadu	56.5	9	36.60	10	35.22	8
Uttar Pradesh	57	10	41.00	11	28.07	12
West Bengal	63.4	14	35.70	8	43.69	6

Note: 'Percentage decrease' is obtained as the decrease in poverty as a proportion of the level at 73-74.

The broad-based reduction in poverty levels is noticed even at a more dis-aggregated regional level (Drèze and Srinivasan, 1996). However, this trend is not shared equally by the different regions. The reduction in poverty at the national level has not been accompanied by a reduction in regional inequalities.

Trends in the Provisionof Education and Health Amenities

While higher income levels are desirable, they are not sufficient to generate better social outcomes. The social development of a nation is also reflected in an important way by achievements in the areas of health and education. In India, the states having a low incidence of poverty are not necessarily the ones with high life expectancy or high literacy rates. For example, Punjab, which has the lowest head-count index of poverty, has significantly lower life expectancy and female literacy compared to Kerala.

Table 8: Trends in selected social indicators

	1951	1961	1971	1981	1991
Population (million)	361.1	439.2	548.2	683.3	846.3
Birth rate (per 1000)	39.9	41.7	36.9	33.9	29.5
Death rate (per 1000)	27.4	22.8	14.9	12.5	9.8
Life expectancy at birth (years)					
Male	32.4	41.9	46.4	50.9	58.6
Female	31.7	40.6	44.7	50.0	59.0
Total	32.1	41.3	45.6	50.4	58.7
Literacy rate (percentage)					
Male	27.2	40.4	46.0	56.4	64.1
Female	8.9	15.3	22.0	29.8	39.3
Total	18.3	28.3	34.5	43.6	52.2
Health and family welfare					
Registered medical practitioners,(per 10000 population	1.7	1.9	2.8	3.9	4.7
Beds per 10000	3.2	5.2	6.4	8.3	9.6

Source: Economic Survey- 1996-97

Trends in the indicators of education and health amenities available to the people of India show improvements in most of them (Table 8). For example, life expectancy at birth has nearly doubled from 32 .4 years in 1951 to 58.6 years in 1991. The infant mortality rate has almost halved since 1951 but still stands at 74 per thousand live births in 1994. In the decade between 1981 and 1991 the female literacy rate went up by 9.5% and the overall literacy rate increased by 8.5%. However, as in the case of poverty alleviation, these achievements are not very impressive when compared with those of many other Asian countries (Table 9). Many other countries, which were at similar levels of social development in the 1960s, have made much greater progress than India. Health indicators for India are generally worse than those observed in the East Asian countries (with the occasional exception of Indonesia for a few of the indicators, such as population per physician). For example, over the period 1960-94, the infant mortality rate (per thousand live births) for India declined from 165 to 74 while it declined from 150 to 43 in China, from 72 to 12 in Malaysia and from 85 to 10 in Korea! In fact, India's infant mortality rate in 1994 is higher than it was in Singapore and Malaysia in 1960! Similarly, life expectancy at birth in India is roughly 10 years lower than the average for East Asia. Moreover, India's maternal mortality ratio is nearly 14 times that in Malaysia and South Korea and nearly 3 times that in China. It should be noted, however, that the impressive record of the East Asian countries in basic indicators of health — infant mortality and life expectancy rates — is not so outstanding given their income levels. Life expectancies in these countries are not much higher than the average for countries having comparable stages of economic development. Nevertheless, the infant mortality rates for these countries are substantially lower than the average for their comparable group — thus Korea, Malaysia and Thailand have infant mortality rates of 10, 12 and 29 respectively in1994 as compared to the figure of 39 for all middle-income countries.

Table 9: Indicators of Social Development: Comparative perspective

Indicators	Indonesia	Malaysia	Thailand	Korea	Singapore	China	India
Human Development Index 1960 and 1994	0.223 0.668	0.330 0.832	0.373 0.833	0.398 0.890	0.519 0.900	0.248 0.626	0.206 0.446
Infant Mortality Rate (per thousand Live births) 1960 and 1994	139 53	72 12	103 29	85 10	36 5	150 43	165 74
Maternal mortality ratio (per 100,000 live births) 1989-95	390	34	N.A.	30	N.A.	115	437
Life Expectancy At Birth (female and male) 1994	65.3 61.8	73.5 69.0	72.2 66.8	75.2 67.7	79.3 74.9	71.1 63.9	61.4 61.1
Population per Physician 1988-91	7143	2564	4762	1205	725	N.A.	2439
Access to safe water 1990-96	62	78	89	93	100	67	81
Access to sanitation 1990-96	51	94	96	100	N.A.	24	29
Population growth rate	2.1	2.6	2.3	1.7	2.1	1.8	2.2

Indicators	Indonesia	Malaysia	Thailand	Korea	Singapore	China	India
1960 to 1994							
Total fertility rate 1994	2.8	3.5	1.8	1.6	1.8	1.8	3.2
Contraceptive prevalence, any method 1987-1994	55	N.A.	74	79	74	83	41
Adult literacy rate, female and male 1994	77.1 89.4	77.5 88.2	90.7 95.6	96.8 99.0	87.2 95.6	70.9 89.6	36.1 64.5
Combined primary, secondary and tertiary gross enrolment ratio (female and male) 1994	59.0 65.0	63.0 61.0	53.0 53.0	78.0 86.0	71.0 73.0	55.0 61.0	47.0 63.0
Women's share of adult labor force (age 15 above) 1970 and 1990	30 39	31 36	48 47	32 39	26 38	42 45	34 31

Source: Human Development Report, 1997

Lessons for development can be drawn not only by comparison with other countries but also by looking at the differential performance of the various states within the country itself. There is a wide regional variation in achievements within the country. Therefore, in Table 10 we present data on infant mortality rates for the various Indian states for 1983 and 1990-92. It is seen that the state of Kerala, where socialist governments have often ruled and have emphasized the provision of social health and education services, has a lower infant mortality rate than many East Asian countries. Table 10 also shows that there has been significant progress in most of the states with a few exceptions such as Karnataka, Orissa and Andhra Pradesh. In fact, in the case of Karnataka, there is a marginal increase in infant mortality rate over the period 1983 to 1990-92! Despite making relatively rapid progress, the state of Uttar Pradesh remains one of the worst achievers. Tamil Nadu and Gujarat made enough progress to improve their relative ranking. Kerala continues to remain on top.

Table 10: Achievement and progress in infant mortality across states

	Infant Mortality Rate 1983	Rank	Infant Mortality Rate 1990-92	Rank	Rate of decrease	Rank
Andhra Pradesh	77	3	71	7	0.0779	13
Assam	94	9	76	11	0.1915	11
Bihar	99	10	72	9	0.2727	6
Gujarat	106	11	69	6	0.3491	3
Haryana	91	8	71	7	0.2198	9
Karnataka	71	2	73	10	-0.028	15
Kerala	33	1	17	1	0.4848	1
Madhya Pradesh	125	13	111	14	0.112	12
Maharashtra	79	4	59	4	0.2532	7
Orissa	126	14	120	15	0.0476	14
Punjab	80	5	57	2	0.2875	5
Rajasthan	109	12	84	12	0.2294	8
Tamil Nadu	88	7	58	3	0.3409	4
Uttar Pradesh	155	15	98	13	0.3677	2
West Bengal	84	6	66	5	0.2143	10

Note: 'Rate of decrease' is obtained as the decrease in infant mortality as a proportion of the level in 1983.
Source: Sen (1993) and Authors' calculations

Education is a key social indicator due to its influence on both income and health levels. Greater educational attainment leads to higher labour productivity and higher income levels. It has been shown that primary schooling affects agricultural productivity through faster adoption of new technologies. Education can also lead to greater labour mobility, which helps the poor to exploit opportunities to improve their standard of living. Social benefits such as reduced fertility rates and lower infant mortality rates are possible through education. States with higher schooling levels appear to have lower fertility rates. A mother's education helps in reducing infant and child mortality. Given the limitations to redistribution of physical capital, through land reforms etc, poverty eradication can ultimately take place primarily through accumulation of human capital through access to better education facilities. Thus, we next consider India's performance in the provision of education to its people.

The data on school enrolment for India suggests that there has been significant progress in educational achievement (Table 11). There has been an increase in enrolment of boys and girls in both primary and upper primary schools. The enrolment ratio for girls, however, continues to be lower than that for boys.

Similarly, although the dropout ratio has been decreasing, it is higher among girls as compared to boys. While education can help fight poverty, it is children from poor households who find it difficult to attend school. For the year 1992-93, national enrolment figures among poor children aged 6 to 14 years were 25% lower than those for rich children belonging to the same age group (World Bank, 1996). This 'poverty gap' is higher in rural areas than in urban areas. Similar to the poverty gap there is a 'gender gap'. For the year 1993-94 it was found that enrolment nationwide among girls aged 6 to 14 years was 22% below that of boys belonging to the same age group. In rural areas the gender gap is higher at 26%.

Table 11: Enrolment ratios (per cent)

Year	Classes I-V (age 6-11)			Classes VI-VIII (age 11-14)		
	Boys	Girls	Total	Boys	Girls	Total
1950-51	60.6	24.8	43.1	20.6	4.6	12.9
1970-71	95.5	60.5	78.6	46.3	19.9	33.4
1980-81	95.8	64.1	80.5	54.3	28.6	41.9
1990-91	114.0	85.5	100.1			
1993-94	115.3	92.9	104.5			

Source: Planning Commission

Note: Enrolment rate is the percentage of children ever enrolled the corresponding age group. The number exceeds 100 in some cases because of the presence of children both younger and older than indicated in the age group for these classes.

Next, we consider how India's performance in providing education to its people compares with that of East Asian countries (Table 12). Many East Asian countries undertook the provision of primary education to a large proportion of the school-age population at an early stage of their economic development — usually by the 1960s. This is particularly evident in the case of Korea and Singapore where primary enrolment ratios were close to 100% by 1965. By 1989, the data show that enrolment ratios in primary education had reached nearly 100% for most countries. However, enrolment data should be used with caution since it may have a limited impact on literacy levels if the quality of education provided is poor. High enrolment ratios do not in themselves indicate whether schoolchildren have remained in school long enough to obtain the cognitive skills they will need for their later entry into the labour force. In India the drop out rate (58%) among children entering primary school is high compared to the East Asian countries where over 80% of children entering primary school complete Grade 4. Specific indicators such as the pupil/teacher ratio can also be used to assess the quality of education. This ratio is very high for primary education in India — nearly three times the average for East Asia. Furthermore, while a sharp decline in this ratio is observed in most of the East Asian countries both at the primary and secondary levels, it has been rising in India, rapidly in the case of primary education and only marginally in the case of secondary education.

Table 12: Indicators of Educational Attainment, 1965 and 1989

Indicators	Indonesia	Malaysia	Thailand	Korea	Singapore	Taiwan	India
Gross Enrolment Ratio Primary, Total (% of school age population)	72 117	90 96	78 86	101 108	105 110	87 100	74 98
Pupils Reaching Grade 4 (% of cohort)	- 90	- N.A.	- 81	- 100	- 100	- N.A.	- 58
Pupil-Teacher Ratio, Primary	41 23	29 21	35 18	62 36	42 29	29 26	42 61
Gross Enrolment Ratio Secondary, Total (% of school age population)	12 45	28 57	14 28	35 87	58 99	45 69	27 43
Pupil-Teacher Ratio, Secondary	25 14	- 21	18	37 28	25 22	25 22	22 23

Note: a. Except in the case of pupils reaching grade 4, the figure here is for 1983.
Source: *Social Indicators of Development*, World Bank.

A better indicator of a country's educational attainment is it's average stock of education, defined as the mean number of school years of education of the working age population. This provides information on the accumulated years of schooling in the working age population of that country. Nehru et al. (1993) obtained estimates of this indicator by summing up the net enrolment at each level (primary, secondary and tertiary). Net enrolment is obtained by excluding the number of returners and drop out's from gross enrolment. Among the five countries that were analysed, India has the least education stock. Korea shows the highest education stock at all three levels (Table 13).

Table 13: Average Education Stock, 1965 and 1987

	Indonesia	Malaysia	Thailand	Korea	Singapore	India
Primary	1.98 3.89	2.85 4.74	3.67 5.00	3.09 5.72	2.56 5.53	1.28 2.48
Secondary	0.05 0.45	0.29 1.38	0.22 0.51	0.41 1.57	0.31 1.53	0.34 0.94
Tertiary	0.01 0.08	0.00 0.08	0.05 0.21	0.10 0.43	0.07 0.27	0.03 0.12
Total	2.04 4.42	3.14 6.20	3.94 5.72	3.60 7.72	2.96 7.33	1.66 3.54

Source: Nehru, Swanson and Dubey (1993)

Table 14: Pupils Enroled in Vocational Education

	Number	Per cent of population	Per cent of total students at secondary level
India (1987)	741715	0.10	1.62
Indonesia (1989)	1349050	0.75	12.00
Korea (1991)	819269	1.89	18.38
Malaysia (1991)	32219	0.18	2.17
Singapore (1980)	9391	0.39	5.19
Taiwan (1993)	513659	2.45	25.07
Thailand (1990)	444218	0.79	18.53

Note: a. Figures in brackets indicate year of data.

Sources: *Statistical Yearbook 1993*, UNESCO and *Taiwan Statistical Data Book 1994*, CEPD.

India fares relatively well with respect to the availability of technical manpower — the percentage of scientists and engineers in the total population (0.29%) and the proportion of tertiary level students in technical fields for India (29%) are comparable to those of other East Asian countries. On the other hand, the number of students in vocational training in India (0.1% of the population and 1.62% of the total number of students in secondary education in 1987) is significantly below that of several East Asian countries (Table 14). This shows the poor spread of basic technical skills among the population in India. It also indicates the 'dualistic' nature of India's human resource development strategy. On the one hand, a large section of the manufacturing workforce in India does not have the background in basic education or the technical skills required for building industrial competitiveness, whereas on the other hand, there is a surplus of technical manpower (in part due to the government's specific interventions in the capital goods sector — see Lall, 1987) which often remains unemployed or leaves the country. As Lall (1990: 51) argues, "India could not have 'done a Korea' even if it had followed export-oriented strategies if its human capital base had remained so small".

Table 15: Achievement and progress in literacy across states

	Illiteracy 1981	rank	Illiteracy 1991	Rank	Rate of decrease	rank
Andhra Pradesh	64.3	10	55.91	12	0.1305	11
Assam		#N/A	47.11	9		#N/A
Bihar	68	13	61.52	15	0.0953	14
Gujarat	47.8	4	38.71	4	0.1902	5
Haryana	56.1	8	44.15	8	0.213	2
Karnataka	53.8	7	43.96	7	0.1829	7
Kerala	18.4	1	10.11	1	0.4505	1
Madhya Pradesh	65.8	11	55.8	11	0.152	9
Maharashtra	44.2	2	35.13	2	0.2052	4
Orissa	59	9	50.91	10	0.1371	10
Punjab	51.9	6	41.19	5	0.2064	3
Rajasthan	69.9	14	61.45	14	0.1209	13
Tamil Nadu	45.6	3	37.24	3	0.1833	6
Uttar Pradesh	66.7	12	58.4	13	0.1244	12
West Bengal	51.4	5	42.3	6	0.177	8

Note: 'Rate of decrease' is obtained as the decrease in illiteracy as a proportion of the level in 1981.
Source: Sen (1993) and Authors' calculations

Data on literacy rates in India show that there has been significant progress in all the states (Table 15). However, the relative positions of the states remains unchanged, as can be seen from their national ranking in the two different time periods. In other words, those states that had high literacy levels to start with are also the ones that have made substantial progress. The states of Kerala, Punjab and Haryana are among the highest achievers of literacy and they are also among the best in terms of the progress made between 1981 and 1991. Women's share of the adult labour force in India is quite close to that in most East Asian countries (Thailand and China are among the countries with very high female shares in the labour force).(3) However, adult female literacy rates in India are less than half of what is seen in the East Asian countries and in China.

In addition to education and health, access to basic services such as sanitation and safe drinking water are essential for human resource development. Lack of electricity in rural areas, for example, can prevent people from benefiting from income earning activities that need electrical power. If we consider the levels of access to basic services like electricity in dwellings, safe drinking water and toilet facilities across the nation we see that as many as 25% of households have none of the three services. Only as few as 16% of households have access to all three of them (Table 16).

Table 16: Access to basic services

	Per cent of households having access to (in the year 1991)				
	Electricity	Safe drinking water	Toilet facilities	All the three facilities	None of the three facilities
Rural	30.54	55.54	9.48	3.9	31.32
Urban	75.78	81.38	63.85	50.4	5.41
All India	42.37	62.3	23.7	16.07	24.54

Source: CMIE, February 1996, India's social sectors

FACTORS RESPONSIBLE FOR INDIA'S SLOW SOCIAL DEVELOPMENT

In the previous section we saw that India's progress in social development has been slow in comparison to the East Asian countries. In this section we explore the various factors responsible for the slow reduction in poverty and the slow improvement in education and health amenities in India.

Factors Responsible for the Slow Reduction in Poverty

Here we consider the main factors responsible for the reduction in poverty in an effort to understand the reasons for the slow reduction in poverty in India compared to the East Asian countries. The Headcount Ratio of poverty (P) is defined as the percentage of the population with income below a given poverty line. Thus, P will generally depend on average income per capita (Y*) and the poverty line (Y), both expressed in constant prices. It will also depend on the income distribution (D):

$$P = P(Y^*, Y, D)$$

Following Jain and Tendulkar (1990), the change in poverty level from period 0 to period t can be expressed as follows (to keep the notation simple we suppress Y, which is constant over the period 0 to t, from P):

$$\Delta P = P(Y_t^*, D_t) - P(Y_0^*, D_0) = [P(Y_t^*, D_t) - P(Y_0^*, D_t)] + [P(Y_0^*, D_t) - P(Y_0^*, D_0)]$$

The first term above is the growth effect, which measures the change in poverty due to the change in average income over the period 0 to t for a given income distribution. The second term above is the distribution effect, which measures the change in poverty due to the change in income distribution over the period 0 to t for a given average income.

Given the fact that the income distribution has remained remarkably stable in India (see Table 2), the above equation indicates that the growth in income per capita has been the main source of reduction in poverty in India. This finding is supported empirically by the work of Jain and Tendulkar (1990), Tendulkar (1995) and Ravallion and Datt (1996a). It is also noteworthy that the decline in poverty was significantly faster during the 1980s when the GDP growth rate averaged over 5% than it was during the 1960s and 1970s when GDP growth averaged about 3.5%. The cross-section data for the different states of India shows that poverty is lower in states with higher state domestic product (SDP). This provides further support to the above finding that (in an environment of stable income distribution) economic growth is the primary channel for poverty reduction.

There are, of course, debates in the literature regarding the channels through which growth reduces poverty. Ravallion and Datt (1996a) argue that higher agricultural growth induces not only higher own-farm productivity but also higher employment and real wages. By contrast, Sen (1996) points out that yield increases in Indian agriculture were accompanied by a decline in the elasticity of labour demand with respect to agricultural output. He stresses the importance of public expenditure on anti-poverty programs in poverty alleviation. Through his time series regression analysis, he shows that rural non-agricultural employment has a significant influence on poverty reduction. He also points out that although government programs constitute only around 5% of the total rural employment, they amount to around 20% of rural non-agricultural employment. In his regressions using pooled time series and cross section of states he shows that state development expenditure is an important variable in explaining headcount indices of poverty, apart from variables such as per capita agricultural output and relative price of food. Tendulkar (1995), on the other hand, suggests that the scale of government rural employment programs is too small and the effectiveness in the delivery of these is too limited to have a big impact on poverty reduction.

In any case, economic growth would still be necessary to generate adequate resources for purposes of direct intervention by the government to reduce poverty by tackling the distribution problem. Even the cross section data for the different states of India show that their development expenditure is positively correlated with the SDP growth rate. Thus, irrespective of the channels through which it benefits the poor, growth has a primary role in poverty alleviation.

Table 17: Employment and Real Earnings in the Manufacturing Sector

Country or Region	Index of Employment in Manufacturing (1972=100)				Index of Real Earnings per Employee in Manufacturing (1972=100)			
	1972	1982	1992	Growth, 1972-92[9]	1972	1982	1992	Growth, 1972-92[9]
INDIA	100	141.0	144.3	1.83	100	101.1	125.2	1.12
Dev Ctry[1] AVG	100	87.7	82.0	-0.99	100	115.4	132.1	1.39
Lat Amer[2] AVG	100	121.7	120.6	0.94	100	222.0	273.2	5.03
South Asia[3] AVG	100	151.9[5]	187.8[6]	3.50	100	109.7	139.2[6]	1.95
East Asia[4] AVG	100	190.4	362.1	6.43	100	153.0	288.8	5.3
Individual East Asian Countries								
Indonesia	100	173.6	465.4	7.69	100	159.0	222.2	3.99
Thailand	100	167.7	277.3[7]	5.67	100	97.0	149.9	2.02
Malaysia	100	233.9	473.4	7.77	100	138.8	172.0	2.71
Korea	100	217.8	303.4	5.55	100	223.3	514.8	8.19
Singapore	100	159.1	206.2	3.62	100	146.8	246.0	4.5
Taiwan	100	178.0	212.2	3.76	100[8]	195.9	405.0	7.77

Notes:
1. Average (unweighted) for Developed Countries (USA, Japan, UK, France)
2. Average (unweighted) for Latin America (Argentina, Chile, Brazil, and Mexico)
3. Average (unweighted) for South Asia (India, Bangladesh, Pakistan, and Sri Lanka)
4. Average (unweighted) for six East Asian Countries (Korea, Taiwan, Singapore, Malaysia, Thailand and Indonesia).
5. The data is for 1981.
6. The data is for 1989.
7. The data is for 1990.
8. The data is for 1974 that is also used as the base year for want of earlier data.
9. Avg. Annual Compounded Growth Rates - they are over shorter periods in a few cases for want of data.

Source: The World Bank, World Tables, 1994-95 (Growth Rates calculated by the author).
Taiwan Statistical Data Book, 1989 and 1994.

Thus India's relatively poor performance in poverty alleviation relative to East

Asia is primarily due to the inadequate growth rate of its GDP. We will not discuss here the reasons for the low growth in GDP. However, India's continued commitment to the Import Substitution regime right up until 1990 could be one of the main reasons. This issue has been addressed in greater detail in, for example, Agrawal et al. (1995; 2000). The ill effects of slow GDP growth have been further exacerbated by an even slower increase in employment. The main reasons for the slow growth of employment are as follows. India's reliance on an import substitution strategy since independence in 1947 until the early 1990s generally led to the use of capital-intensive technology in the industrial sector. Labour laws in India are such that workers in the formal sector have very little incentive to work hard and improve their skills and too much protection against dismissal from their jobs. Since the first point has been discussed extensively in the literature, a brief discussion of the second point follows.

India has achieved very limited success compared to East Asian countries in terms of raising employment levels for workers and improving their real wages (Table 17).(4) Most of the increase in urban employment appears to be in the informal sector. Casual employment rose much more than regular employment. Labour market rigidities in the urban formal sector, including the lack of an exit policy, has led to a situation where firms choose to subcontract production activities to the informal sector (see, for example, Tendulkar and Jain, 1995). Job security laws in India make it very difficult to retrench labour. Firms are unable to rationalize their operations and labour force in response to changing market conditions. Even loss-making firms (referred to as 'sick' firms) are not permitted to close down but are given subsidized credit and other facilities to continue operation. This leads to the locking-up of valuable capital and labour resources in inefficient production. The inability to rationalize the regular labour force in response to changing market conditions has led to an increasing use of temporary, casual or contract workers who do not have any job security or redundancy compensation. However, neither such workers, nor their employers have sufficient incentives to undertake relevant training etc., again leading to an inefficient use of resources.

Although high levels of unionization in the formal sector have resulted in a large share of wages in value added, employment levels and real earnings have been stagnating. The share of wages in value added for the manufacturing sectors in India is high compared to most other countries (Table 18). The share has been around 40% in the developed countries, and is even higher in India (46%), reflecting the strength of unions in India. Among the East Asian countries, Singapore and Malaysia have the highest share at about 33% and 28%. Korea shows an average share of about 26.5%, which is low for its level of development. It shows some improvement in 1988, following a year of major labour strife and wage increases, but the gain has not been sustained into the 1990s. The share of workers' earnings in total value added appears to be very low in Indonesia and Thailand at about 22.5% and 16% respectively, suggesting the very poor bargaining position of labour.

Table 18: Share of workers earnings in manufacturing sector value added

Year	India	Indonesia	Thailand	Malaysia	Korea	Singapore	East Asia AVG[1]	Developed Country AVG[1]	Lat. Amer. AVG[1]	South Asia AVG[1]
1972	54.2	23.50	16.33	29.30	23.50	35.40	25.61	43.80	26.55	36.55
1974	43.6	23.90	16.40	26.90	23.20	30.20	24.12	41.50	22.63	33.94
1976	43.3	21.60	16.33	27.90	24.80	33.10	24.75	42.87	18.90	33.72
1978	48.6	23.80	16.20	26.20	27.10	33.40	25.34	41.77	19.36	33.19
1980	50.7	21.10	15.34	28.00	29.30	29.70	24.69	41.50	20.66	33.83
1982	48.6	25.20	15.54	32.10	27.50	35.10	27.09	41.30	17.70	33.32
1984	50.3	24.00	15.61	28.50	26.30	36.50	26.18	39.33	16.12	32.10
1986	49.4	22.70	15.61	29.10	26.20	31.70	25.06	39.43	15.90	33.23
1988	43.4	22.50		25.90	28.40	28.20	26.25	36.77	15.25	32.43
1990	38.8	19.80		27.00	27.60	31.70	26.53	36.87	16.36	38.13
1992	37.6	19.50		26.90	25.80	33.70	26.48	37.83	8.95	37.60
Average 1972-92	46.4	22.48	15.89	27.90	26.55	32.83	25.74	40.26	18.06	34.04

Note: The developed country average is over USA, Japan, UK and France, the Latin America average is over Argentina, Chile, Brazil and Mexico and the South Asia average is over India, Bangladesh and Pakistan.

Source: ILO, Geneva, *Yearbook of Labor Statistics* 1993, 1985, 1976 and 1966.

Thus, we see that even though India's protective labour laws and strong labour unions have helped obtain a larger share of value added for workers, the growth in employment and earnings has been low. In contrast, the East Asian countries, by emphasizing an efficient and flexible use of labour, have raced ahead in generating employment and increasing real earnings per employee, the things that count most for the working class in a developing country.

Not only GDP growth but also its sectoral distribution is relevant to poverty reduction. Ravallion and Datt (1996b) show that urban growth had very little effect on rural poverty. The increasing share of the tertiary (or services) sector in GDP and the rising percentage of employment in this sector (Table 19) in recent years may change this situation. The breakdown of GDP growth among different sectors indicates that the primary (agricultural) and tertiary sectors have registered impressive growth. These two sectors have a great potential for poverty reduction.

Table 19: Sector wise distribution of workers (usual status)

Year	Primary	Secondary	Tertiary
1972-73	73.9	11.3	14.8
1977-78	71.0	12.6	16.3
1983	68.6	13.8	17.6
1987-88	65.0	15.9	19.1
1993-94	64.7	14.8	20.5

Source: Visaria (1996).
Note: Primary sector includes agriculture, forestry and logging, fishing and mining and quarrying. Secondary sector consists of manufacturing, electricity, gas and water supply and construction. Tertiary sector includes trade, hotels and restaurants, transport, communication, banking, insurance and other services.

Given that most of the poor live in rural areas, increased employment in the agricultural sector through increased investment in agriculture, i.e. irrigation and other infrastructure facilities, will have a positive impact on poverty. Real agricultural wages vary with productivity and it can be seen that real wages in irrigated areas are much higher than those observed in dry regions. Investments in physical infrastructure help induce growth, leading to a sustainable reduction in poverty in the long run. Unfortunately, public investment in agriculture has been declining in real terms since the mid-1980s. However, total investment in agriculture shows an increasing trend, implying that the increase in private investment has compensated for the reduced public investment (Table 20). For example, private investment in tube well irrigation has substituted for declining public investment in additional irrigation schemes. The reduction in public investment is largely due to the diversion of resources from capital to current expenditures, such as subsidies for food, fertilizers, water and electricity. To the extent that public investment in agriculture benefits the poor far more than private investment, this trend is likely to have an adverse impact on poverty. Further, while there had been a steady increase in private investment in agriculture as a percentage of agricultural GDP from 1988-89 to 1992-93, it fell in 1993-94. If this trend continues in the future, the long-term prospects for agricultural growth and poverty reduction could be hampered. Since public investment in rural infrastructure (roads, irrigation, electricity etc.) also encourages private investment in agriculture, there is a need to maintain a certain minimum level of public investment in agriculture. Also, policy measures that can improve the terms of trade in favour of agriculture can lead to greater private investment.

Table 20: Gross domestic investment in agricultural sector (Billion Rupees in 1980-81 prices)

Year	Public Investment	Private Investment	Ratio of Private to Total Investment
85-86	16.37	30.13	0.65
86-87	15.44	28.16	0.65
87-88	15.76	32.04	0.67
88-89	14.82	32.48	0.69
89-90	13.01	34.89	0.73
90-91	13.13	37.67	0.74
91-92	11.43	40.67	0.78
92-93	11.82	46.88	0.80
93-94	13.17	48.03	0.78

Source: National Accounts Statistics, 1996

The slowing down of poverty reduction in rural areas in recent years is sometimes attributed to a decline in non-farm employment, which is mostly generated by public development expenditure. However, it should be noted that employment generated through public expenditure, especially through rural employment programs, tends to be related to agricultural performance and is expected to be high only in periods of low crop outputs.

Table 21: Poverty changes by agro-ecological regions

		Irrigated Areas	Rain-fed Areas
Per cent of poor	1972	42.9	52.7
	1987	31.0	41.0
	Change 1972 to 87	-38.4%	-28.5%
Number of poor (millions)	1972	86.8	90.1
	1987	77.9	89.8
	Change 1972 to 87	-11.4%	-0.4%

Source: Fan Shenggen and Peter Hazell (1996)

Increasing agricultural productivity appears to generate employment, particularly among the poor. This could be one reason why, during the 1980s, the reduction of poverty in rural areas was greater than that in urban areas. While improved technologies and rural infrastructure investments in general can lead to both productivity growth and a reduction in rural poverty, there can be large regional variations in these effects. Fan and Hazell (1996) show that irrigated areas benefited much more from government investments than rain-fed ones. Poverty levels between the early 1970s and late 1980s declined much more in the irrigated areas compared to rain-fed ones (Table 21). However, continued increase in investment in irrigated areas led to diminishing marginal returns. This implies that public investment in irrigation and other infrastructure facilities such as roads has a greater potential for poverty reduction in the rain-fed areas since the marginal benefits to public investment are larger in these regions. Thus, greater reduction in poverty can be expected by concentrating government investments in rain-fed areas.

A large proportion of the total expenditure of the poor is devoted to food. Hence the relative price of food is an important determinant of poverty levels in the economy. This is true in particular for the urban poor who are net buyers of food. Even in rural areas, higher food prices are beneficial only to the large farmers with marketable surplus. The landless labourers and some of the small and marginal farmers are net purchasers of food. An increase in food prices can thus have an adverse impact on standards of living if real wages do not adjust accordingly. A reduction in fertilizer subsidies led to an increase in food prices in 1992, even though they have been roughly stable since then (although at a higher level than that prevailing in the late 1980s — see Figure 1). Higher food prices are partly responsible for the slowdown in the rate of reduction in poverty in recent years. Further, the movement in real wage rates is inversely related to poverty. While there was a steady increase in real wages in the 1980s, they have remained virtually unchanged over the first half of the 1990s, thus contributing to a slower reduction in poverty in the early 1990s.

Public development expenditure and poverty reduction

Government development expenditure is classified into two broad groups: expenditure on social services and expenditure on economic services. Expenditure on education, health, water supply, sanitation etc., comes under the first category. Food, fertilizer, export subsidies and rural development programs fall under the second category. According to the provisions of India's constitution, the state governments assume the major responsibility for providing social services. Since the resource mobilization capacity of the individual states varies, we find a large variation in social-sector expenditure across states. The transfer mechanisms from the central to the state governments through the institutions of the Planning and Finance commissions have not been effective in removing regional disparities.

The need for the protection of the poor in the short run forms the basis for public expenditure on anti-poverty programs, which include rural employment programs to protect the incomes of the rural poor during bad crop years. Expenditure on rural employment programs as a percentage of GDP in the early 1990s has been low compared to the levels in the late 1980s. It was particularly low during 1991-92, the year in which the rural poverty level is estimated to have been the highest in recent years. However, the magnitude of the increase in poverty in this year cannot entirely be explained by this since the scale of these programs is small and their effectiveness limited due to leakage and other factors (see Tendulkar and Jain, 1995). Other reasons include the dip in agricultural production in 1991-92 and the relative increase in food prices. Real wages for unskilled agricultural labour decreased by as much as 6.15% in 1991-92 from its level in the previous year. Expenditure on rural employment programs has, however, increased since 1992-93 to a level higher than in the mid-1980s. Nevertheless, development expenditure as a whole, both capital and revenue, shows a declining trend in recent years.

Figure 1: Trends in Relative Food Price and Real Wages

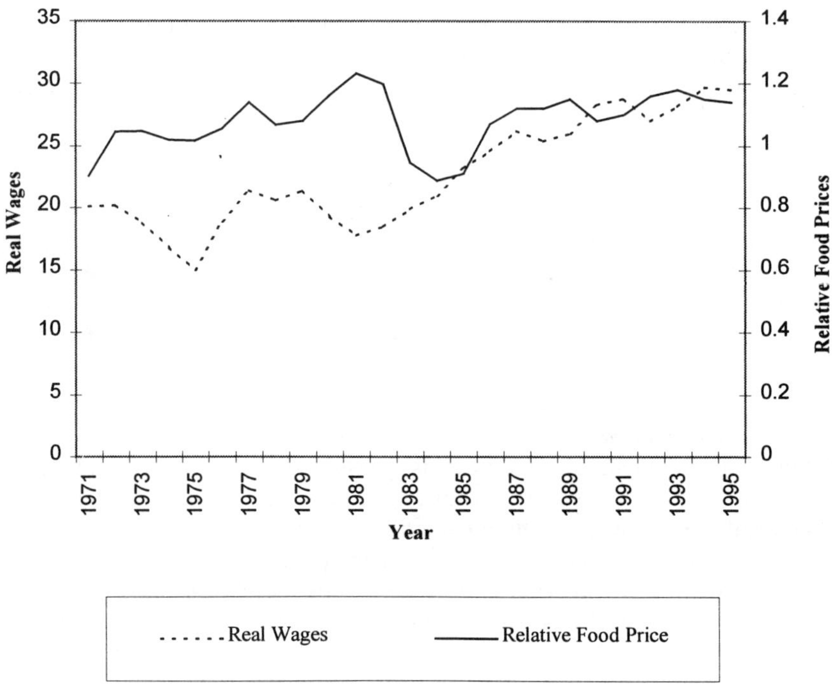

Source:

Relative food price-Economic Survey, different issues
Relative wages-Papnek(1988 and 1996) as quoted in Dev(1997)

Note:

Relative food price is obtained as the ratio of the price index of food articles and price index of all commodities.

Food subsidies are another form of expenditure incurred by the government that have a direct impact on poverty. They are provided by the central government to help maintain buffer stocks to ensure a smooth supply of food-grains in the economy and also to protect poor consumers through the operation of the subsidized public distribution system. As a percentage of GDP, expenditure on food subsidies had been decreasing since the mid-1980s, reaching a minimum in 1992-93 before it started rising again. Although there has not been any significant reduction in food subsidies their effectiveness in reaching the poor has not been impressive.(5)

Since GDP can fluctuate over time it is more meaningful to look at development expenditure in per capita terms rather than as a share of GDP. We see that there has not been any appreciable increase in per capita expenditure on anti-poverty programs and food subsidy (Table 22).

Table 22: Per capita expenditure on anti poverty programs

	Food subsidy (Rupees, 1980-81 prices)	Rural employment programs (Rupees, 1980-81 prices)
1980	9.57	0.00
1981	9.20	0.00
1982	8.44	2.23
1983	8.97	2.01
1984	10.78	6.22
1985	14.70	8.37
1986	16.35	9.85
1987	14.73	10.39
1988	14.68	8.30
1989	14.96	12.69
1990	13.08	10.68
1991	13.00	8.29
1992	11.54	10.49
1993	20.45	14.43
1994	16.67	15.28
1995	16.48	14.29

Source: Union Budget Documents, Ministry of Finance

Although public expenditure is a crucial factor, achievements in terms of social outcomes depend on the cost effectiveness and efficiency with which the various services are delivered. Most of the anti-poverty programs suffer from considerable leakages and inefficiencies in their implementation. They also suffer from targeting errors in terms of excluding the poor and including the non-poor in the list of beneficiaries. For example, the Public Distribution System (PDS), which is meant to provide food subsidies to the poor, is known to suffer from substantial leakage with the subsidies not being effectively targeted to the poor (Jha, 1992; Ahluwalia, 1993; Parikh, 1994). It has not been effective as an anti-poverty instrument. The states of Kerala and Andhra Pradesh are, however, exceptions where the poor have better access to the PDS.(6) Similarly, in the case of the Integrated Rural Development Program (IRDP) the evidence mostly points to the fact that the beneficiaries are not necessarily poor and the effectiveness of this program in alleviating poverty is suspect. Under the IRDP, finance is provided to identified beneficiaries for the purchase of income-generating assets in occupations like dairy farming, small poultry business and other self-employment alternatives. Due to borrower's lack of entrepreneurial skills and capabilities, the default rate on loans has been very high. For these and other reasons it is felt that an employment guarantee scheme might be a better option (Drèze, 1990). The built-in self-selection mechanism in the rural public works programs and employment programs have made them, by far, the best in terms of their outreach to the poor.

In addition, the geographical spread of these schemes is not uniform. For example, there is a distinct urban bias in the PDS. The employment guarantee schemes have so far only been effective in the state of Maharashtra. The midday meal schemes have been successful mainly in the southern state of Tamil Nadu. Land reforms were carried out to a reasonable extent only in Kerala and West Bengal.(7)

To summarize, economic growth has been the main source of poverty reduction in India. In fact, economic growth, measured in terms of mean per capita consumption expenditure explains about 80% of the observed poverty decline over a period of 40 years from 1950 to 1990 (see Ravallion and Datt, 1996). Growth rates in employment, agricultural yields, real agricultural wages, relative food prices, public development expenditure in general and expenditure on anti-poverty programs in particular have also been found to influence poverty levels.

Factors Responsible for the Slow Progress in Education and Health Amenities

We will now consider the main factors affecting the provision of education and health amenities to the population of India in an effort to understand the causes of the slow progress in India in these areas compared to East Asian countries. We have seen that growth in income per capita was the most important factor responsible for the reduction in poverty. One would also expect the indicators relating to education and health to be considerably influenced by either income per capita or its growth rate. This would be due to the greater availability of resources to be spent on education and health amenities in economies with higher per capita income and also due to a greater demand for such services when income levels go up.

To investigate this hypothesis, we examine whether the indicators of poverty, education and health are interlinked, using the data on variations in the performance levels of different states of India. Table 23 shows the matrix of correlation among the various indicators of social development across the various states of India, using data from the 1990s. The correlations in Table 23 are reported in two ways: (a) including the state of Kerala and (b) excluding the state of Kerala. Kerala is a special case due to the unique set of government policies followed there and exhibits comparatively good social development despite relatively low levels of per capita income. When the state of Kerala is included, the data show, in general, a low and insignificant correlation between several social indicators and the State Domestic Product (SDP).

However, when we exclude the state of Kerala, which seems more appropriate since it is a very special case, we find that most correlations are significant at the 5% level. For example, we find that states with lower levels of poverty also have higher literacy rates and lower infant mortality rates as seen from the correlation between various indicators of social development (Table 23). Under-nourishment among children is highly positively correlated with poverty levels. Infant and maternal mortality rates have a significant negative correlation with literacy levels, indicating the importance of education in achieving better health.

Table 23: Correlations among the various indicators of social development across the states of India

	Head-count index of Poverty (1993-94)	Literacy rate (1991)	Infant mortality rate (1990-92)	Under-nourishment among children (1992-93)	Maternal mortality rate (1982-86)	State Domestic Product (1991-92)
Head-count index of Poverty	1.0					
Literacy rate	-0.33 (-.33)	1.0				
Infant mortality rate	0.46 (0.47)	-0.78* (-.58*)	1.0			
Under-nourishment among children	0.65* (0.74*)	-0.62* (-.25)	0.58* (0.27)	1.0		
Maternal mortality rate	0.47 (0.42)	-0.77* (-.79*)	0.58* (0.47)	0.38 (0.18)	1.0	
State Domestic Product	-0.70* (-.74*)	0.35 (0.70*)	-.35 (-0.57*)	-0.33 (-0.56*)	-0.56* (-0.65*)	1.0

Source: Authors' computations.
Note: '*' indicates significance at 5% level, Figures in parentheses give the correlation coefficient when the state of Kerala is excluded. The data for HCR is taken from Table 6 and that for literacy and under-nourishment among children is taken from Prabhu and Kamdar (1998). All other variables are obtained from Dreze and Sen (1995).

To further explore these interlinkages among the various indicators of social development, we also ran several regressions. In our regressions, using the cross section data from the various states of India, we find that reduction in illiteracy (DILLIT) between 1981 and 1991 is positively related to the SDP growth (SDPGR) observed between 1980 and 1990:(8)

$$DILLIT = 24.5 - 0.29\ INILLIT + 3.4\ SDPGR \qquad \text{R-bar Square} = .86$$
$$(-5.9) \qquad\qquad (3.8)$$

(Note: Regression after excluding Kerala from the data set. The t-statistics are given in parentheses.)

We also find a significant negative relationship between achievements in literacy and the initial (1981) levels of illiteracy (INILLIT). Improvements in infant mortality are, however, correlated with income growth to a much lesser extent. In our regression below, the initial level of literacy is found to have a significant influence on reductions in infant mortality between 1983 and 1990-92 (DIMR), although the coefficients of SDPGR and INIMR (initial infant mortality rate) turn out to be insignificant.

$$DIMR = 50.3 - 0.9\ INILLIT + 0.23\ INIMR \qquad R\text{-}bar\ Square = .26$$
$$\qquad\qquad (-2.5) \qquad\qquad (1.4)$$

Note: (The t-statistics are given in parentheses.)

The coefficient of SDPGR is statistically insignificant even after excluding Kerala. The above regression demonstrates the importance of high literacy levels in achieving greater progress in health indicators. Prabhu and Chatterjee (1993: 38) also find in their study that although education outcomes were significantly influenced by per capita revenue expenditure on education, in the case of health outcomes, revenue expenditure on health had poor explanatory power. Some studies such as Murthi et al. (1995) also show that child mortality and fertility outcomes are influenced more by variables relating to women's agency — female literacy and female labour force participation and much less by variables reflecting general development and modernization — per capita expenditure, urbanization etc.

Prabhu and Kamdar (1998) obtained Human Poverty Indices for different Indian states by combining certain deprivation indices such as illiteracy, lack of access to health services and safe water, and under-nourishment among children. They find that public expenditure on social services has significant influence on human poverty, whereas per capita SDP turns out to have no explanatory power.(9) This, however, need not undermine the importance of the income variable since SDP has a positive influence on public expenditure. Nevertheless, there are wide variations across states in per capita expenditure on health and education. Despite the transfer of funds by the central government being based on developmental needs, only those states endowed with greater resources are able to spend more. This could be due to the particular nature of transfers, such as the requirement for states to match central government grants in financing plans.

Public expenditure on health as a percentage of GDP for the East Asian countries is not significantly higher than that for India (Table 24), although their health and education outcomes are far superior. Therefore, a relevant variable for comparison is per capita expenditure on health and not the ratio to GDP. Rapid economic growth leading to higher per capita expenditure seems to be the major determinant of East Asia's better health and education outcomes.

Table 24: Public Expenditure on Health: India and East Asia.

Country	Expenditure on Health as a per cent of GDP for the year:	
	1975	1990
India	2.3	1.3
Indonesia	---	0.7
Korea	2.8	2.7
Malaysia	2.7	1.3
Singapore	3.4	1.1
Thailand	4.2	1.1

Note: a. Figures in brackets indicate year of data.
Sources: *Social Indicators of Development*, World Bank and Statistical *Yearbook 1993*, UNESCO.

The above analysis shows that although growth in income and public expenditure is necessary for improved social outcomes, it is not sufficient. It is not just the quantity but also the quality of public expenditure that determines social outcomes. For example, the quality of health services is acknowledged to be very poor in India. The public healthcare system has a modest coverage and its health centres suffer from inadequate supplies of equipment and shortfalls in key medical personnel. According to most estimates, private health care expenses are very high in India relative to the average income level of the population (Berman, 1996). Furthermore, the private sector operates under very little regulation and not much is known about the quality and effectiveness of these services. Public expenditure primarily supports clinical services and curative care in hospitals with more than 60% of the healthcare budget spent for this purpose. Public health intervention and preventive medicine, which have greater potential in improving health outcomes, have been neglected.

The welfare of the poor depends to a large extent on the consumption of publicly provided services, such as schools, health care, water supply etc. Government expenditure has been steadily increasing over a period of time in several of these sectors. Whether this expenditure will be reflected in favourable social outcomes will depend on the effectiveness with which these services are provided. It is now widely recognized that there is an important link between health and productivity, at least in the case of poor individuals. The question that arises, then, is whether the poor have better access to these services? The link between poverty and access to basic services may depend on the type of service and can vary by region. For example, the urban poor may have better access to some services such as water supply and sanitation compared to the rural non-poor. Studies based on household surveys do not reveal much correlation between poverty and the levels of access to different public services (Table 25).(10)

Table 25: Correlation coefficients between access to public services and poverty and other indicators

	Correlation with			
Access to	Average per capita expenditure	head-count index of poverty	Female literacy	Population density
Electrified dwelling	.20	-.42	.39	-.07
Drinking water	-.15	.08	-.04	.18
PDS rice	-.05	-.08	.64	.45
PDS wheat	-.12	.12	.43	.20
Pediatric care	.06	.24	.51	.43
Pre-natal care	-.05	-.003	.69	.55
Post-natal care	-.07	.07	.52	.43
Family Planning services	-.02	-.07	.59	.22

Source: Srinivasan, 1997

The levels of utilization of health services, such as paediatric, pre- and post- natal care and family planning services, are positively correlated with female literacy. This indicates that the demand for these services rises with improved female literacy, possibly due to the greater awareness that comes with literacy. Also, higher literacy encourages collective action among people for better provision of such services. In general, the utilization of these publicly provided services is found to be low, particularly among the poor (Srinivasan, 1997). Most of the services are provided universally with little or no targeting involved. Thus, the leakage of benefits to the non-poor and the percentage of poor left out are considerable. In most cases the costs of targeting are likely to be high, and under such circumstances the only way to reach more of the poor is through an overall increase in the coverage of these services. Fiscal constraints, however, place limits on expansion towards the universal provision of these services. It is therefore imperative to put greater efforts into resource mobilization.

India's educational achievements are far from impressive. A major reason for India's poor performance in educational attainment is the poor quality of schooling. Expenditure on primary education is thinly spread over a large number of students, resulting in poorly equipped schools lacking in minimum basic facilities and a low standard of education (Minhas, 1991). Several surveys have indicated that rather than economic factors, it is the poor quality of education provided which is principally responsible for non-enrolment among children. The quality of education as measured by the primary school pupil-to-teacher ratio has, in fact, deteriorated over the period 1965-89. India's ratio in 1989 was also much higher than the average of 38 for the comparable group of low-income countries. Shah (1998) observes that the government has been an inefficient provider of education and there is a need to privatize schooling. He compares the performance of the two Indian states, West Bengal and Kerala, and notes that while both of them spend roughly 25% of their respective state budgets on education, the latter's achievements (in terms of literacy rates as well as the proportion of children who enrolled) have been far superior. Kerala ensured good quality education by encouraging competition among schools. The proportion of private schools in Kerala in rural primary schools is the highest in the country at 60%. Competition was generated by providing scholarships and subsidies for transport to the students so that they are not constrained by costs in choosing between schools.

Both demand- and supply-side measures are essential to improve educational performance. Supply-side interventions include the provision of schools with sufficient classrooms and teachers and convenient locations and timetables to suit rural students who are involved in farming activities. Demand-side factors include enforcing compulsory education, removing gender and caste barriers, and special incentives to students from poor backgrounds, such as free school lunches.

Table 26: Public Expenditure on Education: India and East Asia

Country	Expenditure on Education as a per cent of GNP	
	1980	1992
India	2.8	3.8
Indonesia	1.7	2.2
Korea	3.7	4.2
Malaysia	6.0	5.5
Singapore	2.8	3.2
Thailand	3.4	4.0

Sources: World Development *Indicators, 1998 (CD version)*, World Bank.

The relatively lower incidence of poverty in the East Asian countries has also contributed to a faster accumulation of human capital. As the World Bank (1993) argues, the poor in these countries were more capable of investing in their children's education as they were further removed from subsistence levels. This shows that there is a clear role for the government to play in education to take the economy out of this vicious cycle where the low rate of economic growth gives rise to a low demand for education which in turn leads to lower economic growth.

It can be argued that the differing outcomes with respect to human resource development in the case of India in comparison to the East Asian countries can be linked in great part to the different degrees of government intervention in education. East Asia's exemplary performance in terms of accumulation of human capital is mainly due to the great importance given to the provision of basic education in these countries (World Bank, 1993). A large proportion of the education budget was allocated to basic education in these countries. Further, compared to India, public expenditure on education as a proportion of GNP has been significantly higher in East Asian countries (except in the case of Indonesia and Singapore — see Table 26).

One problem with trying to increase public expenditure on education and health is that compared to East Asian countries, India's deficits form a large percentage of GDP. There is thus great pressure for expenditure reduction to keep the budget deficit at reasonable levels. Two major policy recommendations are popular in this context. One is that of reducing expenditure by directly targeting subsidies and income transfers to the poor. The other is the introduction of user fees, wherever possible, for partial or full recovery of costs in the provision of public services. However, apart from political constraints, a major problem with these suggestions is the possibly high costs of implementation. Identification of beneficiaries under targeted programs cannot be assumed to be cost free. With poor administration, cost recovery for services can be difficult, as is seen in the case of the performance of electricity boards in rural areas. It is also not morally appealing to charge users for basic services such as education, health and safe water since benefits from these services are not limited to individuals alone but accrue to the society at large. There is, however, a case for the switching of expenditures between sectors. As has been pointed out in a recent discussion paper of the Government of India (1993), government expenditure can be oriented more towards primary education and basic health. But in the long run there is no alternative to generating more resources by the government. Since the current levels of expenditure on health and education are already so low, expenditure switching alone will not achieve much.(11) In any case, raising expenditure alone will not serve the purpose unless policies are geared towards clearly stated objectives. For example, the quality of schooling has to be improved. Adequate incentives, such as free school lunch schemes should be provided to make it attractive for the children from poor families to attend schools. Absenteeism among schoolteachers needs to be reduced and their performance in schools improved through better administration and improved institutional structures. Similarly, the quality and performance of Primary Healthcare Centres needs improvement. There has been an over emphasis on family planning services leading to a neglect of other healthcare services, including curative care.

Another important feature of public policy in East Asia's human resource development strategy is the role of the government in the diffusion of technical skills amongst the labour force. For example, the Taiwanese government has systematically 'adopted policies for diversifying secondary education to provide technical and vocational education in response to the manpower needs of the late stage of industrialization' (Liu, 1992: 371). Thus, the dispersal of students at senior high school level along academic versus vocational-technical lines was in the ratio 60

: 40 in 1967 but had reversed to 30 : 70 in 1989. Similar stories emerge in the cases of Indonesia and Korea, with the governments in both these countries consciously attempting to alter the academic to vocational ratio in secondary schools towards more vocational qualifications. This has been achieved by building more vocational and technical schools and by introducing vocational studies for students in academic curricula as part of their high-school program (McGinn et al., 1980; Soedijarto et al., 1980). In India, lack of planning in education becomes apparent if one looks at the incidence of unemployment among people with various educational statuses (Dev et al., 1991: 151). The incidence of unemployment among those educated up to university graduation and above is 5 times greater than among those who have completed middle school and 10 times greater than among illiterates. Except for courses in computer software, there are hardly any vocational studies of significance in India.

One of the most important failures of the Indian government has been in the area of population control. Government sponsored family planning programs were introduced in India as long ago as the 1950s. However, the birth rate has merely declined from around 40 per thousand people in 1951 to around 30 per thousand in 1991. While it is expected that fertility rates will go down automatically with development, the pace of economic growth has been very slow in India. This prompted direct government action such as forced sterilization campaigns during the emergency period of 1976-77. The adverse political outcome of this measure drew people's attention to the more fundamental relations between health, education and fertility rates. Better health facilities lead to a decline in infant mortality rates, which reduces the need to produce more children. Female education can prevent teenage pregnancies and reduce the frequency of pregnancies within the childbearing period. Based on Kerala's achievements, Kabir and Krishnan (1996) note that apart from the creation of a healthcare infrastructure it is important to create demand for healthcare by overcoming cultural and social barriers. They feel that people's attitudes and behaviour can be changed through 'social intermediation' measures such as the integration of women in the healthcare system and the promotion of health education in schools. Recruitment and training of women in health professions helps in extending healthcare to women for whom access levels are low due to cultural barriers. Education can not only bring changes in cultural and social values but also encourage informed collective action for securing better health facilities.

CONCLUDING REMARKS

In this chapter, we have analysed India's performance in social development, that is, in poverty alleviation and in the provision of education and health facilities to its people. We analysed this performance using various indicators of social development, such as poverty rates, literacy and infant mortality rates, access to safe drinking water and sanitation facilities. Evidence from the previous three decades suggests that India's progress on these fronts has been rather slow, especially when compared to that of East Asia.

We then tried to understand the causes of this slow progress by examining the various factors that affect poverty and social development, such as GDP growth and public spending on social development, growth rates of employment, real wages and the relative price of food. Economic growth appears to be the main source of poverty reduction in India. It reduced poverty by increasing income per capita and by creating more employment in an environment where the income distribution has remained largely unchanged. In fact, some empirical studies (see, for example, Ravallion and Datt, 1996a) suggest that as much as 80% of the historically observed poverty decline can be attributed to economic growth. Higher growth rates of employment, higher agricultural yields and higher real agricultural wages also help reduce poverty. Given that a large proportion of the expenditure of the poor is on food, lower relative food prices also have a significant role in reducing poverty. Public development expenditure in general and expenditure on anti-poverty programs in particular, also help reduce poverty. However, unfortunately, their scale is too small in India to make much of a dent in poverty.

The slow progress in other indicators of social development, namely those relating to education and health, may also largely be related to the slow growth of GDP as this lowered the government's ability to incur expenditure in these areas. India's public expenditure on health as a proportion of the GDP is comparable to most East Asian countries, but the per capita expenditure is much lower. In the case of education, even public expenditure as a proportion of GDP is lower. This is unfortunate as better levels of education, especially of women, also help improve the health-related indicators by increasing awareness. The poor institutional structure and the prevalence of corruption, due to which even the limited funds available for social development are not utilized effectively to provide health and education services to the poor, further compound the problem.

We did not address in this paper the question of why the GDP growth rate in India has been so low, although the continued reliance on an Import Substitution strategy right up to 1990 is probably one of main reasons. Following the economic and trade reforms of 1991 (which largely abandoned the import substitution regime), the GDP growth rate has increased to the 6–7% range for the first time since independence. However, there are no signs yet of this translating into greater progress in poverty alleviation or social development. One of the reasons for this is that tax revenues have not been buoyant enough and there have been cuts in public expenditure in a bid to reduce budget deficits. The potential for poverty alleviation and social development will be greatly increased if the growth rate can be sustained at a higher level. However, in order to realize this potential, the government has to strive hard to improve tax collection through improved administration and enforcement of tax policies so that more funds can be allocated for health, education and anti-poverty programs and policies. Both the quantity and quality aspects of public expenditure are important. The institutions responsible for social development programs should be made more efficient in order to utilize the funds more effectively.

ENDNOTES

1. These figures are obtained using the official poverty line ofRs 49.09 per capita per month at 1973-74 prices for the rural population andRs 56.64 for the urban population. The estimates are based on the methodology recommended by the Expert Group on Estimation of Proportion and Number of Poor.
2. Poverty comparisons across different groups based on household per capita consumption expenditure or income can sometimes be problematic. For example, partof the household consumption is shared (e.g. lighting, heating etc.) and there can be economies of scale in the consumption of such goods. To that extent by considering per capita expenditure one could overestimate poverty (see, e.g., Lanjouw and Ravallion, 1994; Drèze and Srinivasan,1997).
3. The initial level of the female labour force participation rate is found to have a significant influence on the reduction of poverty over time (Drèze and Srinivasan, 1996).
4. See Agrawal (1997) for a more detailed discussion.
5. See Jha and Srinivasan (1998) for details regarding the cost effectiveness of administering the public distribution system and the various proposals for reforming it.
6. This is due to the fact that until recently PDS was not perceived as part of the government's anti-poverty strategy. It was originally intended to be a price support mechanism for farmers in regions with surplus grain production and a consumer protection mechanism through the transfer of grain from surplus to deficit regions. The recently introduced 'Targeted PDS', which will provide basic foodstuffs to the poor at considerably subsidized rates, is a welcome move toward turning the PDS into a more effective anti-poverty instrument.
7. This, however, does not get reflected in the rural poverty measures of these states.
8. Except for the variable SDPGR, which is taken from Dreze and Sen (1995: Table A.3), all other variables in these regressions are obtained from Tables 10 and 15 of this chapter. The number of observations used in the regression is therefore 15.
9. Dutta et al. (1997), in their time series regressions for each of the Indian states, find in more than half of the cases that public expenditure has a significant influence on achievements in education and health.
10. See, for example, Srinivasan (1997) for a study based on National Sample Survey data for rural India.
11. See Sen (1993) for a detailed discussion on recent trends in human development related government expenditure.

REFERENCES

Agrawal, Pradeep (1997). Do India's Labor policies Harm Indian Workers?A Comparison with East Asia, Indian Journal of Labour Economics, Vol. 40, No. 4, pp. 631-653.

Agrawal, Pradeep, S. Gokarn, V. Mishra, K.S. Parikh and K. Sen, (1995). Economic Restructuring in East Asia and India: Perspectives on Policy Reforms. Basingstoke: Macmillan.

Agrawal, Pradeep, S. Gokarn, V. Mishra, K.S. Parikh and K. Sen, (2000). Policy Regimes and Industrial Competitiveness: A Comparative Study of East Asia and India. Basingstoke: Macmillan.

Ahluwalia, D. (1993). Public Distribution of Food in India: Coverage, Targeting andLeakages, Food Policy.

Berman, Peter (1996). Health Care Expenditure in India, Das Gupta, Chen and Krishnan (Eds.) Health, Poverty and Development in India. Delhi: Oxford University Press.

CMIE (1996). India's Social Sectors, Center for Monitoring Indian Economy, February.

Datt, Gaurav and Martin Ravallion (1996). Why have some Indian States done better than others a treducing rural poverty? World Bank Policy Research Working paper 1594, Washington D.C.

Dev, S. Mahendra (1997). Growth, Employment, Poverty and Human Development: An evaluation of Change in India since Independence with Emphasis on Rural Areas, Review of Development and Change, Vol.2, No. 2

Dev, S. Mahendra , K.S. Parikh and M.H. Suryanarayana (1991). Rural Poverty in India, Incidence, Issues and Policies, Indira Gandhi Institute of Development Research, Discussion Paper No. 55.

Drèze, Jean (1990). Poverty in India and the IRDP Delusion, Economic and Political Weekly, Review of Agriculture, vol. 25, no.39.

Drèze, Jean and P.V. Srinivasan (1997). Widowhood and Poverty in Rural India: Some Inferences from Household Survey Data, Journal of Development Economics, vol. 54.
Drèze, Jean and P.V. Srinivasan (1996). Poverty in India: Regional Estimates, 1987-88, DEP No. 70, STICERD, London School of Economics.
Drèze, Jean and Sen, Amartya (1995). India: Economic Development and Social Opportunity. Oxford: Clarendon Press.
Dubey, Amaresh and Shubhashis Gangopadhyay (1998). Counting the poor: Where are the poor in India? Sarvekshana Analytical Report No. 1, Department of Statistics, Government of India
Dutta, Bhaskar, Manoj Panda and Willima Wadhwa (1997). Human Development in India, in S. Subramanian (ed.) Measurement of Inequality and Poverty. Oxford: Oxford University Press.
Fan, Shenggen and Peter Hazell (1996). Should the Indian Government Invest More or Less Favored Areas? mimeo, Environment and Production Technology Division, International Food Policy Research Institute, mimeo.
Government of India (1996). Level and Pattern of Consumer Expenditure, NSS 50th Round Report no. 402, National Sample Survey Organization, Department of Statistics, New Delhi.
Government of India (1995). A Technical Note on theEighth Plan of India, Planning Commission, New Delhi
Government of India (1993). Economic Reforms: Two years After and the Task Ahead, Ministry of Finance, New Delhi
Hashim, S. R. (1998). Economic Growth and Income Distribution: The Indian Experience of Development, Economic and Political Weekly, March 21.
Jain and Tendulkar (1990). Role of Growth and Distribution in the Observed Change in Poverty, Indian Economic Review, pp 165-204.
Jha, Shikha (1992). Consumer Subsidies in India: Is Targeting Effective?Development and Change, vol. 23(4).
Jha, Shikha and P.V. Srinivasan (1998). On Reforming the Public Distribution System in India, paper presented at the Symposium on Reforming India's Social Sectors: Strategies and Prospects, April, Bombay
Kabir, M. and T.N. Krishnan (1996). Social Intermediation and Health Change: Lessons fromKerala, Das Gupta, Chen and Krishnan (Eds.) Health, Poverty and Development in India. Delhi: Oxford University Press.
Lall, S (1987). Learning to Industrialize: The Acquisitions of Technological Capability by India. London: Macmillan.
Lall, S (1990). Building Industrial Competitiveness in Developing Countries, Paris: OECD
Lanjouw, P. and Martin Ravallion (1995). Poverty and Household Size, Economic Journal, vol. 105.
Liu, P.K.C. (1992). Science, Technology and Human Capital Formation, in G.Ranis (ed.), Taiwan: From Developing to Mature Economy.
McGinn, N. et. al. (1980). Education and Development in Korea. Cambridge: Harvard University Press.
Minhas, B.S. (1991). Educational Deprivation and its Role as a Spoiler of Access to Better Life in India, Technical Report No. 9104. New Delhi: Indian Statistical Institute.
Murthi, Mamta, Guio, Anne-Catherine and Jean Dreze (1995). Mortality, Fertility and Gender Bias in India, Discussion Paper no. 61, Development Economics ResearchProgramme, STICERD, London School of Economics.
Nagraj, R., A. Varoudakis and M.A. Veganzones (1997). Long Run Growth Trends and Convergence Across Indian States, OECD Development Centre, Technical Paper.
Nehru, Swanson and Dubey (1993). A New Database on Human Capital Stock. Sources, Methodology and Results, Policy Research Working Papers, The World Bank: Washington, D.C.
Parikh, Kirit (1994). Who Gets How Much from PDS: How Effectively Does it Reach the Poor? Sarvekshana, vol. 17(3).
Prabhu, K. Seeta and Somnath Chatterjee (1993). Social Sector Expenditure and Human Development: A Study of Indian States, DRG Study No. 6. Bombay: Reserve Bank of India.
Prabhu, K. Seeta and Sangita Kamdar (1998). Human Poverty and Income Poverty: Linkages and Implications, paper presented at the Symposium on Reforming India's Social Sectors: Strategies and Prospects, April, Bombay
Ravallion, Martin and Gaurav Datt (1996a). India's Checkered History in the Fight against Poverty: Are there Lessons for the Future? Economic and Political Weekly, vol. 31 Special Number, September.

Ravallion, Martin and Gaurav Datt (1996b).How important to India's poor is thesectoral composition of Growth? World Bank Economic Review, vol.10, no. 1
Sen, Abhijit, (1996). Economic Reforms, Employment and Poverty: Trends and Options, Economic and Political Weekly, Special Number, September.
Sen, Tapas Kumar (1993). Public Expenditure on Human Development in India: Trends and Issues,K.S. Parikh and R. Sudarshan, eds, Human Development and Structural Adjustment. India: Macmillan.
Shah, Parth, J. (1998). New Education Policy: Choice and Competition, Shah andDebroy (Eds.) Agenda for Change: Action Plan for the Economy, Rajiv Gandhi Institute for Contemporary Studies.
Soedijarto et. al. (1980). Indonesia, in T.N. Postletwaite and R.M. Thomas (eds.), Schooling in the ASEAN Region, Oxford, Pergamon Press.
Srinivasan, P.V. (1997). Regional Poverty and Access to Public Services in Rural India, IRIS-India Working Paper No. 30.
Tendulkar, Suresh D and LR Jain (1995). Economic Reforms and Poverty, Economic and Political Weekly, June 10.
Visaria, P. (1996) Structure of Indian workforce: 1961-1994, Indian Journal ofLabour Economics, Vol. 39, No. 4.
World Bank (1997), India: Achievement and Challenges in Reducing Poverty, Washington, D.C.
World Bank (1996). India: Primary Education Achievement and Challenges, Washington D.C.
World Bank (1993). The East Asian Miracle: Economic Growth and Public Policy, Washington D.C.

GERARD GREENFIELD

CHAPTER EIGHT

THE WORLD BANK'S "EFFECTIVE STATE" IN EAST ASIA

In these turbulent times, the World Bank itself appears to be in transition. For decades the significant role of the state in East Asian economic development posed a serious challenge to the Bank's free market agenda, prompting a struggle over how to explain East Asian economic 'miracles'. The outcome was the Bank's best-seller, *The East Asian Miracle,* published in 1993. It was presented as a new discovery, and though it continued to be a contentious issue within the Bank, it expressed a reluctant recognition that the state played a role in fostering economic growth. While many saw this as a catalyst for change in the World Bank's neoliberal agenda, the changes which followed were very gradual, contrasting sharply with the dramatic changes in thinking and policy that the Bank requires of its debtors under "shock therapy" and structural adjustment. Continuing to work within a neoliberal paradigm, the Bank misinterpreted the development experience in East Asia in fundamental ways. However, this is not simply a matter of getting the facts wrong about the East Asian 'miracles'. The World Bank's particular (mis)interpretation of how countries like South Korea, Taiwan, Singapore and Hong Kong developed largely shapes its lending policies, projects and policy advice in countries such as China, Cambodia, India, Vietnam and the Philippines. For example, as discussed below, the World Bank misinterprets (and misrepresents) the impact of structural adjustment in Hong Kong on working people as a smooth process in which people easily moved from factory jobs to service sector jobs. If we compare this to the Bank's policy advice on labour flexibility in China, we can see that the same logic which underlies its explanation of the Hong Kong experience now shapes the Bank's proposals for labour market deregulation and restructuring in China.

Undaunted by charges of misinterpreting the East Asian experience, the World Bank's World Development Report (1997a), *The State in a Changing World,* constructs a framework for an "effective state" based on what it perceives as the practical lessons of the East Asian miracles. In outlining the tasks of an effective state, the Bank recognizes that, "In nearly all societies the needs and preferences of the wealthy and powerful are well reflected in official policy goals and priorities." References to the involvement of "civic organisations" and "citizen involvement" and the "expressions of voice and participation" throughout the report give the

K.-L. Tang (ed.), Social Development in Asia, 167–186.

impression that the Bank is concerned with rectifying this imbalance. In addition, poverty reduction, environmental protection and the importance attributed to the "social fundamentals" such as health and education are discussed at length. Yet despite these concerns, the Bank asserts that the policy process must be relatively autonomous of civil society, and should only allow direct channels to the private business sector. This is exemplified by the state in East Asia where:

> [p]owerful elite central agencies have been delegated the authority to develop policies that will achieve the leaders' long-term objectives. Although relatively autonomous, these agencies' deliberations have always been embedded in processes – such as public-private councils – that provide input and oversight from private firms (p.83)

Rather than rectifying the problem of the wealthy and the powerful having a greater influence on the policy process, the Bank implies that this should be institutionalised. The primacy of the interests of private firms over and above the interests of other sectors in civil society and the importance of secure exclusive access to the policy process for private firms is a recurring theme throughout the report. There is an inherent contradiction in the Bank's assertion that "the first step toward increasing the state's effectiveness must be to *reduce its reach,"* since this means minimising the regulation of private firms on the one hand, and extending the reach of the state to support the interests of private firms on the other.

What is clear from the Bank's definition of an "effective state" is that it has ignored both the social context and the social consequences of the role of the state in East Asia. In one sense this is inevitable given that *The East Asian Miracle* only dealt with the role of the state as a "a technical policy question". Nonetheless, this has important social consequences, not least because of implicit praise for authoritarian regimes in East Asia. According to the Report, the failure of authoritarian regimes in Africa is *not* because of the absence of democracy and the repression of popular elements of civil society, but because they were *ineffective* authoritarian regimes.

The stifling of independent labour and social movements and the constraints on freedom of association and freedom of speech, restrictions or the elimination of opposition political parties, and the fusion of the interests of the state and large conglomerates, all form part of an effective authoritarian regime. In Taiwan and South Korea severe restrictions on workers' organising, repression of independent trade union movements and extensive controls over trade unions, highlight the entire period of "miraculous growth" (Ho, 1990). In Hong Kong, the colonial regime restricted labour movement activities and denied workers their fundamental rights. In Singapore, civil rights organisations continue to be suppressed, while the trade union functions merely as an extension of the government. However, while the Bank views this authoritarianism as necessary, if not crucial, for economic growth, it was precisely because workers, independent trade unions, NGOs and social movements struggled *against* authoritarian regimes that there has been a redistribution of resources towards health, education and other "social fundamentals" (Hart-Landsberg, 1993).

While ignoring the reality of constraints placed on political and social activities, the Bank attempts to vindicate itself by turning to an explanation common among the political elite in East Asian countries themselves – that they were effective in *persuading* the people to make these sacrifices and to patiently await the long-term benefits of growth. The importance of persuasion for an effective state is a recurring theme in *The State in a Changing World.*

Given that persuasion is an important theme, there is an underlying premise that, when necessary, persuasion may give way to coercion. This is particularly apparent in the Bank's explanations of poverty reduction. In *The State in a Changing World,* the Bank openly declares that attention to poverty reduction reduces social unrest:

> In many regions poverty and inequality are often biased against ethnic minorities or women, or disfavoured geographic areas. Marginalized from public discussion and excluded from the broader economy and society, such groups are fertile ground for violence and instability, as many parts of the world are increasingly learning. (p.4)

Ultimately the Bank appears to be more receptive to what it calls the "lawlessness syndrome", than with poverty reduction and inequality *per se.*

STATE AND POVERTY REDUCTION

Before examining the implications of the Bank's "effective state" for equity and poverty reduction, it is imperative to consider another recent report directly related to East Asia. The report entitled, *Everyone's Miracle? Revisiting Poverty and Inequality in East Asia* (Ahuja et al., 1997), appears to challenge the notion that everyone inevitably benefited from miraculous economic growth in East Asia and argues that while there have been successes in reducing poverty, there has also been a growth in inequality. For the first time, the Bank acknowledges that "growth with equity" – one of the key lessons of the East Asian 'miracles" – is problematic. At the outset the report admits, "it is no longer clear that we were ever entirely justified in claiming that East Asia was so exceptional in its low inequality level" (p.25). Despite this admission, *Everyone's Miracle?* does not attempt to rethink the World Bank's interpretation of economic growth and development in East Asia. The reason for this may be attributed to the fact that there is no understanding *at all* of the experience of inequality, and why this is a problem. In asking "why inequality may be regarded as 'bad'", the report concludes that: " . . [I]ndividuals in a society *may* place intrinsic value in equality. People *might* dislike extreme differences in outcomes, and derive utility from a sense of social cohesion that comes from relative income equality."

Ironically, *The State in a Changing World* itself recognizes the fact that in most societies the wealthy have greater influence over government policy. This could be a useful starting point in making sense of why inequality matters. Regardless of this, the authors of *Everyone's Miracle?* conclude that the real problem is that "inequality may hamper future growth". Unfortunately, rather than exploring the issue of 'growth with equity', and the problem of economic and social exclusion, the report simply argues that growth is inhibited because "greater inequality increases support of the median voter for inefficient redistributive policies, and hence leads to greater efficiency losses and lower growth." (pp.31-32)

In choosing Thailand for its case study, *Everyone's Miracle?* provides a setting in which basic Bank arguments are challenged by actual events. The mass mobilisation of 20,000 villagers and workers in the Forum of Poor in early 1997 was based on their anger over wealth and power discrepancies. The people of the Forum asserted their right to equality both in terms of the much celebrated (though intangible) benefits of economic growth, and also in terms of political equality in determining government policy. The people gathered in the Forum of the Poor were not simply "pressing for immediate short-term action to relieve their plight; they [had] their sights set on addressing structural power imbalances" (Suksamran, 1997). Towards this end:

> [t]he key to their aspiration is actual political reform, since this will open the way for them to have a say on the root causes of their problems. They are making an all-out effort to push for political reform through the writing of a new constitution that will guarantee their rights and participation.

As such, this grassroots social movement challenges the logic of the elite-centred "effective state" and managed "inequality", which the Bank presents as a natural reflection of civil society's interests.

The Bank narrowly defines those needing support from poverty reduction programs and policies as those in *extreme* poverty, and in doing so fails to recognise poverty associated with urban unemployment and with employment that fails to provide a living wage. There are two consequences of this. The first is that by failing to recognise the full extent of urban poverty and unemployment, poverty alleviation programs are being promoted which encourage migration from rural areas to the cities. While this may mean that those in extreme poverty are *less poor*, it adds to a growing unemployment crisis and wage competition in urban areas which is exacerbating the problem of job and income insecurity and is further undermining the capacity of workers to maintain a living wage. The second is that such poverty reduction programs are based on two flawed assumptions: that labour mobility guarantees eventual employment and that unemployment in urban areas is cyclical – or temporary.

A number of contradictions, therefore, become highlighted in the World Bank's approach to poverty reduction. On the one hand is the Bank's promotion of rural-urban migration as a solution to rural poverty, and on the other, *Everyone's Miracle?* indicates that there is trade-off "between the potential benefits of relaxing restrictions on labour mobility, and the costs associated with the possibility of large inflows of poor migrants into China's already overcrowded cities" (p.29). The World Bank's recent report, *Income Inequality in China,* explicitly outlines labour mobility, based on facilitating migration from rural areas to the cities, as the most effective policy for poverty reduction. By promoting labour mobility, "to ensure the poorest residents, and residents of areas where migration has been slower to take hold, have more opportunities to migrate", other poverty reduction programs only need to focus on "the *remaining* poor"(World Bank, 1997b). This has already been translated into practice. Under the World Bank-funded Southwest Poverty Reduction Project, US$486.4 million has been allocated to a labour mobility scheme through which 878,000 people in Guanxi will migrate to urban-industrial areas to find work (South

China Morning Post, 28 April, 1997). There is an implicit assumption that these migrants will be absorbed into a growing industrial workforce under foreign investment schemes, especially in the Export Processing Zones or "Special Economic Zones". Yet the Bank can only present this strategy as logical if the fact that there are already close to 100 million migrant workers searching for work in the 'open cities' and Special Economic Zones is ignored (Han, 1997, p. 6).

Another shortcoming of *Everyone's Miracle?* is the Bank's off-handed, ostensibly independent treatment of the increasing number of East Asia's absolute poor, concentrated in the Philippines, Vietnam, the Lao People's Democratic Republic, Mongolia and Papua New Guinea (p.11). Yet even a brief glance at the World Bank's own Country Assistance Strategy (CAS) reports reveals that these are precisely the countries which have adhered closely to the World Bank's policies and the conditionality of its loans. So while the report points out that since 1993 Vietnam has surpassed Indonesia in becoming the home of the second largest number of absolute poor in the region, there is no mention of the fact that 1993 was also the year in which World Bank projects and policies became fully integrated into the economic reform agenda of the Vietnamese government. This led to the deregulation of the labour market, privatisation of state enterprises and large-scale dismissals from the state sector, widespread decollectivisation of agriculture, and the introduction of fees and charges for public services (Kolko,1997). In the context of rising unemployment, these changes contributed to increases in absolute and relative poverty in both urban and rural areas. In Mongolia, World Bank policies were introduced as a kind of "shock therapy", similar to that experienced in Eastern Europe. The privatisation of state enterprises and the decollectivisation of agriculture, combined with massive cuts to state-provided welfare and public services and dismissals from the state and collective sectors, intensified rural and urban poverty.

The Bank's role in exacerbating poverty and inequality can also be found in the examples of 'success' as cited in *The State in a Changing World.* The Indonesian government's strategy for the eradication of absolute poverty within the next ten years is singled out as a successful case study. The Transmigration Program – involving the relocation of 3.6 million people from Java to the outer islands – is one of four programs to which the Bank refers in the context of Indonesia's 'growth with equity' formula (p.60). The Transmigration Program involves the resettlement of urban poor to less densely populated outer islands where they are given land. In terms of poverty reduction, the program is far from a success. Thousands of transmigrants have been forced to return to the original towns and cities where they lived because the land that they were given was infertile. On their return, they often found themselves facing even greater poverty than before they left (Monbiot, 1989). However, it appears that the primary purpose of the Transmigration Program is not economic, but political. Transmigration is designed to "Indonesianise" regions such as East Timor, Irian Jaya and Kalimantan where local populations are considered to be hostile to the ruling Javanese elite. Rather than combining growth with equity, the Transmigration Program privileges one ethic group above others, creating greater inequity, that aims "to replace the dissenting indigenous peoples of the outer islands with loyal citizens from Java and Bali" (p.29). In the case of East Timor, where there is ongoing suppression of political and social rights, combined with systematic human rights abuses by the Indonesian military, fertile land was taken away from East Timorese villagers and given to the Balinese and Javanese "transmigrants" (Gietzeit, 1989; Aditjondro, 1994). The Transmigration Program, which displaced and impoverished tens of thousands of East Timorese, was directly sponsored by the World Bank (World Bank, 1985).

The displacement and impoverishment of non-ruling ethnic groups has not detracted from the Bank's positive assessment of comparable poverty reduction programs. Similarly, the Bank applauds Malaysia's success in poverty reduction, as well as Prime Minister Mahathir's management of a multiethnic society (p.113). In actuality, however, the situation is a little different. As Tan Pek Leng (1997) observes:

> Non-Malay Bumiputeras, such as the Orang Asli and those in Sabah and Sarawak, complain, that they have been neglected by existing poverty eradication priorities. The primarily non-Malay rural poor on plantations and new villages feel even more marginalised. Similarly, most of the urban poor believe that poverty eradication measures are not directed at them. (p.3)

In fact, it is not just non-Malay ethic groups that are marginalised. Even poor Malays have not been the main beneficiaries of poverty reduction programs:

> In fact, much of what goes on in the name of poverty eradication, even among rural Malays, does not necessarily have a lot to do with reducing poverty. Undoubtedly, provision of rural infrastructure and social services, as well as other efforts to increase rural productivity have gone a long way towards improving rural welfare generally. However, such efforts tend to benefit more the relatively better-off in rural areas – big landowners and the better educated – rather than the poorer rural folks who are generally less well educated and possess fewer economic resources, such as land. Hence, for example, landless rural labourers have benefited little from poverty eradication measures except perhaps indirectly. (p. 4)

It could be argued that Mahathir has in fact adhered quite closely to what the Bank presents as an "effective state" by working in partnership with Malay private entrepreneurs in supporting their interests and aspirations. His 'success' in managing a multiethnic society is also due to a measure of authoritarian practices that the Bank lauds as an important lesson to be learned from East Asia. It is, however, an "effective state" that brooks no dissent. When a Malaysian NGO, Tenaganita (Women's Force), attempted to bring attention to the violation of the rights of Bangladeshi migrant workers in Malaysia, the director of the NGO was arrested and their activities were suppressed.

PERSUASION WITHOUT PARTICIPATION

Resorting to repression and political coercion raises serious questions about the extent to which the World Bank's "effective state" may be considered a democratic state. In *The State in a Changing World*, a section is devoted to "Giving People a Voice". Furthermore, there is also discussion of "informed public debate" and the "participation" of citizens and their organisations in policy-making. However, on closer reading, the emphasis is less on participation than on persuasion, the main objective being to increase "popular trust and confidence in the state" (p.10). By drawing lessons from the East Asian miracles, the Bank concludes that "experience from East Asia suggests that where there is wide-spread trust in public institutions, effective ground-level deliberation, and respect for the rule of law, the conditions for responsive state intervention can be met" (p.116). It is here that the Bank makes a subtle distinction between, on the one hand, the issue of people's trust of the state and on the other, the responsiveness of the state to people's demands. Accordingly, "citizens vexed by state weaknesses have come to insist, often through grassroots and other non-governmental organisations, on transparency in the conduct of government and on other changes to strengthen the ability of the state to meet its *assigned* objectives" (emphasis added, p. 14). Few would disagree with the need for greater transparency and accountability in government. However, the question of *who assigns the state its objectives* remains unclear. As such, "transparency" may simply mean that ordinary citizens can observe what technocrats are doing, without having any means by which to influence the policy process.

One of the weaknesses identified by the Bank in state effectiveness, is corruption. Towards this end, the report again draws on what it deems as positive in the East Asian experience. Fundamentally, the Bank argues that corruption will be resolved through better training and an increased sense of moral obligation among an elite core of technocrats, rather than through the establishment of democratic mechanisms of checks and balances. However, as Dani Rodrik (1994) has argued, while *The East Asia Miracle* claims that the efficient bureaucracies of the East Asian NICs were relatively free of corruption, the reality is that Japan, Taiwan, and South Korea (and even Hong Kong until 1974) have all been plagued by widespread corruption, not least of all in the handing out of government contracts to private firms. The new tigers of Southeast Asia – Thailand, Malaysia and Vietnam – have also demonstrated high levels of corruption in government, particularly in relation to the privatisation of state and public enterprises. Given that the World Bank's "effective state" is based on the mistaken notion in the efficient, corruption-free bureaucracies of the authoritarian regimes in East Asia, the extent to which reliance on this model should be accepted for an effective state, is highly questionable.

The Bank further ignores an obvious alternative, that of genuine democratic processes and popular participation and monitoring, as means by which corruption can be overcome. Conversely, the Bank has a tendency to see parliamentary democracy as an obstacle to an effective state. In *The State in a Changing World,* the Bank laments the fact that important reforms, like increasing value-added taxes (VAT), might require "a vote [in] parliament, implying delays and political compromise" (p.5). Here the link is made with the Bank's praise of "elite central agencies" in East Asia (p.83). The underlying assumption is that there should *not* be open discussion and voting by elected members of parliament on economic policies such as consumption taxes. This leaves the unsettling question of whether the avoidance of delays and political compromise may extend to other laws, when speed and efficiency appear as the overriding objectives. What happened in South Korea on December 26, 1996, is a case in point. The illegal action of the ruling party, where six anti-worker labour laws and the National Security Planning Agency Act were passed at six o'clock in the morning without the presence of opposition party members of parliament, avoided untidy delays and compromises. This supposedly democratic parliamentary procedure took only seven minutes. (Asian Labour Update, 23 November, 1996).

Once decisions have been made in this manner, all that is needed is for someone to persuade the majority that such actions have been implemented in their best interests. Ultimately "an effective state" requires that: "Effective leaders give their people a sense of owning the reforms – a *sense* that reform is not something imposed from without" (p.14). This in turn requires, "the presence of someone who can *convince* the public that the leap is worth making is a potent reform weapon indeed" (emphasis added, p.156). In terms of political and social practice, this reflects what Alexander Woodside has called the "mobilisational myth" of the Asia-Pacific, which "mobilises the poor of the region for economic production without representing or encouraging their political and social claims" (Woodside, 1993, p.24). In other words: persuasion without participation.

This brings us back to criticism of the World Bank's own decisions and actions regarding development projects. In August 1995, an internal report of the World Bank concluded that, "Bank performance on resettlement was not satisfactory" leading to a "resettlement disaster" in the Kedung Ombo dam project in Indonesia. Built in 1989 with a World Bank loan, there were strong protests by hundreds of families that refused to accept forced resettlement caused by the flooding of their homes. But when the dam was built, the homes and farms of 30,000 villagers were flooded. Four years later, a study showed that 72 per cent of those resettled were earning less than those who had refused to be resettled, and more than two thirds of families resettled were worse off then before the resettlement. In its internal criticism of this disaster, it was pointed out that the Bank focused too much on the physical aspects of the dam and ignored the concerns of local citizens' groups. The Kedung Ombo resettlement disaster illustrates how, in spite of convincing farmers to be resettled elsewhere, this decision was, in hindsight, disastrously wrong. Illustrations like this raise serious questions about the credibility of decision-makers, the decision making process and the decision itself before people are persuaded to believe in them.

Of course, this is not an isolated incident. Among the 20,000 demonstrators who joined the Forum of the Poor in Thailand were villagers protesting against forced eviction and resettlement as a result of World Bank-funded dams, such as the Rubro-Thasae, Sirindhorn and Pak Moon dams. Questions remain, however, about other resettlement programs under new World Bank-funded projects, such as the resettlement of 180,000 villagers from the Yellow River under the US$430 million Xiaolangi dam project in China, and the forced resettlement of 5,000 villagers under the Nam Thuen 2 dam project in Laos. In the latter case, the World Bank has gone to great lengths in reassuring private investors and commercial loans. There remain no guarantees for the people most directly affected by the dam.

As mass protest movements like the Forum of the Poor in Thailand have shown, resistance to resettlement is not simply based on demands for material compensation or higher compensation, but express opposition to resettlement itself which will break up their communities, affecting their culture and their livelihood. This does not imply that all villagers would rather stay than be resettled. The main point remains, that there are a variety of responses according to specific cases, and collective decisions must be made on the basis of a community's own interests, over the imperatives of cost efficiency and profit, and the effective implementation of pre-assigned policy objectives. If popular participation is taken seriously and put into practice then nothing can be pre-assigned. Admittedly, real participation goes beyond convincing or persuading, especially through coercion, that the interests served are for the people and that *there are no alternatives*. As one Laotian villager facing forced resettlement as a result of the Nam Thuen 2 dam lamented, *"If we had a choice* we would stay and protect the forest. We feel very sad to lose the forest. But what can we do?"

PRIVATIZATION AND LABOUR FLEXIBILITY

The manner in which issues of privatisation are presented by the Bank, make it easy to assume that there are no other means of economic development. The Indian government's response to World Bank demands that privatisation programs need to be accelerated if India were to become another "Asian tiger", resulted in the announcement that the state-owned textile firm, Gujarat Textile Corporation, would be privatised (South China Morning Post, 11 February, 1997). Undertaken in February 1997, the privatisation resulted in the dismissal of 14,000 workers who were told that there was no other alternative. A simple illustration such as this indicates vividly that the World Bank's primary concern is not a careful consideration of the social costs of privatisation, but how to overcome any resistance to it. The mechanisms by which privatisation programs are being imposed do not allow for alternative forms of state enterprise reform that might even include giving workers greater control over decision-making within the enterprise.

Vietnam provides another example. In 1993, amid massive changes in the state sector which saw the dismissal of up to 80 per cent of the workforce in some state enterprises, there were attempts to reorganise production through increased workers' participation and management of state enterprises. The equitisation of the Refrigeration Engineering Enterprise (REE) in 1993 was based on the workers acquiring ownership of the firm, collectively purchasing over 50 per cent of the shares, while gaining control of another 30 per cent of shares held by the state. But far from considering this as a another possible route towards enterprise reform, the Privatisation Bureau, working in conjunction with the World Bank and United Nations Development Programme (UNDP), warned against the REE example, saying that workers must at a maximum share ownership of no more than 10 per cent (Phong, 1993; Greenfield, 1994). In contrast, the first state enterprise to be equitised under the privatisation program, Legamex International Corporation, was undertaken same year, with voting shares priced at 250 times workers' monthly wages, effectively excluding all but the very wealthy from acquiring shares. This was seen as a success and was promoted as the sound way to privatise (Nguyen,1993). Within a year of Legamex's privatisation, the management was under investigation for corruption and illegal financial dealings. After they were charged, key operations of Legamex were closed. In contrast, REE is still operating profitably.

What these Vietnam examples graphically illustrate is that outright privatisation does not automatically produce efficient management, particularly where the new owners' interests are for short-term profits. An important distinction also has to be made between state enterprise reform as a short-term revenue raising activity to overcome the fiscal crisis of the state, and reform geared towards long-term production. Indeed, as the experience of privatisation in Malaysia has shown, the whole process has very little to do with improving the efficiency and productivity of enterprises. In spite of World Bank's rhetoric, privatisation has been based more on corruption than on fair and free competition:

> The privatisation of public corporations, in particular huge utility establishments, has since proceeded at a relentless pace. One of the key problems of this exercise is that instead of transferring or selling off activities and enterprises which have not been well-run by the public sector, the government seems to be doing exactly the opposite. The better managed public sector activities and enterprises are beingprivatised, leaving the public sector encumbered with the poorly-run and often loss-making concerns. The result will only further strain government revenues and confirm the charges of public sector ineptitude, while enriching those well-placed to gain from the privatisation exercises. Increasingly, these privatisation projects have become the domain of a select group of politically well-connected business tycoons, rendering the Malaysian economy every more oligarchic. More worrisome are the recent moves toprivatise basic services like education and health-care, which had erstwhile been accessible to all at very low cost and comprised importantequalising elements in the social structure. It is invariably the lower-income groups which will be most adversely affected by the attendant rising costs of privatisation. (Tan, p.4)

Despite the complexity of these issues – and a range of possible solutions – the World Bank's privatisation agenda continues to impose its 'one and only' solution, without public debate or participation. This 'one and only' solution has finally become policy in China. After years of insisting that state-owned enterprises be privatised, the World Bank's advice has been realised. In May 1997, President Jiang Zemin outlined a privatisation program which reflected the same recommendations made in the World Bank's report, *China's Management of Enterprise Assets: The State as Shareholder*, which was released on July 25, 1997. In the privatisation program outlined in this report, a "two-track process" of dismissing workers from the state sector (understood in terms of saving money) and "implementing a market-oriented social system such as pensions" is clearly articulated (South China Morning Post, 28 April, 1997). As a result of this policy, up to 50 million workers will be laid off over the next year. There have already been widespread demonstrations by workers faced with the loss of job and income security. In a direct challenge to the new orthodoxy of 'labour flexibility', workers are demanding "the right to work" (China Labour Bulletin, 5 August, 1997).

Although the World Bank is promoting positive prospects of private sector growth and new employment, it is already clear that there will be a massive increase in unemployment. It is also clear that women workers will face greater discrimination and wage inequity in the private sector. In the World Bank's own report, *Income Inequality in China*, it is stated quite explicitly that equal pay for equal work for women is greater in state-owned enterprises. This is despite the fact that recent economic reforms have led to increasing inequality, as well as the forced retirement of women between 30 and 40 years of age. Wage inequality and gender discrimination, however, is recognised as being much greater in the private sector. Moreover, "there is an emerging bias against women of child bearing age" (p.44) in the private sector. As workers' experiences in foreign-owned and foreign joint ventures have shown, there is little means of ensuring equal pay for equal work and freedom from discrimination according to gender. In fact, gender discrimination, discrimination against women over 30, and the systematic undervaluing of women's work, has become part of the private sector ethos. Institutionalised discrimination has become rife in foreign-invested factories, exemplified by the 'economic miracle' province of Fujian, where women workers must present proof of sterilisation, by displaying cards issued by family planning centres when they apply for jobs (Leung, 1997).

In the case of Vietnam, the World Bank describes the sacking of one million workers from the state sector and the government's new emphasis on job creation through the private sector as "a very sensible strategy" (1993). In its report on Vietnam, the Bank describes how workers in the private sector are hired on short-term contracts to "maintain employee motivation and to minimise problems in realising workers if need be." That is, workers can easily be sacked and have no job protection. In spite of the fact that less than 20 per cent of private enterprises have allowed workers to form unions or have signed employment contracts, the Bank concludes that there is "no evidence of abusive labour practices or unsatisfactory working conditions" (pp.63-64). In fact, there have been well over two hundred strikes in the private sector since 1989, with workers protesting against being underpaid, physically beaten and harassed. They have further been the victims of gross violations of the Labour Code, and had their "rights and dignity" abused (Greenfield, 1995). The weaknesses in the protection of workers' rights and the enforcement of labour standards which have permitted these abuses is praised by the Bank:

> For local industry, the labour market is relatively free of distortions. Private entrepreneurs are in a strong position in the currently depressed labour market. Government regulations on overtime and night work, working conditions and the like are not considered major constraints. (p. 61)

Under a system of 'labour flexibility', any notion of workers' rights is perceived of as an unnecessary hindrance. According to the World Bank (1996): "Rigid regulations inhibit private initiative." Based on this understanding, the Bank proposes the removal of all obstructions to private sector development, including collective bargaining, trade unions, minimum wages, and protection against dismissal. The justification by the World Bank is once again based on the East Asian growth experience as seen in its 1996 publication, *Involving Workers in East Asia's Growth.* The importance of labour flexibility and the removal of impediments such as workers' rights, are seen as integral to growth strategy in East Asia:

> The Republic of Korea and Taiwan, China, achieved unprecedented rates of economic growth by letting entrepreneurs manage their workforces as they saw fit. They paid wages that were sufficient to acquire and retain the workers they needed. (p.23)

Abusive labour practices, low wages and long working hours, forced overtime, corporal punishment and physical harassment, the constraints against organising activities and violence against union organisers characterise precisely how managers treat workers in South Korea and Taiwan. Recent incidents include the corporal punishment inflicted on 56 women workers in a Taiwanese-owned factory in Vietnam on March 8, 1997, which left 12 workers hospitalised. Only four weeks later another incident of severe corporal punishment was reported in a Taiwanese-owned shoe factory in northern Vietnam. A year earlier, there was a public outcry over the beating of 15 women workers by a Korean supervisor in a South Korean shoe factory in southern Vietnam. These abusive labour practices are now being exported to countries such as China, Indonesia and Vietnam as well as Latin America.

Involving Workers in East Asia's Growth attempts to reassure its readers that under labour flexibility programs, structural adjustments involving plant closure and relocation overseas "is unlikely to be a source of downward pressure on either wages or working conditions" (p.13). In support of this claim, the Bank argues, for example, that the relocation of industry from Hong Kong to Guangdong did not drive down wages:

> Overall, employment in Hong Kong manufacturing fell from about 900,000 jobs in the early 1980s to only 400,000 by the mid-1990s. Did unskilledlabour in Hong Kong suffer? Individuals lost their jobs in sectors such as garments, but other jobs were being created rapidly, especially in the modern service economy. Average wages have continued to rise, the unemployment rate has remained below 3 per cent, and wage differentials between skilled and unskilled workers have risen. Although wage inequality has increased, the bottom point of the wage distribution has realised substantial increases in real wages. Further evidence of successful transformation of employment opportunities, even for unskilled workers, is that today Chineselabour is imported to work in Hong Kong's construction industry. (p.14)

Omitted from this analysis is the impact felt on workers' families and their livelihood, including the loss of jobs, income security and the control over rights – all of which are meant to underpin this "successful transformation of employment opportunities". The Bank makes the assumption that there is a smooth transition from factory work to work in the service sector and that wages are relatively higher. Far from being a smooth transition, however, the manufacturing sector in Hong Kong saw the disappearance of "30 per cent of the sectoral employment and 13 per cent of the *entire labour force* in less than a decade's time" (Chiu & Lee, 1997, p. 7). In other words, 13 per cent of the entire national workforce lost their jobs in less than ten years. Moreover, jobs in the service sector involved lower wages and greater instability and uncertainty of employment than jobs in the manufacturing sector.

As in most East Asian countries, including Japan, low unemployment figures are the result of restrictive definitions of what it means to be officially considered unemployed. Only those who can prove that they are "active" in the labour market, but without work, are classified as "unemployed". This excludes the long-term unemployed, part-time and casual workers who become unemployed, or those classified as "self-employed", but are without work. This exclusive definition of joblessness hides the true level of unemployment, with the majority of unemployed workers being considered as employed (Greenfield, 1997).

While this sort of flexibility is viewed by the Bank as necessary for "growth with equity", a recent report by the OECD argues that labour flexibility is not a solution to unemployment and poverty. The study of 29 countries by the OECD (1997) shows that there is no link between the existence of unions and low economic growth, and presents evidence that disproves the claim that unions prevent job creation and keep unemployment levels high. In fact, the absence of unions and collective bargaining leads to "poverty pay" and high job insecurity. In the end, labour flexibility means that those in poverty stay poor.

While it is recognised that there are "often fears of rising inequality", this is dependent "on the balance between relative shifts in the supply and demand of different categories of labour" (World Bank, 1996, p. 14). The proposed solution is training which will apparently get workers through the process of "destruction and creation" of their jobs. According to the Bank, this training must be privately funded, which means one of two things: either workers pay for the training themselves, or companies pay for training once workers are employed. The Bank indicates that no training should be financed or organised by governments, arguing that: "In general, evidence suggests that public efforts and resources are best devoted to expanding and improving schooling systems, while leaving the bulk of training to on-the-job efforts by firms or private action." The best form of training, according to the Bank, is "pre-employment training" which is "privately financed by students and job seekers" (p.17).

The social costs of labour flexibility are even greater when the experience of migrant workers in Asia is taken into account. Labour flexibility has been combined with export-oriented industrialization strategies of countries such as the Philippines, Indonesia and more recently Vietnam, where "labour exports" are a major source of export earnings. In the Philippines, the largest "exporter" of migrant labour in Asia, official remittances of overseas migrant workers amount to over a quarter of total export earnings. Forced to leave their own countries due to domestic unemployment, rising costs of living, and impoverishment, migrant workers often work in low-paid '3-D' (dirty, dangerous, and difficult) jobs and are generally excluded from existing labour laws and regulations in the countries where they work. Women in particular are exploited as migrant workers, accounting for more than half of the total number of migrant workers from the Philippines and Indonesia (Azu, 1996). Migrant workers face extremely difficult living and working conditions, with 3,016 recorded cases of distress (including rape and sexual harassment, psychological trauma, trafficking for prostitution, death or suicide, arrest or detention, maltreatment, or forced repatriation) in the Asia-Pacific region in 1995 alone (Alcid, 1996).

It is ironic that so much of *The State in a Changing World* concerns the role of the state in guaranteeing protection from risk and uncertainty. Unfortunately, this only applies to the protection of property rights of private entrepreneurs and minimising the risk and uncertainty they face in their business dealings. There is nothing in the report about the uncertainty and risk faced by workers in flexible labour markets. It is this ideology that, more than anything else, demonstrates the fact that an "effective state" is not everyone's state.

WHOSE STATE? THE SOCIAL FUNDAMENTALS RECONSIDERED

The question, then, is "Whose State is it?" The answer lies in *The State in a Changing World*. Towards the preparation of the report, interviews were conducted with 3,600 private entrepreneurs in 69 countries. There are no interviews with social workers, teachers, workers, farmers, street traders or the self-employed in the informal sector. This is justified by the casual comment that: "The best way to understand the problems holding back private sector development is to ask entrepreneurs directly" (p.13). We are thus reminded that in the discussion of the successful example of authoritarian regimes in East Asia, the Bank identifies the primary "stakeholders" in society as private firms. In fact, the very definition of an "effective state" is based on the privileging of private business, where the state must be "engaged in a productive partnership with the private sector"(p.163).

The East Asian growth model is once again invoked by the Bank to argue that "public-private deliberation councils" that link policy-makers directly to the private business sector form an essential part of the functions of an effective state:

> In successful countries policymaking has been embedded in consultative processes, which provide civil society, labour unions, private firms opportunities for input and oversight. In East Asia public-private deliberation councils – such as Korea's monthly export promotion meetings, Thailand's National Joint Public and Private Consultative Committee, and the Malaysian Business Council – have provided mechanisms for feedback, information sharing, and co-ordination. (p.11)

Noticeably, these "consultative processes" favour big business to the exclusion of popular social organisations such as independent trade unions, peasants' associations and NGOs. Only the government controlled Federation of Korean Trade Unions (FKTU) was permitted to participate in the Korean government's export promotion meetings, while Malaysian Government's public-private deliberations with the Malaysian Business Council excluded labour unions altogether (Asian Monitor, 1988).

Based on these examples from East Asia, such consultative processes, rather than facilitating popular participation in decision-making, act as precisely that mechanism which enhances "the political clout of the more affluent in society" (p.4) which the Bank itself sees as marginalising and excluding the less well-off in society. It should also be noted that the World Bank promotes "public-private partnerships" in its projects such as the Nam Thuen 2 hydroelectric project in Laos, where it works in partnership with Transnational Corporations (TNCs) involved in building the dam. The effect of such partnerships is to increase public risk for the sake of private profit (Hildyard, 1996).

Understanding *whose state* this is allows us to understand the Bank's explanation of the regulatory functions of an "effective state". On the one hand, the Bank claims that the state lacks the capacity to regulate and tax private firms, particularly foreign investments since "countries cannot hope to tax corporate or personal income at rates much higher than global norms and still attract investment" (p.48) On the other hand, it proposes that an effective state *should not* attempt to impose regulations – even environmental regulations – on private firms. Citing an example of "successful" environmental activism in Japan, the Bank argues that "voluntary agreements" adopted by companies is the most effective form of regulation (p.71).

It is necessary to point out that the limited capacity of the state to regulate private capital has only *become limited* as a direct consequence of the neoliberal agenda of governments and the World Bank and International Monetary Fund (IMF). Given the three elements of "good policies", "avoiding price distortions" and "liberalizing trade and investment" (p.46), there is very little scope for protecting the "social fundamentals" in society. Far from being a natural outcome of globalisation, as the Bank suggests, this diminished capacity of states to regulate capital has been orchestrated by international institutions such as the World Bank and IMF. New instruments for restricting states and freeing capital are thus actively being created. In relation to TNCs in particular, the Multilateral Agreement on Investment (MAI) severely restricts the capacity of the state to regulate activities and limit the social and environmental costs wrought by international private capital. While the World Bank recognizes the environmental costs of growth and proposes "citizen participation" in regulation, it is clear that this is not possible given the actual practice of Bank-funded projects, and the limitations imposed by "good policies for growth" and an effective state's partnership with private firms.

This reduction of the regulatory functions of the state to voluntary standards, and offering incentives rather than enforcing protective measures such as environmental and health and safety standards, raises questions about the priorities of private firms. Will considerations of cost efficiency based on competition and profit-motivation really produce the sort of standards and self-regulation that this implies? There is a plethora of examples of major industrial accidents and environmental disasters in the region in recent years to refute such claims. The death of 189 workers in the Kadar Toy factory fire in Thailand in 1993, and the death of 87 workers in the Zhili toy factory fire in Shenzhen, China, in the same year, occurred under conditions where existing regulations were simply ignored by the factory owners.

Ultimately the short-term interests in company profits will not act as a sufficient regulatory mechanism for protecting the longer-term interests of society. This is illustrated by the collapse of the Highland Towers, a 12-storey condominium block in Selangor, Malaysia, in 1993 in which 48 people died. The accident was caused by environmental degradation, primarily hill and land clearing for property development. The 1995 collapse of the Sampoong Department Store, built only in 1989, which killed more than 400 people in Seoul, South Korea, further illustrates the contention. The rapid pace of property development has led to a number of similar accidents (Tan, 1997). Finally, the 1984 poisonous gas leak at the Union Carbide Corporation plant in Bhopal, India saw the instantaneous deaths of 4,000 people and the subsequent deaths of over 15,000 more, reminds us that the protection of people and their communities simply cannot be left to private corporations.

Securing the "social fundamentals" such as health, education, environmental protection and poverty alleviation requires a tremendous leap from rhetoric to reality. The reality is, that of the US$26.8 billion in World Bank loans to China, less than nine per cent is designated for health and education. At the same time, free market reforms in China and Vietnam, and economic liberalisation in countries such as the Philippines, have led to the removal of state subsidies, cuts in government spending, and the closure of public schools. This has led to deterioration in the quality of education provided, as well as a drop in participation rates among children from poor and low-income families.

These changes have also seriously affected teachers, in terms not only of their wages and working conditions, but also their capacity to provide their students with a sound education. In China, economic liberalisation and the promotion of profit and competition has led to the degradation of public schools, especially in rural areas, which are treated as "low profit" activities. Teachers on low wages struggle under rising living costs and extremely long work hours. Any attempts they make to improve their own qualifications often leaves them heavily in debt, as vocational training centres become more and more commercialised under market reforms (China Labour Bulletin, 26 May, 1996).

Like education, access to health care is becoming more and more restricted, as commercialisation and cuts in government spending turn this "social fundamental" into a luxury commodity. Ironically, the Bank observes that: "Evidence from Vietnam confirms that wealthier groups benefit disproportionately from hospital care: the richest fifth of the population are estimated to enjoy some 30 per cent of the benefits of hospital spending, while the poorest fifth get only 11 per cent" (p.53). The World Bank recommends increasing privatisation and commercialisation of health care systems as a means of overcoming inequality. This follows existing situations of economic liberalisation and *de facto* privatisation of health care where, under market reforms, fees have become the norm in a number of hospitals and clinics. It is this system which excludes the majority of people from having access to quality health care in the first place as exemplified by reforms in Vietnam (Kolko, 1997).

In spite of the discussion of unequal access to education and the under-funding of "social fundamentals" in *The State in a Changing World*, the Bank fails to come to the logical conclusion. The Bank seems unable to acknowledge that education and health are always the first sectors to be affected when indebted governments are forced to implement fiscal austerity programs and cut corporate taxes to attract investment.

It is now clear that the problem of poverty and increasing inequality in East Asia, as identified in *Everyone's Miracle?,* will be exacerbated in two ways. First, by the World Bank's "good policies" of economic liberalisation and privatisation, and second, by the Bank's definition of an "effective state" based on a partnership between private firms and elite central agencies under authoritarian political regimes. The book does not seriously challenge the World Bank's neoliberal agenda. Instead, its recognition of the role of the state in East Asian economic growth has merely led to the integration of the repressive functions of the state and its exclusionary institutional links to private firms into this agenda.

CONCLUSION AND RECOMMENDATIONS

1. The Social Welfare Functions of an Effective State

We live in societies where the majority of the wealth and resources are concentrated in the hands of a minority. As such, we must assert the right of the urban and rural poor to receive public assistance to secure their livelihood, a living wage and the right of equal access to public services, especially health and education. Therefore, social welfare, health and education should not be privatised, but be available to all. Corporate taxation and progressive taxation systems can generate the revenue necessary to undertake public assistance and social welfare. This is a more viable means of revenue raising than selling off state assets and cutting services to solve short-term fiscal crises. An effective state must ensure equity and social justice by guaranteeing welfare rights as fundamental rights. Increased corporate taxation and progressive taxation systems will provide the revenue necessary for an effective state to ensure these rights.

2. Enhancing the Regulatory Capacity of an Effective State

It is necessary to renew the capacity of the state to exercise capital controls and protect its citizens from the social, cultural and environmental costs imposed by the unregulated activity of private firms, particularly transnational corporations. The long-term interests of society cannot be left to the short-term interests of profit or cost efficiency. Only through strict enforcement and monitoring by the state, and the direct participation of local communities in the planning and implementation of policies and projects, can the social and environmental costs of growth be minimised. An effective state must be based on a comprehensive system of regulations and social standards which will minimise the social and environmental costs imposed by private corporations and protect the longer-term interests of society. Enhancing the regulatory capacity of an effective state also requires the formulation and implementation of a long-term national economic development strategy based on democratic processes and popular participation.

3. Re-regulation of Labour Markets and the Protection of Workers' Fundamental Rights

Labour market deregulation and 'labour flexibility' involves extensive social costs for society, by undermining the job and income security of working people, generating even higher levels of unemployment and exacerbating the constraints on the fundamental rights of workers. Labour markets must be re-regulated in order to provide job and income protection, to actively engage in the creation of jobs and to institute and enforce laws which protect the collective and individual rights, health and safety, and livelihood of all working people. This re-regulation of labour markets must be based on an environment which allows freedom of association and the right to organise, and not re-regulation based on new restrictions and state control of trade unions. An effective state must guarantee the fundamental rights of workers and trade union rights embodied in International Labour Conventions, particularly the right to organise and bargain collectively, have freedom of association and freedom from discrimination.

4. Alternatives to Privatisation

The social costs created as a result of privatisation are immense. These include mass retrenchments and the destruction of job and income security for millions of workers. Privatisation often involves the creation of private monopolies out of public monopolies, and further weakens the capacity of the state to enforce social, labour and environmental regulations. Clearly there is an urgent need to reform state-owned and public enterprises, to increase the democratic processes, and to increase the transparency and accountability of public enterprises. However, privatisation only serves to close off these possibilities and exclude workers and their communities. There must be open debate and popular participation in the reform of public and state enterprises and recognition that privatisation is only one among a wide range of strategies for reforming public and state enterprises. An effective state must increase the social value of public and state enterprises, including their capacity for employment generation and the role they can play in ensuring equal and fair access to goods and services.

5. Democracy and Participation

While welcoming discussion and debate about the role of the state, and the development of an "effective state", we strongly reject the notion of an effective state based on authoritarian political regimes and elite central agencies. Neither is 'persuasion' a substitute for participation. Persuasion is simply a strategy for suppressing popular protest and resistance, while failing to address the reasons for this resistance. We must work towards building an effective state that is effective in its responsiveness to the demands and interests of the people. As such, it must be based on democratic policy-making and administration that gives substance and true meaning to citizenship rights and participation.

REFERENCES

Aditjondro, George (1994). In the Shadow of MountRamelau: The impact of the occupation of East Timor. Leiden: Indonesian Documentation and Informater Centre.

Ahuja, Vinod, Bidani, Benu, Ferreira, Franciso, & Walton, Michael (1997). Everyone's Miracle? Revisiting Poverty and Inequality in East Asia, Washington DC: World Bank.

Alcid, Mary Lou (1996). The Costs of Labour Exports. Asian Migrant Forum, 11, November.

Asian Monitor (1988). No-Jo, Min-Ju South Korea's New Trade Unions: The Struggle for Free Trade Unions. Hong Kong: Asia Monitor Resource Center.

Azu, Masumi (1996). Labour Imporation Schemes: Human and Labour Rights Havoc? Asian Migrant Forum, 11, November.

Berger, Mark T (1997). The triumph of the East? The East Asian Miracle and post-Cold War capitalism. In Mark T. Berger and Douglas A. Border (eds), The Rise of East Asia: Critical Visions of the Pacific Century. London and New York: Routledge.

Chiu, Stephen W.K. and Lee, Ching Kwan (1997). Withering Away of the Hong Kong Dream? Women Workers under Industrial Restructuring. Occasional Paper No. 61. Hong Kong: Hong Kong Institute of Asia-Pacific Studies.

Chronology of a strike. Asian Labour Update, 23, November 1996-March 1997, p. 4.

Forum on Human Rights and Development (1995). Stability and Unity on a Culture of Fear: Indonesia 50 Years After Independence. Bangkok: Forum-Asia.

Gietzelt, Dale (1989). The Indonesianisation of West Papua. Oceania, 59(3), pp. 201-21.

Globalisation Thriving on Women Migrants, Asian Migrant Forum, 11, November 1996, p. 40.

Greenfield, Gerald (1994). The development of capitalism in Vietnam. In Between Globalism and Nationalism, Socialist Register 1994. London: Merlin Press.

Greenfield, Gerald (1995). Between discipline and dignity: Strikes in Vietnam. AsianLabour Update, 19, August-October.

Greenfield, Gerald (1997). Governmental Livelihood Assistance & Non-governmental Assistance for Day Labourers and the Homeless: Perspectives on Poverty Alleviation Strategies in Japan.A Report for the Study on Alternatives for Poverty Alleviation in Hong Kong. Hong Kong: Department of Applied Social Studies, Hong Kong Polytechnic University & the Hong Kong Social Security Society.

Han, Dongfang (1997). Workers: The great losers in China's reform process. In At What Price?Workers in China. Hong Kong: Asia Monitor Resource Center.

Hart-Landsberg, Martin (1993). The Rush to Development: Economic Change and Political Struggle in South Korea. New York: Monthly Review Press.

Hildyard, Nicholas (1996). Public risk, private profit: The World Bank and the private sector. The Ecologist, 26, July - August, pp. 176-178.

Ho, Shuet Ying (1990). Taiwan - After a Long Silence: The emerging new unions of Taiwan. Hong Kong: Asia Monitor Resource Center.

Kolko, Gabriel (1997). Vietnam: Anatomy of a Peace. London and New York: Routledge.

Kwan, Shek Ping (1997). China's labour safety and health standards. Change. June.

Leung, Apo (1997). Labour Rights in the Pearl River Delta", At What Price? Workers in China. Hong Kong: Asia Monitor Resource Center.

Monbiot, George (1989). The transmigration fiasco. The Geographical Magazine, 61, May.

Naowarat, Suksamran (1997). Claiming the right to have a say. Bangkok Post, February 11.

Nguyen Ngoc Chinh (1993). Legamex equitisation showing early success. Vietnam Investment Review, July, pp. 12-18.

OECD (1997). Employment Outlook. Paris: OECD.

Phong, Thang (1993). Business undertaking a motive of production", Vietnamese Trade Unions.

Proceedings of the International Conference for Toy Workers' Health and Safety, January 9-10, 1996, Hong Kong. Hong Kong: Asia Monitor Resource Center, 1996.

Rodrik, Dani (1994). King Kong meets Godzilla: The World Bank and The East Asia Miracle.In A. Fishlow, C. Gwin, S. Haggard, D. Rodrik and R. Wade (Eds.), Miracle or Design? Lessons from the East Asian Experience. Washington: Overseas Development Council.

Syed, Hussein Ali (1995). Economic Take-off: Trade unions in Malaysia. In Henk Thomas (ed.) Globalisation and Third World Trade Unions: The Challenge of Rapid Economic Change. London: Zed Books.

Tan, Pek Leng (1997). Capitalist Growth in Malaysia. In Vinod Raina, Aditi Chowdhury and Sumit Chowdhury (Eds.), The Dispossessed: Victims of Development in Asia. Hong Kong: Asian Regional Exchange for New Alternatives.

Teaching in China: A Crisis looms. China Labour Bulletin, 26, May 1996, pp. 1-4.

Vinod, Ahuja, Benu Bidani, Francisco Ferreira and Michael Walton (1997). Everyone's Miracle? Revisiting Poverty and Inequality in East Asia. Washington: World Bank.

Woodside, Alexander (1993). The Asia-Pacific Idea as a Mobilization Myth. In Arif Dirlik (ed.) What is in a Rim? Critical Perspectives on the Pacific Region Idea. Boulder, Colorado: Westview.

World Bank (1985). The World Bank Annual Report 1985. Washington: World Bank.
World Bank (1993). Vietnam: Transition to the Market. Washington DC: World Bank.
World Bank (1995). World Bank Development Report 1995: Workers in an Integrating World. Hong Kong: Oxford University Press.
World Bank (1996). Involving Workers in East Asia's Growth. Washington: World Bank.
Work Bank (1997a). World Development Report 1997: The State in a Changing World. Hong Kong: Oxford University Press.
World Bank Country Operations Division, China and Mongolia Department (1997b)Income Inequality in China. Washington: World Bank.

Social Indicators Research Series

1. V. Møller (ed.): *Quality of Life in South Africa.* 1997 ISBN 0-7923-4797-8
2. G. Baechler: *Violence Through Environmental Discrimination.* Causes, Rwanda Arena, and Conflict Model. 1999 ISBN 0-7923-5495-8
3. P. Bowles and L.T. Woods (eds.): *Japan after the Economic Miracle.* In Search of New Directories. 1999 ISBN 0-7923-6031-1
4. E. Diener and D.R. Rahtz (eds.): *Advances in Quality of Life Theory and Research.* Volume I. 1999 ISBN 0-7923-6060-5
5. Kwong-leung Tang (ed.): *Social Development in Asia.* 2000 ISBN 0-7923-6256-X

KLUWER ACADEMIC PUBLISHERS – DORDRECHT / LONDON / BOSTON